Larry H. Miller

BEHIND
— THE —
DRIVE

BEHIND

— THE —

DRIVE

99 Inspiring Stories from the Life of an American Entrepreneur

SHADOW
MOUNTAIN

Unless otherwise noted, all photographs courtesy of the Larry and Gail Miller family.

© 2015 Bryan J. Miller

Visit us at ShadowMountain.com

Library of Congress Cataloging-in-Publication Data
Larry H. Miller—behind the drive: 99 inspiring stories from the life of an American entrepreneur / Bryan Miller.
    pages cm
    Summary: Ninety-nine stories about Larry H. Miller told by those who knew him well, including family members, NBA players, childhood friends, governors, senators, neighbors, employees and business competitors.
    ISBN 978-1-62972-094-4 (hardbound : alk. paper)
    1. Miller, Larry H., 1944–2009. 2. Automobile dealers—Utah—Biography. 3. Businessmen—Utah—Biography. 4. Mormons—Utah—Biography.
    HD9710.25.U62M554 2015
    338'.04092—dc23
    [B]   2015018653

Printed in the United States of America
Publishers Printing, Salt Lake City, UT

10 9 8 7 6 5 4 3 2 1

CONTENTS

CONTENTS

CONTENTS

LEADERSHIP

INTEGRITY

PASSION & PLAYFULNESS

COMPETITIVE SPIRIT & COURAGE

CONTENTS

FOREWORD

Governor Mitt Romney

During a GOP presidential debate in 2007, I was asked what I dislike most about America. I was at a loss for words, and I found myself instead naming the things I love about our country. I told the moderator that what makes America the greatest nation in the world is the heart of its people: hardworking, innovative, risk-taking, God-loving, family-oriented American people.

I could have been describing Larry H. Miller. Larry was all of those things, the embodiment of the American spirit.

I met Larry in downtown Salt Lake City in 2000, a year after I had been hired to lead the organizing committee for the 2002 Winter Olympics. Everyone in Utah knew Larry. He had a reputation as a skilled businessman, a passionate owner of the Utah Jazz, and a great-hearted donor to everything Utah.

Larry was also an enthusiastic supporter of the Olympics. When I asked him and his wife, Gail, to serve as chairmen of the Delta Center venue—which hosted figure skating and short track speed skating events at the Games—they graciously agreed. I was grateful to have their leadership at such a high-profile venue.

Over time, I learned that Larry and I had much in common. We shared the same deep belief in our Mormon faith. In fact, Larry famously chose not to attend Jazz games on Sunday, even missing the last game of the 1998 NBA finals against Michael Jordan and the Chicago Bulls.

We each married our high school sweethearts, had five children, and stayed married for the course of our lives. My wife, Ann, has always been my chief counselor and confidant. Larry and Gail had that same bond; they were partners in life and in business, sharing equal ownership in each venture they undertook.

Larry and I also have a strong connection to the auto industry. I'm a son of Detroit, born and raised in Michigan. My father served as president of American Motors, and at one point my dream was to be the head of a big automobile company. Larry found his path on the dealership side, working his way up from a parts manager until purchasing his own Toyota dealership in 1979. Today, the Larry H. Miller Group owns fifty-four dealerships, sells more than 100,000 automobiles annually, and employs 10,000 people nationwide.

Success like that doesn't come easy. I've never met a successful entrepreneur who didn't like to work. Larry loved to work and did so right up until his passing in 2009. My father used to say, "The pursuit of the difficult makes men strong." Larry pursued the difficult. He worked hard, innovated, took risks, and served God and his family—all the things that are at the heart of the American people.

On the morning of the Opening Ceremony for the 2002 Olympic Winter Games, the torch relay made its way through Salt Lake City. Each runner had his or her own torch, so the flame was passed from one torch to the next. Fittingly, Larry Miller passed his flame to Gail. Never one to hide his emotions, Larry wiped tears from his eyes. His job done, he extinguished his torch, and the flame carried on.

INTRODUCTION

Bryan Miller

About a week before my dad, Larry H. Miller, died, I sat at his hospital bedside, reminiscing with him. His health had deteriorated enormously—an incredibly intense work schedule and the decades he'd spent overpowering every task, project, and problem through sheer willpower had finally caught up to him.

His long work hours, poor diet, habit of skipping breakfast and often lunch, lack of exercise, not visiting the doctor, getting little sleep, and living constantly under high stress had taken their toll. He'd survived a heart attack and a heart stoppage—but just barely—and (without ever complaining) he'd lived for years with many ailments, including diabetes, retinopathy, kidney failure, gout, arthritis, sepsis, intestinal bleeding, and a rare, painful, and incurable disease called calciphylaxis. But now, however, it was clear that the end was near.

Sitting alone in his hospital room, we fondly recalled family vacations, special meals we'd shared, and jokes we'd told one another. It didn't take long to exhaust the supply of happy memories we'd created together, because he'd spent so much more time working than he had with me.

If you've ever found yourself trying to figure out what to say to a person near the end of his life, you know how challenging and uncomfortable it can be.

Wanting to connect on a deep level, I said, "Dad, it's been a privilege to have been your son, and I want you to know that I will spend the rest of my life practicing lessons I've learned from you and also teaching those lessons to others." He lay with his head on his pillow, eyes closed. He didn't say anything, but I sensed that he'd heard me. I went on, "But I know that as I do, I will also spend the rest of my life comparing myself to you."

A few moments passed in silence before he responded, "Don't. Don't measure yourself against me. I don't know if you're more than I am or less than I am—I really don't—but it's not important. Measure yourself against yourself. It is enough."

He passed away a few days later. He was sixty-four years old.

This book is one of the ways I've endeavored to fulfill the promise I made to my dad before he died—to both live and share the lessons I learned from him.

It contains ninety-nine stories about him from every aspect and era of his life, told by those who knew him best, from family members to NBA players; from childhood friends to governors and senators; from neighbors, employees, and softball teammates to even his business competitors.

My dad told his incredible life story in his autobiography, *Driven*, but after reading it I knew that there were many more stories about him and my mom that were worth telling. I realized that if they didn't get written down, they'd be lost.

So, with the support of my family, I made a list of about five hundred people who were likely to have an entertaining or otherwise worthwhile story about my dad and proceeded to contact each one personally.

In the course of collecting stories about my dad, I learned of hundreds of acts of service that he had performed for people. Some of these were small, like buying a refrigerator for someone or paying for a car repair or medical bill. Others were large, such as paying off a mortgage or giving or lending money to people to save them from bankruptcy. His generosity extended beyond money, though; he gave of himself, sharing freely of his time and advice and frequently performing personal acts of service for others.

As I collected story after story, I wondered, *When did he have time for that? Was it in between negotiating NBA players' salaries and building new automobile dealerships?* My dad never told me of these acts of service—I figure he was either too busy performing them or too humble to share.

It hit me that providing service to others isn't something my dad did *after* he became successful. Providing service to others—always with my mom as his partner—is *how* he became successful. It's *why* the two of them became successful.

Larry was full of paradoxes (I often switch between calling him "Larry" and "Dad" because most people knew him as Larry and because I feel that he belonged to all of us). He was a college dropout who funded hundreds of college scholarships. He was an intense competitor, but he was willing to share his knowledge and practices with his rivals. He was at times intense and tempestuous, but he was also capable of exceptional kindness and thoughtfulness. He was an ordinary man who accomplished extraordinary things.

I think that Larry was also an artist, despite most people considering him a businessman. Instead of paint or marble, business was his medium. He was a philosopher, and he taught that "even more important than the action is the philosophy behind it." He was a teacher, a citizen, a philanthropist, and a man of great faith. He was a visionary, a builder, a dealmaker, an entrepreneur, and a family man.

I hope this book does three things. First, I hope it helps to preserve Larry's memory by standing alongside *Driven* as a lasting testament to the manner of man Larry was. In turn, I hope that example inspires and uplifts future generations of students, leaders, and entrepreneurs as well as members of the Miller family and employees of the Larry H. Miller Group.

Second, I hope it inspires you to live your inherent greatness by following the simple-yet-powerful formula I believe Larry used to achieve his incredible success: use your natural strengths, gifts, and talents doing work you love; strive to get better at it every day; and see that your work serves others.

Third, I hope this book encourages you to protect and preserve your health. Before he died, my dad had his legs amputated below the knee due to complications from diabetes. When I saw him in the hospital following his surgery, I asked myself, "Is this man successful? Is this the price of success?"

It changed me. It is easy to see the outward aspects of my dad's success—the money, the NBA team, the other businesses and accomplishments—but what's not as visible are the sacrifices and tradeoffs that he made. I'm convinced that if my dad had taken better care of himself, he could have lived another two or three good decades. I hope that as you read these stories, you'll also think carefully about what it means to live a healthy, balanced life and that you'll take the time to define success for yourself.

When I viewed my father's body in the mortuary, I was dumbfounded by its lifelessness. I'd seen corpses before, but it was particularly strange to see my dad's body devoid of its vigor and vitality, because he'd always been so powerful. He was the kind of guy whose presence you could feel—if he was in a room, you knew it, and you knew that he was in charge. He was so passionate and intense about everything. He was so *alive*.

It occurred to me that although each of us is animated by a spark of life, some people, like my dad, seem to possess a *second* spark. I often think that he packed two or three lifetimes into one. As the proverb says, "The star that burns twice as bright burns half as long." If my dad had slowed down, taken better care of himself, and lived a more balanced life, he'd probably still be here. But then I realize that if he'd done that, he wouldn't have been who he was.

Though George Bernard Shaw wrote these words, they could have just as easily come from Larry: "I am of the opinion that my life belongs to the community, and as long as I live, it is my privilege to do for it whatever I can. I want to be thoroughly used up when I die, for the harder I work, the more I live. Life is no 'brief candle' to me. It is a sort of splendid torch which I have got hold of for a moment, and I want to make it burn as brightly as possible before handing it on to the future generations."

It's been a privilege to collect these stories about my dad, and I'm grateful for the opportunity to share them with you. This project has allowed me to get to know him in a way that I never would have otherwise. I hope that as you read this book, and as you get to know Larry (or get to know him better), his example will ignite a spark in you. I also hope that you will be inspired to carry out his final admonition to "Go about doing good until there's too much good in the world."

Bryan Miller

Sandy, Utah
May 2015

✆

The Larry H. Miller Group of Companies has donated $100,000 to support the American Diabetes Association® Stop Diabetes® movement.

HARD WORK

THE GUY FROM THE PARTS DEPARTMENT

David Stern

On April 15, 1985, I sat with members of the NBA Board of Governors at the Waldorf Astoria in New York, waiting to meet the guy who had purchased half of the Utah Jazz just a day earlier. The room was full of some of the league's most important owners who constituted the Advisory/Finance Committee; among them were Jerry Buss (Lakers), Bill Davidson (Pistons), Alan Cohen (Celtics), John Krumpe (Knicks), Abe Pollin (Bullets), Larry Weinberg (Trailblazers) and William Wirtz (Bulls). We were there to vet this potential new owner, and in walks Larry wearing a pair of chinos and a shirt that barely had a collar.

Someone on the board said, "What's your story?" Larry proceeded to tell us about how he'd been the head of the parts department at a Toyota dealership. People were shaking their heads. Sam Battistone had been trying to sell the Jazz for a while, and prior to Larry, he had brought us many successive candidates who did not pass muster. So now it was like, "Oh, gosh, this is the last person on the list. Sam has gone down to the bottom of the barrel. He's brought in this guy from the parts department."

But there was this quiet determination to Larry that he was going to get it done, and he was going to do it his way. He couldn't have been prouder of his ability to make a purchase of the Jazz.

Larry had bought fifty percent of the team, with an option to

3

purchase fifty percent more. He told the board that he planned to pay off the loan sooner than his contract required. That had people scratching their heads and saying, "Hey, you're not supposed to do that. As long as you're satisfying the loan and you're not paying too much interest on it, you shouldn't pay it off early."

But Larry said, "No, I don't like to have debt."

I really think people were saying, *Boy, who is this rube?* But Larry was utterly delightful and very serious about professing certain values. In the end, he was approved by the board. Larry impressed me that day as a simple person. Not a simple*ton*—I mean a simple person. He was a man of few words and certain precepts, and he was going to live his life and conduct his business that way, unfettered by what the world around him thought. He was not offensive about it; he was very accommodating to people. He had his own set of beliefs and procedures to live by.

Over the years, Larry and I developed the kind of relationship where he would call me, or I would call him, and we'd say, "Just checking in, got a minute?" And then we would spend the better part of two hours on the phone. There was a certain intimacy to it. I tend to be plainspoken, and if I like somebody and I think I can help him, I tend to tell him what I'm thinking. Larry would do the same. He'd tell me what he liked and didn't like about the way the league was running. And he would call and talk a lot about Karl Malone and John Stockton. But Karl was the one who was driving him crazy. Always. Like an extra kid.

In the late '80s we talked a lot about his plan to build what was then the Delta Center. I told him I thought it was crazy to build because rather than being a trophy, it might become a tombstone, incapable of being moved. I admired it, but I said, "There's no flexibility once you build a building. Your club is going to be worth a small fortune, and it could be sold and moved anywhere at a monumental price. But here you are; you're going to build a building and cement it."

I was the loyal opposition, and I think he sort of enjoyed it, because it gave him the sense of opportunity to bear witness to the fact that he was staying and that this was what he was going to do. He said, "I bought this team to keep it in Utah. And I am going to keep it in Utah."

So he built it. Larry was like the foreman, scurrying all around the construction site. It was surreal to me, because you almost felt like he was going to get a hammer and start pounding nails in. I used to call him the little engine that could. That was just Larry. It was fun to see.

Today, there's only one building in the world that has a beam with my name on it. I don't like heights. I don't like buildings when they're being built; I like them when they're finished. But I got up there, with a hard hat on, and wrote my name on the beam that topped off the Delta Center, because if my pal Larry was going to build that building, I was going to be there for the topping-off ceremony.

Under Larry's direction, the Jazz personified what we wanted an NBA team to be. They were in a spanking clean building that was always being improved. They serviced all their customers. Larry knew the fans well. He was deeply involved in everything having to do with the team—maybe too much sometimes, like when he wanted to climb over the bench and punch someone in the nose or when he wanted to walk over to the visiting team's huddle. I once called and said to him, "Larry! Stop it! I'm not going to suspend you now, but after the season tickets come out next year, if your seat isn't next to the home bench instead of the visitors' bench, I'm coming out to Salt Lake to get you."

But everyone in the community knew that the Jazz and Larry were there for them. That's what we wanted for basketball. If there's an essence of a franchise—a face of a franchise—Larry was it.

My relationship with Larry was sufficiently close that it didn't feel out of character for me to say, "Larry, you're killing yourself. You have diabetes, you're overweight, you're working too hard, you're stressed, you're agitated, whatever." That's not usually the commissioner's role, but he was always good-natured about it. Then one day, after a very long hospitalization, he called me and said, "This is

Larry. I just want you to know I'm leaving the hospital to go home to die."

I'll take that moment to the grave with me. I'm not sure what I said, because I was so beside myself. Shaken. Stunned. I just said something like, "Oh, stop it, Larry. I'll call you when you get home. We'll talk."

I never spoke to him again. He knew exactly what was happening. I knew that he had decided it was time, and he was giving up the ghost. I don't know how many people he called to say goodbye to. I'm sure it was more than me, but it couldn't have been a long list. I felt honored to have received the call.

Larry was an important inspiration to me on this level: be who you are, and learn how to feel more comfortable with it. That's hard for me; growing up in New York, going to a New York City school and university, and practicing law in New York, there's a certain level of sophistication—real or perceived—by which you conduct yourself.

But here was a guy who, in his own way, was sort of like the Warren Buffet of Utah. You live by a certain value and you conduct yourself that way. Most people are not as comfortable with themselves as Larry was. I don't think I ever, ever saw him in a tie. I used to tease him when I caught him in a jacket, but I don't remember a tie. And it wasn't some style-affected approach. It was just who he was. Larry taught me that you can be very successful, you can be a good parent, a good husband, a good member of the community, and you can still be yourself.

Great American Success Story

Governor Jon Huntsman Jr.

Somehow, despite all we know of Larry Miller's contributions to the state and citizens of Utah, there are still untold stories about the many ways he made his home state a better place. There are so many examples of the impact Larry had on the communities and people in the state he cherished. One story that is known by few is the invaluable counsel he gave to me before and during my administration as the sixteenth governor of this great state.

Our relationship, though, started long before I was sworn in. I first met Larry in the mid-1980s when he came to visit my dad, Jon Huntsman Sr., about possibly buying the Utah Jazz. My initial impression of Larry was that he was a hungry, dynamic entrepreneur. He had great confidence and optimism in his direction, and failure wasn't an option. I had heard a little bit of his story, and I loved it: the way he worked his way from the parts desk to a successful business leader. It all served as an early education for me on who Larry was and was a primer for my later interaction with him.

Despite both being very public people, Larry and I developed a genuine friendship that was somehow out of public view. He was a good friend to my father and beloved by all of us. When I began to prepare for the 2004 Utah gubernatorial election, I decided to seek out Larry's help.

Utah's economy needed a boost, and as part of my campaign,

I wanted to create a plan to change the taxes and regulatory environment to get the local economy firing again. I needed help in creating my ten-point economic development plan, and I asked for Larry's support and input. Larry wasn't much interested in politics then; even though he was deeply patriotic, he was wary of politicians and thought that state government usually achieved very little useful output. I told him things that I thought we could do for the state of Utah that would represent a better pathway, and I eventually won his support. His counsel in crafting an economic plan for my campaign was crucial.

Ultimately, I won the election, and it was time to think about governing. I had never been elected to any political office before, but I knew where I wanted to go and what I wanted to do. I needed some people around me who could give me advice as I prepared to transition into office and build my administration. As governor, you report to the people who elected you, but you don't really have a director or boss. Coming from the corporate world, I wanted to have an outside board that I could vet things with, who would be honest with me and not be shy about telling me what I was doing wrong.

I asked Larry to serve as a vice chair to my campaign's transition team along with a number of other leaders such as Senator Jake Garn, local business leader Dinesh Patel, humanitarian Pamela Atkinson, and others. I put each in charge of looking at a department within the government, examining the bureaucracy, and recommending ways we could make improvements. I wanted each department in the state government to be reviewed independently from a financial standpoint, a leadership standpoint, and an efficiency standpoint. I asked Larry to oversee the transition of the public safety department, one of the biggest departments I had. He loved it.

He got very engaged and really enjoyed the work. He interviewed senior staff, listened as people described obstacles, and made recommendations regarding improvements and budgets. I think it was the first time Larry had ever been involved with a government assignment, and I like to think it changed the way he thought about state government. We implemented many of his recommendations, and we were off and running with the new administration.

But the experience with the vice chairs had been so positive that I wanted to keep that concept of an external board of directors with whom I could consult about whether or not we were living up to expectations. I wanted to hear voices from outside of government. Once again, I created this outside board that included Larry and several other trusted advisors, and we met each month to figure out what we could be doing better.

Larry was an invaluable advisor to the administration and me and once again became engrossed with the work. Few will know the extent of his work because it was never made public, but he brought such perspective to these discussions. Larry saw the world in different shades than anybody else I was around. I always found that to be totally refreshing and stimulating because he could look at a problem or an issue and see it far differently than anyone else sitting around the table. He always saw it in passionately human terms. It wasn't just an inanimate budget item or a number in a vast bureaucracy. He could see and articulate how things impacted people. I always thought that he was right on in terms of the way he saw things and the way he prioritized his thinking. I learned a lot from that, and I learned a lot from the way he saw the world.

He was also a great listener in those settings because he had an unquenchable thirst for knowledge. He was one of the keenest, most inquisitive learners I've ever been around, constantly absorbing information and endlessly curious about the world. We used to swap books about Thomas Jefferson and Abraham Lincoln because we both had a great love for history and the hardworking souls who founded our republic.

That's not the only passion we shared, however. We also talked a lot about racing, and he knew my passion for motorcycle racing. After he finished the Miller Motorsports Park complex, he invited me out to see it. When the supermoto track opened, I went out there on the first or second day and rode a dirt bike, going over all the jumps. Larry was excited and incredulous, saying, "I never thought I'd see the governor of the state in full riding gear, ten feet in the air on a racetrack doing crazy things."

"Larry," I replied, "that's not nearly as crazy as running for public office."

Larry is the epitome of the great American success story, the ultimate example of someone pulling himself up by the bootstraps through hard work, dedication, vision, and passion. His name will obviously be remembered, but his real legacy is the human connection and the story of a passionate entrepreneur who pursued what he loved to the highest degrees of success.

FIRED BY LARRY

Franklin T. Ferguson

Construction projects are stressful under the best of circumstances. But these weren't the best of circumstances.

As founding partner of FFKR Architects, I was placed in charge of design for one of the most aggressive construction projects in Utah's history: the Delta Center, which was to become the long-term home for Larry Miller's Utah Jazz.

By May 1990, Larry had secured the approvals and funding to greenlight the arena. But changes to the NBA's collective bargaining agreement meant we'd be working on a short clock. The new agreement called for escalating salaries starting in the 1991–92 season, and if Larry didn't have the new arena ready by then, he would lose millions of dollars each season. So our almost-impossible deadline was set. The Delta Center doors would open along with the '91–'92 season. We had sixty-six weeks from start to finish.

Because of this aggressive timeline, the project was fast-tracked. Larry told us, "We've got to build while we're designing," and that's exactly what we did. We built while we planned, with the planning and design for each phase happening just one step ahead. Bulldozers were on site and foundation concrete was being poured, yet we were still making numerous design decisions daily, both large and small. We were spending $200,000 daily on construction, but we were still making design decisions along the way.

11

I met with Larry almost daily to get his approval for proposed design features. With his approvals in hand, our production team would work with the contractor and building officials to propel one part of the project while we turned our attention to the next set of design questions.

It was during this stressful period that I was sitting in my office one day, about to be dealt a huge surprise. Only rudimentary graphic computers existed in those days, so my office and drafting tables were littered with hand-drawn sketches and hand-built cardboard models, and there was a general sense of controlled chaos that matched the feeling of the project itself.

That was the scene Jeff Fisher walked into one afternoon. Jeff led our production team, and he had just gotten to our office after a meeting at Larry's Chevrolet dealership. He was as white as a sheet when he stepped into my office.

"Larry has fired us!" he announced. "He just told me we have received our last check."

For a moment, I just stood there, stunned. Finally, I gathered my wits, grabbed my keys, and headed for the Chevrolet store. It was after hours by the time I arrived, but I ran up the stairs to Larry's office. The waiting room was empty except for Larry's assistant, Marilyn, who was clearly surprised to see me.

"I have to see Larry," I announced.

She said he didn't want to see me. I implored her several times to tell Larry that I was in the waiting room. Finally, she called him on the office intercom and told him I was present. He told her to show me out. I refused to leave.

After an hour or so, Marilyn left for the evening, and on her way out she said, "Well, good luck!" Now I was alone in the waiting room. My stomach was grinding.

After another hour or so, the door to Larry's office opened. There he stood. When he saw me, his eyes narrowed and he shot me the most intense, angry stare imaginable.

I didn't know what to do so I simply started talking—babbling, really.

Eventually, Larry grudgingly began to talk, and we were having a two-way discussion about the design of the Delta Center and the construction schedule.

Larry's sudden change in tenor emboldened me a bit, so I blurted out, "Larry, you cannot fire us! Firing us would hurt you and it would hurt me. More important, it would also hurt the project, perhaps irreparably. We started this project as a team, and we have to finish it as a team."

The words "hurt the project" sank in. He could tell I cared about the arena, and it was an emotional moment. When he responded, his voice broke, and soon he began to cry. At that point I knew we were going to be able to go ahead together.

Larry and I talked for another two hours about the project and about anything else that came to mind. By the time we walked out into the night, we were like old friends again.

Working together, we finished the arena in under sixteen months. The Jazz opened their 1991–92 season in the Delta Center as planned. The project became noted as the fastest construction of a major arena in the United States.

Some months later I was talking to Scott Williams, the manager of the Delta Center both during and after construction. I told Scott of the day Larry fired our firm and of the sit-in I staged in the Chevrolet dealership lobby to get rehired.

"Oh, Larry fired you many times," Scott responded. "You simply were never told."

The Delta Center (now Energy*Solutions* Arena) has been the region's premier sports and entertainment venue for almost a quarter century now. Over that time, I have reflected many times on my day-to-day experience with Larry. My respect and affection for him have only grown during that time.

He was deeply committed to his work, particularly to the design of the Delta Center. He was loyal to his team and listened intently to advice and counsel from all angles. If he ever exploded in anger— like with Jeff that day—he was always able to back up, reconsider, and then ultimately move forward with renewed energy.

13

He never once penalized me for openly disagreeing with him as I did from time to time. In such an environment I felt entirely free to speak my mind, which was vital in keeping our project on track.

To this day, I still don't know why Larry fired us. But I know that he rehired us, and there's a 19,911-seat arena that stands as evidence.

GENIUS WITH A
YELLOW PAD

Mayor Ted Wilson

By 1990, I had spent enough time around Larry Miller that we were generally pretty relaxed and comfortable with each other. That's why it was odd when my phone rang that summer and I picked it up to find a rather anxious-sounding Larry on the other end of the line.

"Ted, can you spend an hour with me this afternoon at my office?" he asked. As mayors often are, I was rushing out the door to some official luncheon. We figured we'd both be free by two o'clock.

As I drove toward Larry's office, I wondered what the deal was. A lot of thoughts were swirling through my head about the meeting that awaited me, but the one I kept coming back to was, *never underestimate this guy.*

I had already made that mistake once, several years earlier.

It was 1985, and Utah Jazz owner Sam Battistone was in a quandary. Team finances were muddy, and Sam was considering all options, including an out-of-town sale. It broke my heart to think of the Jazz leaving town; Utahns had become excited about being in the big leagues, and even though the crowds were still small, the team was gaining followership and financial viability. I spent a lot of time with Wendell Ashton, publisher of the *Deseret News,* and Fred Ball, president of the Salt Lake Chamber of Commerce, seeking an

15

investor to save the day and keep the team in Utah. None of us could quite believe just where the savior would come from.

In stepped this car salesman clad in a golf shirt a couple of sizes too small and possessing no slick sales pitch. He sported an alarmingly common demeanor, with the grin on his face the only sign of self-confidence. Larry arranged a meeting with Fred, the governor, and myself with a plan to buy Sam out.

Larry, to say the very least, did not sweep us off our feet. We had too many questions. Who is this guy? Does he have the cash? Would he be able to convince the NBA elders that he could handle ownership of a franchise?

On the way out of the meeting, I whispered to Fred, "Do we have any other choice?" Fred shook his head.

Of course, that was the first time I underestimated Larry. He went on to defy our expectations and the Jazz became Larry's team, a solid NBA franchise. Larry had become a hero in his own town.

So here I was, years later, with that self-admonition in mind. I parked outside in Larry's car lot and rushed up a flight of stairs, where I was greeted by Larry holding a sack of hamburgers.

"Sorry, Larry, I just finished lunch," I said.

Larry shot back, "Eat one, you never know when there will be another meal, I've learned."

I smiled at the lesson and then obliged, downing a burger because this guy always worried about the future. I even polished off the fries.

"Ted, I want to build an arena."

Stunned, I mumbled something about people never building arenas; that's normally done by states, counties, cities, and such. Larry just smiled over his burger. Without knowing it, I had just played right into Larry's purpose for the meeting.

Stammering on, I tried to approach reality for him. "You'd better get someone to run some numbers for you," I advised, sure that when Larry found out what an arena would cost him he would back off quickly. I did not want this genuine guy, our Jazz redeemer, faced with an economic situation that would send the team packing. We'd had enough of that suspense.

"What's wrong with the Salt Palace, Larry?" I posed.

"Twelve thousand seats is what's wrong!" he bellowed back. "NBA Commissioner David Stern tells me we have to have almost 20,000 seats to keep a small market team in business."

"Look, Larry, I'll be glad to talk to the county commissioner for you, and even the governor. We might be able to put a package together. We do need to upgrade our convention facilities, and we can make it multipurpose."

With that inimitable smile he always had when showing confidence, Larry explained to me that he thought the governor, the county, and the city had good people running government, but he could never trust a public solution to work. "Too many people involved, and it will take too long," he said.

"Well, get those numbers together and see what you might do," I said in serious retreat.

It was then that he reached into a desk drawer and pulled out a yellow pad. This wasn't a flat pad of paper; it was fat, the way a pad gets when you use it over and over, rumpling the pages a little with each use. It was obvious that Larry had been employing this pad pretty heavily, filling it with number after number, regression math, projection math, amortization schedules, and who knows what else.

Armed with the pad, he looked at me and said, "Here's what I want from you. I need about twenty million from the Salt Lake City Redevelopment Fund."

The chips were on the table now. Time to show our hands. This was my turf—I was chairman of the city redevelopment fund, a fund that grows over the year from captured property taxes and can be used in developing economic activities in areas of urban blight.

My first sidestep was easy work for Larry. "I don't know if we have that much money in the fund," I said. Larry just grinned and showed me the budget of the fund and the amount expected in coming years. He had done the research and knew exactly what it was.

I tried again. "Well, the funds may be available, but we can't just give them to a private venture like you are proposing."

Larry grinned again and said, "I don't want it for my building on my property; it's for the city-side improvements. The underground utility vaults, the curb, and gutter. It's only right the city pay for those improvements."

"What about the urban blight requirement?" I had been knocked down twice by this dynamo and his yellow pad, but I was sure this rebuttal would work.

He flashed the grin again. "This is one of the most blighted areas of town. We're looking at the block between South Temple and 100 South, and 300 and 400 West. If I build an arena there, it will be an incentive for surrounding businesses, for restaurants, for retail, for enterprise. Do you have a better blight plan than that?"

I gave up. The match was over. I stumbled out of his office, my stomach rumbling with hamburger, dazed. Before I got back to City Hall, I had thought through the yellow-pad logic and was a convert. Using those numbers and those arguments, we were able to secure approval from the Salt Lake City Council, which managed the redevelopment funds.

Larry was right. Despite having avoided a lot of formal education, he was a genius. He had learned to think things through, to prepare carefully, to anticipate counter arguments, to have answers for everything. And, in the final analysis, he had the rare skill and the soothing grin to convert others to his thinking.

Larry went on to build his arena in record time. He was on the job watching construction almost every day. He did his usual mortgage-the-farm routine and somehow managed over $600,000 a month in payments to creditors for the place.

As for the city, I know of no other redevelopment project that accomplished what Larry did. The Gateway, an outdoor mall complex, grew nearby. The restaurants and services appeared. Property values shot up, and an area of serious blight got a big kick forward.

About a year after the arena was completed and the Jazz were now solidly the long-term pride of our town, I found myself talking to David Stern on one of his trips to Salt Lake City. David and I reminisced about the details behind Larry's bold move. Stern admitted that he was not optimistic about the project, that not even Larry could make it work, and that the Jazz would unfortunately reside elsewhere.

We smiled at each other, as if we were trying to copy Larry's grin, and said almost simultaneously, "Never underestimate Larry Miller."

DROPOUT

Grant Cannon

It makes me sick to think that the smartest person I've ever known is spending his time working in a gas station when he could be going to college. What a waste of a great mind. These were my thoughts about my good friend Larry Miller as I was preparing to start at the University of Utah following high school.

I had known Larry since kindergarten. We lived in the same Salt Lake neighborhood growing up. He seemed to be a typical kid, with one exception: he was completely *consumed* in his passion for things he liked and felt no remorse for ignoring the events that didn't stimulate his interests. This was tolerable in elementary school when we were playing at recess, but it wreaked havoc with the teachers who tried to guide a class and with his parents at home.

In the fourth grade, Larry would bring a novel to class to read while the teacher taught. It seemed like he spent more time in the principal's office than in the classroom. In spite of this, he was able to learn the material and pass the exams. I marveled at how in the world he was able to get away with it all. I had always been taught to respect my elders and people in authority; it made me feel very uneasy whenever Larry was about to get in trouble. It seemed most teachers and administrators at school were aware of Larry's potential and extraordinary IQ, and they tried to understand him and channel his passion in a positive manner. As peers, we just weren't aware of it. He was simply one of the guys.

The boys in our neighborhood were competitive, and baseball was a particularly favorite sport. We didn't have a ball diamond in our neighborhood, so we would go to the capitol grounds to play. There was a triangular piece of property on the west side of the Utah State Capitol that we used for a baseball field. The only problem was that we had no backstop or fence, and it paralleled Main Street, so we were constantly chasing balls into traffic and dodging cars. Finally, our mothers went to the city council on our behalf and convinced them to build us a small baseball field on property just north of the capitol building.

We had several great players, and most of us lived in the same LDS ward, so it was only natural to put together a fastpitch softball team to play in church tournaments. We had a dilemma, though. We didn't have a softball pitcher. That problem presented an opportunity for Larry, who took it upon himself to learn how to pitch softball, which was a different motion than in baseball. With the same mania that brought him success playing marbles as a youngster, he was driven to conquer pitching softball as a teen. He would convince us to catch for him for hours on end. When we weren't available, he would throw the ball against the wall, over and over.

Within a year, Larry was a well-respected softball pitcher. He led our team to a fifth-place finish one year and to third place another time in the young men's All-Church Softball Tournament, which included teams from all over the country.

But Larry wasn't satisfied with just playing church ball. He participated in county recreation leagues and eventually moved up into the big leagues of softball, launching a part-time career. Eventually, he was inducted into the International Softball Congress Hall of Fame.

With time, our lives drifted in different directions. That was especially true when Gail entered the picture. One day after our careers were well underway, Larry invited me to see the new basketball arena he was building to house the Utah Jazz. I met him after work just before the roof was to be placed on the new Delta Center. We climbed up the steps to the top of the upper bowl, which didn't have any chairs installed yet, and sat on the cement. I was flabbergasted as Larry told me the story of getting the financing for the stadium. I was amazed that he knew every detail of the financial world and building industry, including how many cubic yards of cement went here and how much rebar went there. He knew everything about the building in great detail—things that only a contractor would normally comprehend. Larry understood it all.

While we chatted, I was astonished at the level of debt Larry was taking on with a young NBA team and with financing a new arena.

"How are you able to sleep at night!?" I asked.

His simple answer shocked me.

"I've been poor before and survived," Larry said, "so I could be poor again."

It wasn't money that brought him fulfillment. It was accomplishing something that only a few special people have the ambition, daring, and drive to pursue. At that point, I realized just how wrong my impression from long ago had been. This was not the waste of a great mind. It was the manifestation of what true genius coupled with a driving desire can accomplish.

LESSONS FROM
AN IRATE CUSTOMER

Dave Hoer

Larry came by my store to chat one afternoon. He would often stop by after teaching at BYU or speaking at Utah Valley University. This day, he had driven his blue Cobra.

"It keeps me humble to drive an old car—helps me remember my roots!" he would joke.

As he was parking, a group of three young men gathered around the car, obviously enamored by the classic. Larry calmly got out of the Cobra, showed them a crisp $50 bill, and promptly tore it in half! He gave them one half of the note.

"I'll give you the other half when I come out—if no one touches the car, including you," he told them.

We visited for a short while, and then Larry went over to the window to have a look outside. The boys were physically screening people away from the car with outstretched arms. He laughed and said he had better go save them. He went out and gave them the other half of the $50, as promised, and drove off with a little squeal of the tires, to the delight of the boys.

Larry enjoyed making people smile. Every time he would call my office, he had a peculiar way of identifying himself before he was transferred to my phone.

"Just tell him it's an irate customer!" he'd joke.

I would know immediately who was calling, but my employees

rarely caught on. I would answer the phone to his laughter. Larry seemed to find joy in shaking me up a little.

I first met Larry and Gail in 1992 as a young twenty-nine-year-old entrepreneur. I was the owner of American Coin and HUR Jewelers in Orem, Utah. I had made a name as an expert in copper coins, particularly Indian cents and two-cent pieces. Out of nowhere, I received a phone call from a person identifying himself as Larry Miller. He said he had been doing some research, and everyone was telling him he needed to talk to me.

I thought it was a prank call. He assured me he was indeed Larry Miller and was interested in putting together a set of certified Indian cents. The next day, Larry and Gail came down to the store. It was after closing time. My wife and kids were there. While we talked coins, Gail must have been a little bored. She played "Ring around the Rosie" again and again with my little girls. I was mortified, but they had a blast. Gail said it was like watching kids in the nursery at church again. Larry just laughed.

Gail and Larry became very real people in that moment. Celebrity and public persona were gone. They became instant friends. I have always cherished that memory, as have my daughters.

That was the beginning of a special relationship with Larry Miller. Although we discussed business some of the time, I felt that it was more of an escape of sorts for him to just talk about coins or cars or life. I was naturally drawn to those individuals who were successful in their business ventures. I viewed Larry as the prime example of how to do it right. I was in the habit of "picking his brain," as he called it. He would tell me, "If you want to succeed at something, ask the person who did it, not the one who failed."

There are always plenty of people who can tell you how to fail, how *they* failed. He would surprise me with how candid he was concerning the cost of his success. As we visited one day, I mentioned that I was considering expanding my business ventures. He stood up out of his chair, putting both hands flat on my desk.

"Get a piece of paper," he said.

Larry then drew a line down the middle. He told me to write

down my business goals and aspirations on one side and what was truly important to me in life on the other. As I wrote, I could see that Larry was somewhat emotional. He pointed straight at me, leaning over the desk, and asked what I was willing to sacrifice on the right hand to succeed on the left.

"Success never comes without a price," he said. "By the choices you make, you determine the cost."

He went on to talk about his family and children and how much he felt he "missed out" on much of what he knew now was so important. He asked me to consider the question posed in 3 Nephi, "What manner of men ought ye to be?" (3 Nephi 27:27).

"What is truly important to you? What are you willing to give up? Your time? Your family? Your faith?" If not, he begged me to reconsider my business goals.

"*This* is what really matters," he said, pointing to my paper. "Listen to me, David. Don't be like me."

I was speechless.

I wanted to be like him. Here was my business idol, whom I greatly admired. Here was my mentor, my friend, with tears in his eyes, pouring out his soul.

So, of course, I followed his advice. It was clear that Gail and his family were truly important to Larry.

Years after I'd made a beautiful diamond ring for their anniversary, Larry was determined to get an exact duplicate made of a pearl ring he'd given to her.

There must have been some great significance to this ring. I recall it was special to Gail because Larry had given it to her early in their marriage. Now it was lost. Larry would admit that he seldom gave Gail much in the way of jewelry.

In an effort to duplicate the pearl ring, he brought in old photos, close-up images, detailed drawings and specifications. He was on a mission. We custom made patterns for his inspection.

"It has to be exactly the same!" he kept saying.

Weeks later, we finally had it right. Larry was almost giddy with excitement. I had never seen him like this. "Gail is going to love it!" he beamed. Apparently, she did. The last time I saw Gail, she was wearing the pearl ring.

I will be forever grateful to Larry for his direct, yet kind, guiding words. Over a decade has passed, but I have not made a single major decision without asking myself and my wife, "What is truly important?"

Not a day goes by that I don't miss my friend.

Details

Jim Brown

P eople who know some of the lore and legend about working for
Larry Miller are often curious to hear my perspective. They've heard
about Larry's idiosyncrasies, manias, and intensity, and they want to
know more.

What was he really like? Was the job extremely demanding?
How could I keep pace and meet expectations? They're fair questions. Working closely with Larry brought some challenges, especially
as a young general manager. But Larry had a lighthearted side, too,
and often used his humor and playfulness to teach the importance of
attending to even small details that he believed added up to success
or failure.

Early on, I ran the Chevrolet store in Murray, working in the
same building where Larry had his office. He would notice minute
details and point them out to me and then follow up to see where I
was in the process of correcting them.

It wasn't quite what I expected from my CEO. I had envisioned
having conversations about big-picture items, such as overall staff-
ing or total inventory dollar amounts or perhaps the net profit on
the financial statements. I knew Larry was a numbers fanatic, so
maybe we'd engage in high-level conversations about forecasting
sales volume or profit figures.

None of that happened from a big-picture perspective.

If he asked about vehicle inventory, it was about one specific model series and how many of that particular model we had in stock. It was important to Larry that you knew at the time of the discussion, without having to rely on guesses or broad ranges. If he asked how many new units you sold yesterday and you answered with the total sales of new and used combined, he would be frustrated. I learned to listen to the question and answer it specifically without delving further. (I've adopted this practice elsewhere in my life, including with my kids, who say it drives them crazy.)

While working in the same building as Larry, I learned how important it was to him that everything on the lot was clean and orderly. He called me one afternoon and asked me to meet him outside in four minutes. The instructions were specific, almost as if I were being sent on a highly sensitive mission: I was to meet him on the south side of the dealership, at the entrance nearest the parts department. He was never vague on directions. I met with him at that precise place and moment, and he then asked me to look at the trash receptacle. It was the type that held sand at the top for extinguished cigarettes.

He said, "Well, what do you think?"

I looked all around for trash that may have fallen out. I circled twice. I knew I had to look for the smallest of details. I crouched down and asked Larry to join me so he could see what I was seeing. He could tell I was missing the obvious as I leaned close to the sand.

"There are far too many cigarettes in that area!" he finally exclaimed.

"You mean the cigarettes here in the sand, where they are supposed to be?" I retorted. He seemed unmoved by my counter, so I waved for him to step closer and look at the way they were arranged in the fine sand. "Have you ever noticed that cigarette smokers don't just place their butts in a random pattern?" I said. "They put them in rows like crops of corn, in perfect symmetry."

This drew a laugh from Larry, who thankfully moved on. But the message was received, and I took care of what Larry viewed as the excess butts.

That very next winter, Larry called me and opened the conversation with what almost seemed like a riddle: "Jim? This is Larry. Your window of opportunity is closing!" I wasn't sure which window of opportunity he meant, and when I asked, he simply answered with another question. "Do you know at what temperature snow melts?"

"32.1 degrees," I answered confidently.

"And what temperature is it outside?"

"Thirty-four degrees?" I ventured.

"It is thirty-five degrees!" He proceeded to explain that the snow banks left by my plow were too large, and they were taking away valuable space that could be used for customer parking or inventory display. I told Larry that I already had a remedy in place: I had contracted to have the snow piles removed that very evening by a front-end loader and a dump truck for only two hundred dollars.

"That's way too expensive," he said. "What you need to do is take your plows and break down the snow piles. Spread it two and a half inches thick the width of the service drive from the entrance all the way to State Street."

Confused, I asked, "Wait, you want me to put the snow *back* to the same place I just removed it from?"

"You are missing the point! Snow melts in thirty-five-degree weather, and if you spread it out before the temperatures fall, the vehicles coming in will trample it down and make it melt!"

I saved two hundred dollars that day, and I got my first experience with *un*plowing snow.

It wasn't my last experience with Larry's unique brand of management. Even when I moved across the street to the Lexus dealership, I was still under Larry's watchful eye. He called me one afternoon and asked if I had a mobile phone. I said yes, and he replied, "Great. Walk to the north side of the lot and call me back. I'll give further instructions."

Like a kid on a treasure hunt, I complied with this first directive and called him back. "Okay, now walk one hundred paces directly north of where you are standing," he told me. It was obvious now that he was watching me and enjoying the game. I counted every step out loud as I went, which made him laugh quietly as I carried out the instructions.

I kept counting: " . . . ninety-nine . . . one hundred. I am here."

"Do you see that light pole you're standing directly underneath?" he said, revealing the end of my scavenger hunt. "It has two lights, one on the north side and another on the south. The south side light bulb is out. Do you think you could get it replaced sometime soon?"

I had plenty of these playful moments with Larry. But he could also move from playful to a whole other set of emotions at lightning speed. If you weren't aware or prepared, you could be caught quite off guard. You had to be on your toes with Larry, but it was nice to know you could expect an unfiltered take and know exactly where you stood.

That's what it was like working for Larry. Yes, it was intense, and detail-focused, and at times stressful. But I felt proud to be a part of his team and to carry out what was most important to Larry in my day-to-day work.

MY FIRST SCOOP

Chris Thomas

At the ripe old age of twelve, I experienced my first watershed moment—a significant experience that set in motion a series of events that would have an indelible impact on my life's passion, education, career, and future.

I vividly remember every detail of when I arrived home from school and first turned on the radio—from the sloppy peanut butter sandwich, to the cold glass of milk dripping onto my faded Converse high-tops, to my eyes fixated on the microwave flashing 12:00 in the kitchen as I listened to the countertop radio.

"The Jazz are staying in Utah. The team has been saved. Car dealer Larry Miller has agreed to purchase half of the franchise," the distinctive voice of afternoon-drive personality Danny Kramer reverberated through the muffled speaker.

It is truly a miracle, I thought.

For several weeks, I had intently followed every development—watching the nightly news, listening to the radio, and even waking up early to be the first to read the latest headlines before folding and delivering newspapers in my neighborhood.

For me, the prospect of the Jazz leaving Utah was akin to my best friend moving to Omaha. The situation had grown so bleak that my parents had begun to prepare me during countless discussions after school and at the dinner table for what appeared to be

31

the inevitable. Utah would lose its major league franchise. The small market team, the little guy, was about to be quashed, leaving in its wake no chance for legitimacy or any type of redemption for generations to come.

For me, the likelihood of the Jazz leaving Utah represented the loss of something even greater. That explained why upon hearing the news, instead of jumping or screaming or dancing around the room, I hurried to dial 4-6-7-4-0-1-4 on our beige rotary phone.

"Grandpa, did you hear? Did you hear the news?"

Watching Adrian Dantley, Mark Eaton, Darrell Griffith, and "The Fastest of Them All" Rickey Green; listening to Hot Rod and debating the nuances of the game helped forge a special bond with my father and my grandfather that only comes from the shared experience of sports.

"Grandpa," I interrupted as he tried to respond. "We have to go to the game tonight. My dad is working. I'll pay for the tickets with my paper route money. Grandpa, can you believe this? When can you pick me up? The game is sure to sell out and we have to be there. Grandpa . . ."

My grandfather had taken me to my first Jazz game when the team moved to Utah from New Orleans in 1979. We watched games when they were televised on KSL and listened on the radio to Hot Rod painting a vibrant picture—with his "leapin' leaners," "frozen ropes," and "cowhide globes hitting home."

While my grandfather drove us to the Salt Palace that evening in his late-model pickup truck, the wheels in his head began turning. Grandpa was passionate about learning and was always looking for an opportunity to creatively expand his grandchildren's horizons.

"You're a reporter, aren't you?" he quizzed. "Ready for your assignment?"

"Not really, Grandpa," I responded. "I have only written a few stories about teachers, hot lunches, and assemblies. That's all we write about. The school paper doesn't cover sports."

"Well, maybe it's about time it does," he retorted.

At the next stoplight, Grandpa opened the glove compartment,

32

pulled out a small notebook, and handed it to me along with a ball-point pen.

"Tonight, if you agree to be on assignment, I'll pay for the tickets."

"It's a deal," I said, somewhat reluctantly.

I took careful notes at the game, especially when announcer Dan Roberts enthusiastically introduced Larry Miller and then when Sam Battistone, the previous Jazz owner, threw him the game ball. I tried to capture the sight and the emotion in words. It was challenging. At the same time, I saw the event through a new lens.

When we returned home, my grandfather had me recount my experience and review the largely illegible notes with my parents.

"I have an idea," my mother interjected. "Why don't you call tomorrow and interview Larry Miller for your story?"

"That would be cool," I said enthusiastically, "but I don't think he has time to talk with a twelve-year-old kid. He just bought the Jazz and has a lot of work to do."

The developments of the day were underscored by the fact that Larry Miller had been a longstanding example to our family of the value of hard work. My father grew up in a neighborhood a few miles west of Larry's. My uncle Joe played on one of Larry's softball teams. I remember my father pointing out Larry's dealership and telling the story of how he built his success. Any time there was a Larry H. Miller Toyota ad on TV or the radio, my parents and grandfather would remind me that with hard work anything was possible. The fact the Jazz had been saved by Larry further illustrated their point and, more important, elevated Larry to hero status in my mind.

Early the next morning, my mother helped me find the dealership's phone number and coached me on what to say. The call rang through. I was petrified. I stumbled through the script once and then was transferred to Larry's secretary. I tried again. This time, my voice cracked a little less, and I was mostly coherent.

"What is your name again? Who do you write for?" his secretary asked. "Wait. How old are you?"

I answered her questions, and then she said, "I'll see what I can do and call you back."

"At least she didn't say no," I explained to my mom.

The vigil started. I sat on the kitchen floor guarding the area near the phone, refusing to get dressed or eat breakfast. I began drafting possible questions while listening to the radio and waiting for the phone to ring. A press conference to officially sign the deal had been scheduled for late morning, radio personality Tom Barberi reported.

As the minutes and then hours passed, I knew my chances were dwindling. Finally, the phone rang.

"Hello?" I answered somewhat abruptly.

"Did Larry Miller call you back?" Grandpa asked from the other end.

"No," I said with great intensity and a dose of preteen attitude in my voice. "You are tying up the line. He might be trying to call at this very moment."

As the morning dragged on, my mother suggested I get ready and go to school. She promised to come and get me immediately if Larry called. I adamantly refused.

Shortly before the press conference was scheduled to begin, the phone rang.

"Hello, this is Larry Miller. May I speak to Chris?"

I found myself in a state of shock even greater than when I had first heard the news the afternoon prior.

"Yes, this is he," I responded before becoming tongue tied.

"I understand you want to interview me for your school paper. What questions can I answer?"

"I'm sure you are really busy, so I'll be quick," I promised.

"Take your time," Larry said. "The other reporters can wait."

The interview lasted about ten minutes. After nervously reading a couple of questions about why he had purchased the Jazz, I began to feel a little more at ease. The interview slowly transformed into more of a conversation. As we were concluding, Larry informed me that my story was a "scoop."

34

"I gave you the first interview because you asked," Larry said. "Never forget the power of working hard, and don't be afraid to ask. You never know where it will get you in life."

This sage advice has served me well. The "scoop" resulted in my first cover story. It ignited in me a love of writing, journalism, and hard work. I continued to write, covering sports in high school and earning a journalism scholarship to attend Westminster College. Upon graduation, I worked in public relations and eventually ventured out and built my own communications firm.

In 2012, I became acquainted with Linda Luchetti, then senior vice president of communications for the Larry H. Miller Group of Companies. One afternoon while I was traveling, Linda and I were emailing back and forth about some PR issues the company had recently encountered. I told her I would jump at the opportunity to help her.

"I've actually been wanting to talk with you about hiring your firm," she responded. "How is your schedule for a meeting next week?"

I forwarded the email to my wife with the subject, "I think I am going to cry."

More than twenty-five years later, Larry's advice had not only served me well, but it had come full circle. What to Larry had most likely been an insignificant few minutes on the phone with a kid reporter was for me a life-changing event that has had a reciprocating effect.

While I have been very fortunate to work with many high-profile individuals, projects, and companies during my years in the communications arena, very few experiences have come close to matching the excitement and fulfillment of my first "scoop."

I will forever be grateful to Larry for his kind gesture. As a result, I frequently look for opportunities to follow his example and pay it forward.

EXCELLENCE

LARRY THE JESUIT

John Stockton

It was the mid-'80s; I was a young, quiet player just trying to make it in the NBA, and our financially struggling team had just taken on a new owner in the form of polo shirts and sneakers. We had just suffered a humiliating home court defeat to the L.A. Clippers—who weren't very good at the time. As we sat licking our wounds in the locker room, the entire team was startled by this sudden and terrible scream we heard from outside. We peeked out the door, and sure enough, it was the new owner coming at us. He charged into the locker room, huffing and puffing like a rhino, snorting with his arms crossed. I thought, *What kind of madman just stampeded into our lives?*

What I didn't know was what a blessing had just begun to grace our lives.

When I arrived in Utah in 1984, the world was pretty small. I didn't talk very much, and I didn't worry about much outside the basketball court lines of ninety-four feet by fifty feet. The Utah Jazz owner was Sam Battistone, a debonair and wonderful man in sharp suits who didn't say much himself. Sam was very much on the periphery, at least from my standpoint. He sat across from our bench with his family, and he certainly never came into the locker room. That made sense to me. I grew up with the understanding that the locker room was sacred ground that belonged to the players and coaches. Nobody else came in.

Soon, though, there was a new sheriff in town. Toward the end of my first professional season, Larry Miller became part owner of the team, and later he'd become a full owner, rescuing the team from possible relocation. But he had a different approach, and it wasn't something that was entirely comfortable at first.

Larry wanted to be in the locker room all the time. He was even on the court before the game, rebounding for the guys, giving suggestions and pumping us up for the game. He went out and played defense—*real* defense—while players did their pregame routines. He'd get his body up on players, bumping and fouling them a little bit, even trash talking. That was quite a bit different for me. I'm not sure I was excited at first about the way Larry stormed onto the scene.

A year or so later, it was time to renegotiate my contract. I hired an agent to do all the wrestling with the Jazz, but things were progressing slowly. So one day I called Larry, whom I still didn't know very well except that he was the guy who came out and gave me elbows during pregame warm-ups or who occasionally stormed around after a loss.

"Would you be interested in talking about the contract a little bit?" I asked.

"Sure," he said. "Come on in." I went to his office at his Chevy store, just to hear his terms and understand his thought process a little bit.

We talked for a couple of hours until finally he suggested, "Hey, John, why don't you write the number down that you think is fair? I'll do the same, and we'll exchange them, and we'll just see where we're at."

We each wrote down our numbers and then passed the papers across the table. As it happens, each was the same number, and just like that, the contract negotiation was over. I felt such a sense of relief to have it done. Just as important, I felt lucky to have crossed swords with this seasoned negotiator. In the time it took me to hand my paper across the table, he probably had the whole contract amortized out over four years in his head. He could have cut me to ribbons at any time, yet he didn't.

That was the first occasion when we spent significant time getting to know each other. It certainly wasn't the last. Our relationship grew naturally over time, and eventually he was a friend and a boss, a mentor and a leader.

From then on, I negotiated directly with Larry, and not just on financial terms. As I was advancing in my career, my kids were growing up, and I was worried about missing opportunities to do fun things with them due to the many restrictive clauses in the NBA contract. Because of injury risk, the uniform player contract says you can't skydive, white-water raft, or ski, among other things.

Finally, I said to Larry one day, "I want to be able to play with my kids without worrying about my contract being voided out." He asked what I wanted to do about it. "I want that fixed," I told him.

"Well," he said, "write it in."

I wrote a paragraph that went something like: "Mr. Stockton is heretofore authorized to participate in any activity, including waterskiing, snow skiing, skydiving, and the like, notwithstanding Paragraph 13, and pursuant to Part A of Paragraph 14, as long as it is with his kids."

Larry accepted it with a smile and sent that contract into the league.

As a practicing Catholic, one of the very oldest leadership models I've learned was developed by the Jesuits some 450 years ago. Every school I ever went to was founded by the Jesuit Order of Catholic Priests, and a 2005 book called *Heroic Leadership* does a great job describing the basic principles of leadership behind the world's largest religious order.

The first principle is self-awareness: know yourself within the worldview, and know where you fit into it. The second point is ingenuity: be creative, have new ideas. The third one is love and caring with a connection to community: recognize the potential in people and have faith in them. The final principle is heroic ambition: dare greatness and dream big, and believe you can do it.

As I reflect on Jesuit leadership and think back upon the life and career of my friend Larry, I realize he would have made one heck of a Jesuit priest. He's the epitome of leadership as defined by these principles.

First, he was very aware of his standing in the community. He was comfortable and confident with the responsibilities that came with that. Second, nobody can deny that he did things differently and better. His love for the community is unparalleled, and his commitment to believing in others and helping build bridges is unimpeachable. He did things with the goal of making people's lives better simply because he cared. And he was certainly a heroic and ambitious risk-taker who believed in the impossible and made it happen.

One time I asked Larry, "How do you get all this work done?"

He looked at me and he said, "I don't talk about it. I just do it. I just get it done."

I think that is his secret to success.

We didn't get a Jesuit out of Larry Miller, but we certainly got a peerless leader and a visionary man. Larry enriched the lives of countless people. He improved and enhanced the community and made life better for people. He achieved, taught, gave, and loved. I'm honored to have had Larry first as a rampaging boss and ultimately as a friend.

Beyond the Numbers

Clark Whitworth

Larry would always say to me, "If you don't measure it, you can't manage it." Precision was more important to Larry than to anyone else I ever knew, and he relied on numbers for almost everything. This was a lesson I learned early on when I first started working for Larry nearly thirty years ago.

I first came into contact with Larry in 1984, when I was working for one of his competitors, Rick Warner. I met Larry when my company wanted to set up a reinsurance division for our service contract business. Larry had already successfully done this within his own organization, so my boss asked if Larry would sit down with me to explain this process.

I knew right away that I was learning from an incredible, brilliant businessman and a gifted, talented person in general. Larry was clearly willing to be a teacher. We sat and shared our experiences, and he offered me his know-how about setting up a reinsurance company, despite my working for a competitor.

While we were talking, Larry said to me, "It's really great because I can even do mortgages."

I laughed a little and replied, "Well, that's interesting because I'm looking for a mortgage."

To my surprise, he said, "Great. I'll do you a mortgage."

"I also am in the building process, and I need a construction loan," I added, not thinking he'd take me seriously.

"I'll do that, too. Here is my card. Call my assistant and get this set up."

Needless to say, I was overwhelmed at the generosity of this man, offering me not only trade secrets into his business but also helping me with a personal favor.

I worked for Warner for another two years and then went looking for opportunities elsewhere. Larry knew I'd been looking, and one day he called me to say, "Why don't you try looking at this project with me?"

"Great!" I replied. So I came and met with him. I dove straight in and started doing evaluations for the Top Stop convenience stores. During this project, Larry offered me a job doing additional special consulting.

I came to work for him full time, and it was always interesting to see how Larry understood numbers. Not only did he calculate them, but in a way, he could "feel" them. That was very different for me. Numbers helped Larry make some of his best decisions. He understood what it took to sell a car, what had happened in his stores the day before, how many customer were seen, and more. He understood what each of these numbers meant—the stories behind each one and everything it took to arrive at that number.

He could understand the needs and emotions of the person on the other side of every negotiation he ever made. Being fair was important to him. He wanted to understand not only how something was being done but why it was being done. And he carried his integrity throughout his actions. Numbers and negotiations never compromised how he felt about humankind.

This proved to be true when relocating the Utah Jazz's home court from the Salt Palace to the Delta Center. When the arena was finally completed, it turns out that someone from the county uncovered some breakage fee in the lease between the Jazz and the Salt Palace. It totaled around three hundred thousand dollars, but Larry went ahead and quietly paid the fee to the county. It was important for him to honor his agreements.

Larry would always throw everything he had into his work, and he wanted to make sure no one could ever question his character. He would give 110 percent all the time. Tasks were great to him. Accomplishments were great to him. They brought him joy.

In the case of building the arena, Larry cared primarily about how the Jazz impacted the community and never wanted to burden the public. All his financial advisers counseled him against building it, but Larry had a plan and knew that it would work. He had a feel for the numbers of seats that could be sold, the number of suites he could lease, and so on.

I'll be the first to admit that Larry wasn't always easy to work for—he demanded a lot of people's time and would often criticize others for taking vacations. It wasn't his intent to dominate in such a way; it's just that most minds don't operate with the same focus that he had. However, that's not to say he wasn't thoughtful of others. The best way Larry often showed he cared was when he would simply talk to someone and ask about that person's life. When it came to both numbers and people, for Larry, the complexity was always getting to the simplicity.

He also had a very humanizing spiritual side. Larry belonged to my same faith, and he would often confide to me, "Clark, some mornings when I pray, by the time I get done I've already perspired so much that I have to change my shirt." I believe that he often wrestled with the Lord. But as much as he had faith, it never affected him how he dealt with different types of people. They were all the same to him. He didn't look down on anyone. He saw beyond the image of a person, much like he saw beyond the image of a number, and looked for the story behind each one.

After Larry passed, I once found myself holding the last balance sheet that Larry ever completed, which led to a very spiritual experience for me. It was sheet number 339, completed right before he had his heart attack. To this day, it still serves as a reminder to me to always look at the bigger picture behind what each number says on paper. Larry taught me that there is spirituality in everything.

I'm not the same person I was when I first started with this company. My knowledge and understanding then compared to what I know now is entirely different—for the better. And I know that the reason I'm not the same person is because of my interaction with Larry.

YOU KNOW THIS GUY

Scott Anderson

In the early 2000s, the Larry H. Miller dealerships were running a heavy schedule of TV and radio advertisements with the tagline, "After all, you know this guy." And the truth of the matter is that most people in Utah, and particularly the Salt Lake Valley, did know Larry. If they didn't know him personally, he was certainly among the most recognizable people in our community. In fact, evidence of the reach of Larry's influence wasn't limited to our state or even our country.

Several years ago I traveled with my wife, Jesselie, and our three children to Africa. Amidst the African wildlife of elephants, hippos, cheetahs, leopards, flamingos, and lions, and the beautiful Great Rift Valley and Lake Naivasha, we were introduced to the fascinating people and culture of the Maasai tribe. We conversed through an interpreter with a Maasai warrior, and he learned that we were guests from Utah. Without hesitation he nearly shouted, "Do you know Utah Jazz?" Here we stood nine thousand miles from home, in the middle of the remote East African wild, and people knew about Larry's Jazz.

The reach and legacy of Larry are seen far and wide. We all see the impact locally as we drive around town—from dealerships to movie theaters to the Utah Jazz, the Salt Lake Bees, and the Miller Motorsports Park, Energy*Solutions* Arena, and countless other projects that bear his fingerprints. However, we don't often fully appreciate the impact of his reach across the world in creating a positive image for the state of Utah. The advertisements weren't exaggerating: even in places as far away as South Kenya, people knew this guy.

Nevertheless, even at the height of this "You know this guy" media barrage, Larry encountered a Zions Bank employee who bucked the norm and apparently didn't "know this guy." As president and CEO of the bank, I heard about this story later from Larry himself.

One afternoon, Larry pulled up to the drive-thru window of the Zions Bank office in Murray. The office is located on the same street as the flagship Toyota dealership that started the Larry H. Miller empire of dealerships, as well as several other dealerships that bear his name. When he presented a check to the drive-thru teller, she asked him for identification. He realized that he had left his wallet at the office, but he was certain the young teller would recognize who he was and would complete the transaction.

The teller maintained that Larry needed to present identification before she could cash his check. Larry responded by saying, "If you look out the west window of your branch you can probably see my picture in the advertising on the windows of my dealership." Yet, the new teller stuck to procedure and insisted that Larry needed the proper identification to cash the check.

Frustrated and slightly embarrassed, Larry retrieved his check from the teller and said he would return with the requested identification. He did return a short time later with a copy of his driver's license and a full-page newspaper ad featuring his picture and the tagline, "After all, you know this guy."

Larry shared this experience with me shortly thereafter, and we shared a laugh. I was slightly embarrassed that our employee hadn't recognized one of the state's most recognizable faces, but Larry simply congratulated me on the thoroughness of our fraud prevention training.

Interestingly, the reason Larry even shared the story with me was to come clean on something. In his frustration and haste to leave the bank's drive-thru, he momentarily lost focus and drove his truck over the curbing. He did a bit of damage to the underside of his car, but fortunately knew a good service department who could repair it for him. But in case there was any damage to the curbing and landscaping, Larry reached out to me to offer to take care of any repair costs.

Larry's unwavering honesty was one of the things I loved about him. He was committed to being truthful, as he was in 2007 when I presented Larry with a gift.

Larry and Gail had just established the Miller Scholarship at Utah's Waterford School to be provided to an upper-school student who exemplifies a commitment to family, community, and learning. At the time of the establishment of this scholarship, an event was held to pay tribute to Larry and Gail. To help show our appreciation to Larry for all he had done for Waterford, I commissioned a painting of Larry's family ranch in Idaho. The artist, Ken Baxter, visited the ranch and completed much of the beautiful oil painting on-site to ensure he accurately captured the image and the feel of the ranch.

As I proudly presented the painting to Larry, he thoroughly examined it from one side to the other. He was admiring the beauty of the painting but also noticing some details. "This is a beautiful painting," he said, "but it's not my ranch. I know exactly where this ranch is, but, it's not my ranch."

He then expressed deep gratitude for the thoughtful and personal gift. Where many would have just silently accepted the gift and never disclosed my error in identifying the location, Larry's commitment to honesty wouldn't let him do that. He was unfalteringly honest, even at times when others might rationalize that it was okay to say nothing at all.

Larry did express his appreciation and commented on how

much he loved the gift. That painting, despite depicting someone else's ranch, still hangs in the Miller home today.

I am grateful for the opportunities I had to get a small glimpse into Larry Miller's reach, influence, and integrity.

After all, I knew this guy.

THE PASSENGER

Greg Miller

When I was about six years old, a stranger approached my father in a downtown Salt Lake City parking lot, asking for a ride. I don't recall much of what this stranger looked like, except that he had a beard and reminded me of a lumberjack. He wasn't someone I was necessarily afraid of, but he wasn't the type of stranger I wanted to ride with, either.

But my dad did this man one better: he didn't give him a lift—he lent him a car for an entire day! In this day and age, something like this would seem crazy, but my dad had a big heart and always wanted to help others.

He helped me throughout my entire life, and sometimes he left his biggest impressions without realizing it. The day before I married my sweetheart, Heidi, I went over to my parents' house in Sandy to mow their lawn. As I was walking the mower down the driveway to start cutting the front grass, I heard the roar of an engine. I looked up and saw my dad driving his cherished blue 427 Cobra. He pulled into the driveway, looked at me, and said, "Are you busy?"

"Not anymore!" I replied, instantly forgetting about the lawn.

With him at the wheel, we drove up to Wasatch Boulevard, overlooking the Salt Lake Valley. As we neared the freeway, he suddenly pulled over. At first I wondered if the car was overheating or something. But then he looked over at me and said, "Don't burn your legs on the exhaust pipe when you get out."

What he was really saying was, "Your turn to drive, son." For the first time, Dad would ride in the passenger seat.

I shifted the car into gear and drove us up through Emigration Canyon all the way north to Morgan, Utah. It was the most special day I'd ever spent with my dad. For once, he didn't have any kind of agenda and wasn't out to teach me anything. It was just the two of us in his car. Although he didn't state it specifically, it was his way of letting me know that I was grown up and about to start my own journey. On the way home, we stopped at my soon-to-be in-laws, and he let me take each of them for a ride. Not only did I get to spend a little quality time with my father on that day, but he also let me know that he trusted me with a car he'd spared no expense in restoring.

I continued working for my father after I was married. I'll be the first to admit that Dad wasn't always the easiest person to work for, mainly because he wanted to do everything himself. He loved his company dearly and wanted to make sure everything ran the way he thought it should. I think he had a hard time trusting others to do the job for him.

Sometimes he'd call me and say, "Greg, I need you to call so-and-so about X and Y. Call me when you have that handled."

So I'd hang up the phone and dial the number. No answer. I would leave a message, and within a few minutes they'd call back to say, "Sorry I couldn't talk to you. I was on the phone with your dad. He was asking about X and Y."

It's how he ran things. If he'd had it his way, he would have torn every ticket at every usher stand at the stadium and theater, handled every concession order, sold every single car personally, and turned the wrench on every auto we repaired. Eventually, this hands-on approach and his heavy work schedule took its toll on his physical health. This is when I began to transition to running the company as CEO.

Near the end of his life, when his physical condition deterio-rated, he was hospitalized for fifty-nine days, and many of his man-agers were uncomfortable making decisions because he'd always made them. It was an atmosphere with a lot of anxiety and frustra-tion. So I started prioritizing decisions, and I started saying, "Okay, you do what you think is best on this one." We just started working through it, and eventually the logjam broke. That was the period when I learned that delegation is an important aspect to running a company and balancing work with a personal life.

I think my ability to navigate this situation stemmed from one of the greatest lessons my dad ever taught me: the importance of making a decision. When I was young and we were still living in Colorado, I was at softball practice with him. Practice was heating up, and my dad handed me a quarter and asked me to buy him a Coke at the vending machine. But when I put the quarter in, I saw the orange light on the button that indicated the Cokes were all sold out. So I did what I thought was the next best thing: I bought him a Tab.

He wasn't happy. "I don't want a Tab!" he yelled, telling me what an idiot I was. Of course it hurt my feelings, as I was just a kid, but on the drive home he turned to me and said, "You know, I owe you an apology. You at least made a decision, which is more than I can say for most adults I know."

That moment still reminds me of the importance of being decisive and moving things forward. My father taught me many of these lessons. For example, I spend a lot more time with my children and grandchildren than he was able to. I want them to understand the significance of the sacrifices he made to build this incredible foundation that blesses the lives of so many, particularly our family.

My father didn't give me a lot of material possessions, but when he passed away, he left me that 427 Cobra. The car is now on display at Miller Motorsports Park, and each time I see it, I have that same special feeling of the day when he finally let me drive. It helps me to remember him not as a businessman, but as my father, a man who let his heart guide him and who always put others first. Whenever I think of the acts of kindness he performed throughout his lifetime, I'm as awestruck today as I was when I was just six years old.

The Number of Happiness

Steve Starks

We have a lot of people with gray hair in our company. I'd like to build the bench so that we have people to step in and take over when the people with gray hair decide to move on."

That's the most specific Larry ever got when he hired me to work for him in February of 2007. He didn't talk about money. He didn't talk about a specific position or job duties. He only said that he'd love to have me join the organization and that my primary duty was to show up at nine o'clock on the Monday that we'd agreed on. He said that I would work with him directly, and through that process, I'd get to know the company and the people within it, and over time my natural position would emerge.

That's how Larry operated. I'd met him in the fall of 2004 when we'd worked together on the transition team for Utah's incoming governor, Jon Huntsman Jr. Larry was one of the community leaders involved in that process, and I was immediately impressed by how approachable he seemed to be. I felt like he was as genuinely interested in conversations with me as he was with anybody, regardless of their status or standing in the community. He was a real person.

Larry later became the chairman of the board that hired me to help improve the way state government was being operated. For two years I reported to Larry. We became more familiar with each other, and when I started applying to business schools, I asked if he would write me a letter of recommendation.

He agreed to, but he also proposed an alternate path for me, which was to come work for the Group. We met for what I would later discover was a typical Larry lunch; it lasted two and a half hours, during which he spent a lot of time explaining the history of the organization and the culture and a lot of the philosophies behind the business and how all of it came to be.

At the end, he made me the offer to show up and start working. No discussion of salary, title, or responsibilities.

I arrived on that Monday in February 2007. The receptionist had no idea who I was. Larry got off the elevator and greeted me and asked me to follow him to his office. He just opened his brief-case on his desk and began to check messages.

After about half an hour, he took me around the tenth floor, popping in and out of individual offices as he introduced me to people. Usually, employees came to Larry, not the other way around, so I think they were as surprised to look up and see Larry as they were to find out that I'd been hired.

After about two weeks on the job, I asked Larry about my salary. My wife and I had been married only six months, and although I trusted that Larry wasn't going to put us in a situation to fail, money was certainly on our minds. I said, "Larry, we never had a chance to talk about compensation. How should I go about doing that?"

That question led to one of the best conversations I've ever had on the topic of money, and it taught me more about compensation and what matters in life than any other conversation. He asked how much I had been making and what my goals were. He gave me a number. Then, he just started to talk philosophically.

"You know," he said, "I've discovered in life that when you make enough money to provide for your family, to put a little bit in savings so that you can replace the refrigerator when it goes out, and you have a little bit of money to take your family on vacation, that is the stage where you are getting as much enjoyment from money as you're ever going to get. Everything above that, while it may make you more comfortable in life, it doesn't add to your enjoyment at all."

After our conversation about salary, Larry told me to go introduce myself to Lynda Jeppesen, the vice president of human resources. He said, "Tell her that this is what we've talked about, and this is how much you'll make, and this is what you'll be doing."

The next day, I went to Lynda and introduced myself and said I'd been hired and told her how much I was making. She was kind of taken aback. I think she wanted to say, "Excuse me?" But she was very polite. She said, "Have you filled out an application?"

"I have not filled out an application."

"Do you have a job description?" she asked.

I described my job based on how much I knew about it. She got everything together and tried to throw together a quick employee orientation for me. I was now officially an employee.

For the next several months, I would just follow Larry throughout the day and go to meetings with him. It was a chance to observe a true genius at work. It was fascinating, although he had so many things going on inside his head that it was hard to always follow how he got to a conclusion. To me, it didn't feel very linear. As I came to understand him better, I realized that he could see things along the way so much quicker than I could. He saw things that I didn't even know existed. He would skip to that point, whereas I had to have the foundation to get to that point.

Larry also didn't carry a cellphone. He would sit at his desk and call people from memory. He would try them at their office. If the office line didn't work, he'd try their mobile. If that didn't work, he would dial their home phone number. All from memory. One day, after working with him for about eight months, I said, "Larry, how many phone numbers do you think you have memorized?"

He said, "You know, that's a good question. I have to think about it."

The next day, he said, "I thought about your question, and I think it's about 270."

He cared about knowing things that I took for granted. A lot of that was because he didn't use computers, but part of it, I think, was because he wanted to master something so well. And he truly mastered the details. His company, especially in the early days, wasn't left to chance. He understood the details so well that it wasn't a guessing game for him. He knew what would work, and he put those systems in place and surrounded himself with very good people who never let off the gas.

And he certainly never let off the gas, right up until the end. In February 2009, two years after I'd come to work for him, Larry called me on a Monday morning at around nine o'clock and said that he was passing away that week. "This is it," he said.

"What do you mean, *this is it?*" I said.

"I'm passing away," he said.

Larry wanted me to gather the advisory board and meet at the hospital at ten thirty that morning.

You're never prepared to hear those words, but I was able to convey how I felt about him and express my gratitude. It was very personal to me. He had taken the time to get to know me, as someone in his twenties who didn't have great credentials, or pedigree, or any worldly standing at all. But Larry took time to get to know me and took a risk on me. I was truly grateful and I expressed that to him.

At the end of the conversation, Larry said, "Before you hang up, do you have the booked and boarded reports?" He wanted to know how the dealerships had done over the weekend.

"Yes, I have them," I said.

"Okay," he said. "Tell me the numbers."

MEETING THE MAN BEHIND THE LEGEND

Greg Johnson

Unlike many employees of the Larry H. Miller companies, I learned about the Group by working for it. I didn't know who Larry Miller was when I joined his team in Boulder, Colorado, in 1992, and I didn't get to meet him for another five years.

I imagine that Larry Miller was already a recognizable name in Salt Lake City by 1992, but not in Nebraska, where I grew up and went to school. That's where my automotive career had started, but then I started looking to branch out. I had sent some résumés out to dealerships around the region, and at one point was actually on my way to interview in Arizona, when Darrell Wells called me. Darrell was a partner of Larry's at Boulder Toyota and had received my résumé. I figured I would stop by on my way to Arizona for a quick interview in Boulder. I ended up really liking Darrell, so I went to work for Boulder Toyota. That's how I became a part of the Larry Miller Group.

For those first few years, I learned about Larry from other people. We would see his handwritten notes of appreciation every time we exceeded a performance target or set a new record for sales or service, and those were very important to us. But, beyond that, I knew little about him. In that sense, Larry was a bit of a man-behind-the-scenes figure. Because of that, stories of just how intense he was probably got blown out of proportion.

That reputation was in my mind when I finally went to meet Larry in 1997. I was being given an opportunity to possibly run the Lexus store in Salt Lake City, and part of the interview process for general managers was to sit down with Larry. I was nervous about meeting him; at that point he was more of a legend than anything, and the operations guys played into that. "Don't say anything stupid," they'd tease. That admonition was still in my head as I sat outside Larry's office waiting for him.

When I finally got in his office, I was amazed at how easy he was to talk to. He was obviously very intelligent, and I could tell he was sizing me up a bit, but I was quickly put at ease during our casual conversation.

One of the questions that stood out from that conversation was when he asked me what he could do to help me be a more effective leader in the store. Considering everything I'd heard, I said, "I'll do my best work if you don't yell at me, if you just kind of coach me and send me in the right direction." I knew things would come up, but I wanted us to be able to talk through any issues.

"Okay," he said. "I can deal with that." In hindsight, this was probably a somewhat unfair request. I was asking him to operate outside of how he'd normally act. Asking him not to be an emotional leader was like asking him not to be Larry. That's what he was all about. But he respected the request, and he kept the promise . . . except for one time.

There was a time when sport-utility vehicles were in short supply and hard to get. I wanted to find one for my dad to purchase at a discount, but I didn't feel right using one of mine, taking away the opportunity for the store to make a profit. So I reached out to a regional manager I had become friends with and we went outside, bringing a vehicle in from outside the region, all the way from Cincinnati.

When Larry found out about this, he called me and really let me have it. He was steaming hot. I tried to come back and explain that I had gone well outside the region, that it was an extra vehicle, and that I hadn't even sold it for too steep a discount. Larry didn't want to hear any of that. He was very upset, and we didn't talk for a few weeks after. He just didn't call me, and I certainly wasn't going to call him.

Soon after, we were at the general managers' leadership conference in Hawaii, and Larry pulled me aside. "I'm really sorry," he said. "I made you a deal that I wouldn't manage you that way. I went the wrong way." Obviously he remembered our conversation from the initial interview.

I answered, "Hey, I need to apologize. You were right. Ultimately, it was an extra vehicle and incremental profit, but we could have made more by selling that vehicle to someone else. I understand that now, and I didn't at the time."

It's the only time he ever got that intense with me, and I'm glad he did. I learned a lesson on that deal, and then we went right back to the pact we made in his office in 1997.

Coincidentally, it was also on a trip to Hawaii that I had one of my most memorable and humorous exchanges with Larry, but also one that says a lot about him. While boarding a plane to return home from the week-long conference, I noticed Larry carefully placing some hanging garment bags in the overhead compartment. I hadn't remembered seeing him in anything other than his usual khaki pants and sport shirts, so I wasn't sure why he was carefully handling what appeared to be nicer clothes.

"I noticed you were being very careful placing those hang-up bags in the overhead," I ventured. "Did you buy some clothes in Hawaii?"

He said that he was flying to Japan for a Toyota Dealer Council meeting. "While you all are connecting in Los Angeles for the flight back to Salt Lake, I'll be heading to the international terminal for a flight to Japan. I'll need the suits there."

"So you had to carefully carry those suits all the way to Hawaii and back?" I asked. "You've had to carry them between hotels and now bring them all the way back without letting them get wrinkled?"

"Yeah," Larry answered, "I did. On the layover on the way here,

I stopped to check out the airport. There was a set of lockers that were probably going to be on my way to the international terminal that would have worked for the suits. But you know what? They wanted six bucks a day for those lockers!"

I was just floored and amused at the irony of this successful man who would rather drag his suits across the Pacific Ocean and back than pay six dollars per day for an airport locker. Larry had just hosted an all-expense-paid seven-day meeting in Hawaii for all the general managers, with all of our spouses. It is fascinating that he would see the value of a weeklong leadership meeting including the spouses but balk at spending $42 on a convenience for himself.

Working for Larry was a unique opportunity and one I'm glad I had. As I conveyed to Larry, he's done so much more for me than I could ever bring to the company. He was a true legend and genuine person. His is a company that is focused on enriching the lives of others. I'm fortunate to be a part of an organization with that type of mission.

ONE OF THE GOOD GUYS

Bryant Henrie

In 1986, Larry Miller was negotiating to purchase what would be his seventeenth dealership. Owen Wright was selling his Cadillac and Oldsmobile store in Midvale, Utah, and Larry was expanding his operations. Ultimately they reached a deal, but as the two negotiated over the final price, Owen reportedly said to Larry, "You're not just getting the dealership; you're also getting Bryant Henrie."

Larry told this story more than five years later as I celebrated my service anniversary with the Miller Group. Larry held yearly service award celebrations to recognize people as they hit significant milestones with the Group. As he would call people up, he'd share a personal memory or thought about each person. This particular year, we were holding the celebration in the 100 Club at the newly constructed Delta Center, and that was the story Larry shared about me as he thanked me for my first five years with the company. It was important for me to hear him say that. More than two decades have passed since that moment, and I still feel the same emotions when I think back to that day.

Shortly after Larry and Owen finalized their deal, I had my first opportunity to meet Larry personally. He came to introduce himself to our team on December 28, 1986, but he arrived fifteen minutes early to meet with me. He had been in the news a lot after becoming full owner of the Jazz just months earlier, so I knew who he was and was excited to meet him.

Right from that first interaction, Larry was teaching me. I was the finance manager at the time, and Larry was really focused on the financial revenues. We started talking about selling product from the finance office. Coming from a stand-alone dealership, I had nothing to compare myself to and didn't know how I was doing. As I visited with him and shared the specifics, he instructed me to seek out a particular finance manager of another store who excelled at selling. "If you'll listen and learn the process from him," he said, "you'll be very good."

I eventually became the general manager of the Cadillac-Oldsmobile dealership, and I was really excited. Not long into my tenure, we had a Group sales meeting with the sales teams from the other stores, and I was enthusiastic to show off my team and represent what we were doing. We Cadillac guys put on our suits and ties, arrived early, and sat right in the middle section of the eighty-person meeting. All morning I was on an incredible natural high because of the meeting and our participation, and then suddenly came the lowest of lows. That's when my operations manager reminded me that I had missed something.

He told me that Larry had been to the dealership and found that it wasn't open. In my haste to have everybody there and looking good, I had forgotten to go to the dealership and open up the showroom. I went to grab my things so I could run to the store, and as I came back out of the meeting, Larry was just hitting the top step. He curtly said a hello, and then he continued into his office.

Mortified, I quickly decided the best thing to do was to get it over with, face the music. I went into his office and said, "Do we need to talk about something?"

He said, "No, I'm okay," and he shut the door.

About thirty minutes later, I was sitting in the sales office of the dealership when the phone rang. "You're probably sitting there worrying about your job, aren't you?" It was Larry. "Look, we pay a lot of money for these dealerships. Plus, we need to take care of the customers. When we tell them we're going to be open, we need to be open."

I acknowledged that he was right, and then he went on, "I know what you were trying to do. I know where your heart was. I don't want you worrying about your job. We would need to have many, many visits like this before you ever had to worry about your job." He gave me the confidence and support and trust that I was trying to do things the right way. I never felt as though my job was on the line, and I was grateful for that. Most important, I am grateful for all the teaching moments and his belief in me.

I was also proud to work for the Group because of Larry's integrity and generosity. If he made a commitment to somebody, he kept it. He never went back on a commitment, never stepped out of bounds from an integrity standpoint. Oftentimes, a call would get directed to me from a local LDS leader who had a young man wanting to serve a Church mission but who needed help funding it. I don't know how many missions Larry funded, but there were many. He did these things very quietly, but he was proud to do things like that.

One time, he took me and a couple of colleagues to Lindon, Utah, where a sculptor was creating a bronze statue for the This Is the Place Heritage Park. The park is a historical site with monuments celebrating the entry of pioneers into the Salt Lake Valley, and Larry was proud that he and his wife, Gail, had been able to be involved, financially and otherwise. While we were there, he said, "You know what? I get to do things like this because you guys go out and do your jobs well and generate the revenue so that Gail and I have the opportunity to give back." It was special to be involved and to see what Larry's real mission was. It was truly about what he and his family could create for others through their success.

But the most personal conversation I ever had with Larry was also the last. I was at the arena enjoying the circus with my grandkids but stepped away when a call came in from Larry, who had just been released from one of the hospital stays at the end of his life. He was returning my call, but I informed him that I hadn't called—perhaps it was a little divine intervention that got us on the phone.

Our conversation was purely personal—no talk of cars or transactions—and I asked him, "So really, Larry, how are you doing?" He told me he was able to walk more, but also that he had a hard time getting up the six-inch steps because his legs were so weak. It was a revelation for me that he was really struggling, and I took it as an opportunity to share some of my heart with him, something I hadn't done in more than twenty years at the company.

"This experience for me has been far more than just putting in an honest day's work for an honest day's pay," I said. "It's been way beyond that." I thanked him for all he had done and we reminisced.

Then he said, "You know what, Bryant? You've always been one of the good guys."

The comment took me back to my five-year anniversary when Larry found a unique way to show me how much he appreciated me. It reminded me of all the great moments over twenty-two years working for Larry. It reminded me that he, too, was "one of the good guys."

A Confession

Lane Beattie

As president and CEO of the merged Salt Lake Chamber and Downtown Alliance, I enjoy interacting with Utah's leaders. When rubbing shoulders, I usually inquire as to how they achieved their many successes. Larry H. Miller was one of those people. I first met him when I was in the leadership of the Utah State Senate.

In the mid-2000s, just a few years before he died, the two of us were driving to see the new Miller Motorsports Park west of Salt Lake City, near Grantsville. Passing the time with conversation until we got there, I matter-of-factly asked about his stunning achievements and how he had been able to accomplish all he had done in his life. He hesitated a few moments before sharing some of those professional successes and phenomenal opportunities.

I inquired if he had any regrets. At that point, he got emotional.

"You know, Lane," he responded, "I would trade all the successes I ever had for the chance to be a better father."

I sat, shocked both by his candor and willingness to share something so personal. He wept as he related how much he admired and appreciated his wife, Gail. He talked about what an incredible partner she was, how unfair it was that she had had to raise their children almost on her own and how she deserved full credit for shepherding the kids.

"Because of that, I'm now missing out on more personal

relationships with my children," he said, emphasizing I should never forget that.

I haven't.

Here next to me was a highly successful individual embracing the fact that the most important part of life is family. With so many career endeavors, he certainly had plenty of potential for regrets. To single out his devotion to his wife, his love for his children, and his regret for not having been a better father says it all.

I have always felt strongly about the importance of family. Sitting next to one of Utah's greatest business leaders as he wept over not having been a better father impacted me greatly. Before me was a man who seemingly had everything except for what truly counted. My family always has been important to me, but Larry brought home how absolutely critical legacy is. I want my children and grandchildren to know that what is important to me is *not* my material success but my personal legacy. My family is the number-one priority. I don't want to end up telling a friend the same story Larry told me.

Other aspects of Larry's life are easier to discuss. His business acumen was second to none. About eight years ago, then-Jazz president Dennis Haslam described to a group of Utah CEOs how Larry Miller had built one business upon another, and a third business upon those two businesses, and so on until he had created an empire. Haslam called Larry a mastermind who understood all that it takes to build a business.

The Chamber of Commerce honored Larry two years before he died with the Giant in Our City award, an honor our Board of Governors periodically bestows on leaders for exceptional public service and extraordinary professional achievement.

In the spring of 2015, the Giant in Our City went to Gail Miller, Larry's partner on so many levels. This marks the first time a husband and wife have been separately singled out for this prestigious recognition.

How fitting.

Dogs, Brats, and Barbecues

Mark Stedman

While leading the catering and food service businesses for the Larry H. Miller Group of Companies, I often had the privilege of both serving Larry and watching him serve others.

As the general manager of All-Star Catering, I was given the opportunity to work side by side with Larry—literally. He was passionate about creating a memorable experience and completely unafraid of rolling up his sleeves to make sure we were delivering exactly as promised. He didn't simply pass the assignment along to me or my team; he was personally engaged.

Nowhere was this more evident than in the recognition lunches Larry held for construction workers at his various project sites. In 2003, Larry called me and asked if my team would feed the construction crews working on the Zions Bank Basketball Center and the Super Ford Store.

We set up a large tent with tables and chairs and served a barbecue lunch each Friday. Larry and some of his other general managers would arrive each week to visit with the workers. He would walk through the dining area, shaking hands and thanking each of the workers for their hard work.

It was an incredibly unique gesture and something Larry did because he felt it really made a difference in the commitment and workmanship of the teams. His construction schedules were usually placed against very aggressive timelines, and he knew that people were working hard for him. This was his way of showing people that he thought of them as an important part of the team.

As I would clean up after each event, rounding up plates from satisfied laborers, I'd hear terrific comments of gratitude from people who had worked many similar projects before for other companies but had never been treated this way. It was obvious that the gesture wasn't lost on the crew, who would then go back to work happier, full, and with a greater sense of connection to Larry's purpose and mission. I'll never forget the smiles and appreciation.

We had so much fun and success in doing this that Larry decided to continue the effort for his future projects. So again at Miller Motorsports Park, at the Megaplex 20, and at many other sites, we showed up on Fridays to feed and thank the hardworking crews who were helping to literally build the Miller empire. Larry even had the idea to park a Coca-Cola trailer on site so that drinks were available for them every day during construction. Impressed by Larry's generosity, I was happy to provide the service.

Larry enjoyed the meals, too, but his favorite was a good hot dog or bratwurst. The best thing you could do for Larry was hand him a hot dog and a slice of apple pie.

Hot dogs and brats were the two menu items I knew not to change without Larry's input and approval. Larry had a passion for quality hot dogs—he was a connoisseur—and I knew I would get valuable input in the selection process.

Occasionally, I would get a call from Larry explaining that he had missed dinner in the Jazz 100 Club, and he'd ask if I would send a hot dog down to his seat on the arena floor during the Jazz game. We didn't have in-seat service, so heads would turn as I walked down the aisle with his hot dog and drink in hand.

When I began to approach the task of creating a new signature hot dog for the ballpark, I asked Larry to be a part of the taste test. On the appointed day, Larry showed up with Gail and other family members and GMs.

We tried a number of different combinations in search of

the great hot dog, and everybody voted with their taste buds. Ultimately, we crowned a winner: a foot-long hot dog with bread and butter pickle chips, fresh tomato strips, red and green bell peppers, purple onion, and a jalapeño pepper jack cheese over the top. We had successfully created the "All-Star Dog."

Larry also enjoyed a good bratwurst. One day I sent a case of a variety of bratwurst home with him to try and let me know which type he liked best. He fired up the barbecue grill on his deck and then realized he didn't know the best way to proceed.

He picked up the phone and called me. "How do I cook these darn things?" I gave him a brief explanation of the best way to cook them, and he went to work. The next day he called to tell me that the beer bratwurst was his favorite. I knew it all along. We sell that same brat to this day.

Larry had a unique way of congratulating me on those successes, too. We had a similar experimentation with dinner rolls, another item Larry was particular about. Shortly after our deliberation yielded a winner, there was a recognition dinner for people who were reaching service milestones with the company. At the end of the evening, his parting words to the five hundred people in attendance were, "Thanks for coming. Even Stedman got the rolls right tonight!"

The fun times we shared tasting and creating were quite memorable. It was one of those things we enjoyed together, something that bonded us.

It was a privilege to be able to occasionally serve this great man a hot dog. It was an even greater honor to watch from up close as he served and thanked others.

Reflections on
Larry H. Miller

Governor Gary Herbert

I first met Larry in 2004 when I was running for governor of Utah, and unfortunately for me, Larry had endorsed one of the other candidates. At the time, I was a Utah County Commissioner campaigning for governor along with seven others, including Jon M. Huntsman Jr. I observed Larry's commitment to good government and his desire to see Utah succeed. Even as busy as he was as a very successful businessman, he wanted to be involved. Needless to say, the Larry Miller endorsement was a coup for soon-to-be Governor Jon Huntsman Jr.

Huntsman and I eventually combined our efforts when he asked me to run as his lieutenant governor, and we went on to win the election. It was in this position as lieutenant governor that I had the opportunity to get to know Larry on a much more intimate basis. Once a month he would host the Huntsman/Herbert kitchen cabinet luncheon meeting in the Delta Center. The meetings were mostly informal, and we were able to discuss Utah's important issues of the day, such as politics, the economy, education, civic involvement, and many more topics, including the Jazz.

Larry always began every meeting with, "My job is to welcome you all. So, welcome," after which he would turn the time over to Governor Huntsman. Larry always contributed insight and wisdom to the discussion, choosing topics to which he felt he could add value. But I noticed that when he spoke, everyone listened. Because of his remarkable background and successes, he had tremendous credibility.

It was easy to like Larry. He had a humility that drew people to him. He had street-smart wisdom. He had a deep love for Utah and for America and its founders and founding principles. His love for Utah and her people made it important for him to keep the community strong. He stuck his neck out to keep the Jazz franchise here. I always admired Larry for sacrificing himself financially for so many years and taking a risk to save a struggling sports franchise for the sake of the public. That effort and success put him on my personal list for admiration long before I'd ever met him.

I got to know Larry more personally by staying and talking to him after our kitchen cabinet meetings concluded. We would spend a few minutes talking one-on-one, chatting about whatever came up. Larry would tell me, "You know, I really like talking to you, Gary. I think we see things similarly." I realized then that I had gone from a fan to a friend. That was a nice awakening for me.

Larry and I were both passionate about education. Larry had never been a conformist in much of anything, including schooling, and he didn't consider one universal school model to work for everybody, believing that we all learn in different ways. He valued home schools, private schools, and charter schools just as much as he did traditional public education.

A political controversy arose regarding a piece of legislation that passed during the 2007 legislative session regarding a government-subsidized voucher program to help families pay partial tuition at private schools. The issue didn't sit well with the UEA, PTA, and others, and it was taken to the public for a referendum vote. Larry had asked me to personally speak with him about the voucher program and explain why I supported them.

Our conversation led him to take out a full-page ad in the local papers to support the voucher legislation. I quickly asked how that might affect his business, reminding him that many people in the state were against the vouchers and might not buy another automobile from a Larry H. Miller dealership, or they might not attend his movie theaters; perhaps they would even boycott Jazz games. He demonstrated outstanding courage and principle when he told me, "I may lose some business because of this, but I think it's the right thing to do."

He spent a significant amount of money to purchase those ads in the Sunday editions of the *Salt Lake Tribune* and the *Deseret News*. It was an open letter to the public regarding his support for the vouchers. It was impressive to see a man, so visible to the public, take action on his principles. He put his own business profitability at risk, which, whether or not you agreed with him, reflected the character of a man who wanted to do what he felt was right. There are too few today willing to take the same kind of action.

The vouchers ended up being rejected by voters. Larry never did tell me how much business he lost, if any. I suspect it probably had less impact than we feared. I hoped that if people saw that he had the kind of character to stand up for his beliefs on education, they'd expect his business dealings to have that same kind of integrity.

You could tell he was on a mission to do things, and always more than one thing at a time. He was compelled to be successful and to take on the hard task to do something that would say to most of us, "You can't do that; that appears impossible; that's too tall of a mountain to climb." But not to Larry. He was truly driven.

Along with his business acumen and a compulsion to get things done, he had a soft side. He was very genuine. He was a humble and tenderhearted man, a person who believed he was extraordinarily blessed (he always said "there are no coincidences in life"), maybe even beyond what he felt he was worthy of. Particularly later in his life, he was looking for opportunities to give service, to put his resources to work on behalf of the people of Utah and others. He wanted others to understand that even a guy from his very humble circumstances could become extraordinarily successful.

He was also very appreciative and grateful for his family. He recognized the outstanding qualities of his wife, Gail, as she demonstrated patience and love in her support of Larry's ambitions—during both the good and difficult times. He also knew he had been blessed with wonderful children and was thankful for each one. If he were here today, he would tell us to make our families our number-one priority. His family would be his greatest achievement.

I miss the opportunity I had to meet with Larry on a monthly basis and enjoy a little small talk. When I think about all the success he had, it was really about people and wanting to serve them, coupled with hard work. What he was saying to all of us was: "You, too, can participate in this American Dream if you will avail yourself of the opportunity."

On behalf of all Utahns, I pay tribute to my friend Larry and offer thanks for his contributions, his love of country, his great example . . . and thanks for the memories.

WHO IS THIS LARRY MILLER?

Blake Andersen

I didn't know what to expect when I was called into the Midtown Manhattan office of my company president.

I'd been working for Loews Cineplex Entertainment, the second-largest theater chain in the world at the time. We were headquartered on Fifth Avenue in the historic Coca-Cola Building, right in the heart of New York City. I got the call that Michael Norris wanted me to come to his seventh-floor office, and I was a little nervous.

Michael told me he had asked to see me because he knew I was from Utah and asked how familiar I was with the market there. I explained that I had grown up in Utah and worked in many of the movie theaters along the Wasatch Front. He then asked me a very strange question.

"Blake," he said, "who is this Larry Miller?"

I smiled and told him that I did not know him personally. I explained that he owned the Utah Jazz and several car dealerships, that he was a well-known entrepreneur.

"Well, do you know he's building a theater called Jordan Commons in a place called Sandy?"

"Yes, I heard a rumor of that," I said. "I've even seen the building going up."

"Well, what are we going to do about that?" he asked.

He asked if Larry had the Hollywood connections or if he knew how to get films. I told him I didn't believe he knew anything about the theater business.

"Okay, then," he said, "so you are telling me that we do not need to worry about this Jordan Commons complex?"

I answered confidently. Nobody in Hollywood or in Utah thought it was going to work. Newcomers don't just step into the industry and succeed. It doesn't happen. "I predict it will be just a flash," I averred. "It will go away. We'll probably own the building one day."

I was dead wrong. In the decade and a half since that conversation took place, the Larry H. Miller Megaplex Theatres have become one of the premier independent theater chains in the country. They frequently top the country in opening-weekend grosses, and they've become a model for the theater industry in many ways. And, in a twist of irony, I am now the president of the Megaplex chain.

Several years ago, I came back to Utah to interview for a position with the Megaplex group. That day, I met Larry for the first time as I happened to share an elevator with him and Kathy Farrow, the HR director who was conducting the first part of the interview.

There was an aura about him that was casual yet powerful. With his polo shirt and off-the-cuff demeanor, he didn't look like the entertainment executives I had worked with back in Manhattan, which put me a little at ease. The sheer power of knowing who he was and what he had done was admittedly a bit intimidating, but at the same time, there was warmth to him. I had never met anyone quite like that.

Ultimately, I was offered and accepted the job, and that gave me special insight into the secret of Larry's success in the theater business. At first, Michael and I were right: he probably knew nothing about how to get movies or make the connections that are important to succeed. But he did his homework and was a very good student. He asked a lot of questions and listened intently. He made himself an expert on everything about the effort, and then he took the risk simply because he felt good about it.

What he did know was that he and his wife, Gail, liked going to the movies, and he thought he could create a great experience for people. He pushed people to take care of all the little details that make a great guest experience.

He genuinely felt success started with the small things. He was huge on cleanliness. A cleaning team waited at the doors as each movie ended, ready to get the theater ready for the next showing. He wanted every showing to feel like the first one of the day. That wasn't standard practice for theaters, and it wasn't even something guests expected. But that was Larry.

Another example was popcorn buckets. The entire movie industry had moved toward wax-lined paper bags for popcorn. They were more cost effective than buckets, easier to store, and easier to dispose of. But Larry knew that guests liked the buckets better. It's nice to hold a bucket and it's easier to share, and much less noisy during the film. So Larry insisted on bringing back those popcorn buckets, and it's now becoming the industry standard again. Larry changed the industry just by thinking about what the guests liked and what made the best experience.

His passion for excellence stemmed from his desire to make going to the movies a better experience. I truly believe that's the case with all of Larry's efforts. He didn't do things for the pride and vanity or to just make more money. He wanted to make a difference in people's lives, make the world better.

Very few people have that kind of vision and the kind of magnitude to carry it forth, let alone the commitment and resources to follow through.

His motto was, "Go about doing good until there's too much good in the world." I'm not sure if it's even possible for there to be "too much good," but I understand Larry's message. You just keep trying, you keep giving. His legacy was to make a difference in people's lives, and it's remarkable the number of different ways that legacy has manifested itself. I know that I've been blessed, and countless others have been blessed, because of the difference Larry made.

Who is this Larry Miller? Now, I know. And I'm glad I do. He was a lot more than I ever imagined, and every day I strive to carry on his vision and dreams. He set the standard very high. It is humbling and awesome to see his vision as I walk through any of the now eighteen theaters across Utah and Nevada and think that it all started with a guy building a theater in Sandy, Utah, creating waves clear across the country to Manhattan.

STEWARDSHIP & SERVICE

THE AMERICAN DREAM

Peter and Nataliya Serdyukov

There was a time when I did not believe in miracles. I came from the former Soviet Union, where people believed only in Communism. But two things happened that changed my mind forever. First, I had a chance to come to this country in 1987; very few Soviet people could do it at that time. Second, and this is the real miracle, I received a gift from above, personified in the great Larry.

Larry came into our life in the fall of 1991, when I was a visiting professor at Utah Valley Community College. I was organizing an educational program for a group of new Soviet business people coming to Utah. We asked Larry to present his business as an example of a successful capitalist enterprise. He immediately agreed to host the group.

Larry met us at his old Chevrolet dealership on State Street and shared his rich experiences and knowledge. All the Soviet visitors—the USSR would officially dissolve in December of that year—were very much impressed with Larry's profound expertise, wit, and manners. He was very open, accessible, and kindhearted. He often joked and laughed together with the visitors. His way of communicating was new to this group: he was knowledgeable, requiring attention and respect, but also unpretentious, humorous, and hospitable, which was very unusual for a person of such a caliber.

From that first meeting, my wife, Nataliya, and I soon became

friends with Larry and Gail and their family. That's when the miracles began to happen.

Nataliya, whom we all affectionately call Natasha, was diagnosed with breast cancer in 1994. We were living back in Ukraine,
and at that time there was no opportunity to save her life there.
One day in December, at about 6:00 a.m. Kiev time, I heard the
telephone ring. Still mostly asleep, I picked up the receiver.

"Peter, what's up with Natasha?" It was Larry. He had learned
about Natasha's illness through someone else. He proceeded to ask
me many detailed questions, as was his habit, and then said that
there was a famous oncologist in Salt Lake City, Dr. Kushner, who
could examine Natasha. For most people, it was very difficult to get
an appointment with Dr. Kushner. But not for Larry.

We came to Salt Lake City on January 10, 1995, just a few
weeks after Larry's phone call. Natasha was thoroughly examined,
and the doctors found out she had a very advanced stage of cancer,
which necessitated immediate surgery and treatment. The doctor
called us into his office, where he explained the gravity of the situation and possible ways to save Natasha's life.

Dr. Kushner explained that he could offer different treatments
for her, but the effectiveness of each was proportionate to the cost.
There was a 20% chance of recovery if we did the $40,000 option,
40% if we did the $90,000 option, and so on. To do all that was
necessary to have a 95% chance of surviving, the cost—as I remember well—was $300,000. Clearly, coming from Ukraine, we did not
have the insurance or the money to pay for the treatment.

After we'd heard it all, we thanked the doctor and left his office.
Larry, who had spent the entire day with us, was sitting in the waiting room. He asked about the result of the meeting, but we were too
overwhelmed to relate it to him. We suggested that he talk to the
doctor himself. He spent at least half an hour in the doctor's office,
and when he came out, we got in his car and drove to his house.

On the drive, Larry asked me, "What are we going to do?"

"Even if I could sell everything I had in Kiev," I said, "it would
not make even ten percent of what is needed for the treatment

to save Natasha." I paused, and then added, "But not to treat her would mean death." I did not know what else to say.

Larry responded in a way I can never relate without tears. "When I promised to help you," he said, "I did not say I was going to help for five thousand dollars. I am going to help, whatever it costs." That was Larry. He always did everything very thoroughly, taking complete responsibility for all he undertook and bringing every action to a successful ending. I realized Natasha would have a chance.

The treatment lasted ten months, during which time Larry and Gail took care of Natasha: she lived in Larry's grandma's apartment; she was provided with food and everything else she needed. Larry often called Natasha and talked with her about everything. Once, she mentioned that the doctors had recommended she drink Ensure shakes. That very night, the doorbell rang. Natasha opened the door and there was Larry, holding a case of Ensure.

In November 1995, Natasha was discharged from the hospital and allowed to go home. Going back to Kiev was like returning from another life. We celebrated and had a feeling we were starting a new life—a life that was a gift from Larry.

Two happy years passed quickly, and then Natasha suffered another blow. She started dying of something nobody in Kiev could understand. She was losing her strength, could not go up stairs, could not walk, and then finally, could not even lie down to sleep. She was short of breath. Her pulse was 160 beats a minute and barely audible. I took her to the best hospitals and doctors in Kiev, but nothing worked. I did not know what else I could do to save her. One doctor advised, "In Ukraine, we do not have the technology and medications she needs in her situation, and may never have. If you want her to live, you must go to the United States."

There was nothing else to do but contact our angel-savior Larry again and tell him what Natasha was facing. And, as before, he offered his help without a second thought. He contacted the same hospital and requested that they send an invitation for Natasha to come to Salt Lake City for treatment. The doctors at the University of Utah suggested a new, experimental treatment. It would require that Natasha be located near the hospital where she could be under continual observation and control. The treatment would last for at least five years. It meant that we would have to give up on our life in Kiev—our home, jobs, relatives, and friends—and begin a new life once again.

I forever remember the day of September 25, 1998, when we had to make the decision that turned our world upside down. It was definitely one of the toughest decisions in our lives. But we had no choice. The price was Natasha's life.

Now, eighteen years later, Natasha and I are both full professors at National University in San Diego. Our son, who thanks to Larry earned a bachelor's degree at the University of Utah and later got his MBA at Yale, is now a financier in New York.

Larry made it all possible. How could a busy man, who spent at least a hundred hours a week on the job, find time to know of other people's troubles and help them? It is a mystery, but we know now that he had a motto that drove him: "Go about doing good until there's too much good in the world." Larry lived according to his principles, and his good deeds will forever stay in many people's lives and hearts.

There is never a single day we don't remember Larry and thank him for what he has done for us. He made the American Dream come true for our family. When we are alone, Natasha tells me she often talks to Larry, and she believes that he hears her.

MODERN PIONEER

Ellis Ivory

Larry always struck me as unusual, but in a good way. He had a spirit and drive that I'd never encountered before. In many ways, he reminded me of a Mormon pioneer, always personifying courage, vision, and success in creating and enhancing the community.

In the early years of Larry's ownership of the Jazz, Ivory Homes became a sponsor. In those days when the Jazz played at the Salt Palace, tickets weren't worth a lot. Their salesman, Larry Baum, reached out to me and asked me if I would be interested in drumming up some excitement by sponsoring free throw contests during the games. I agreed to meet with him in my office, and he brought along Larry Miller.

Larry was interested in meeting me due to his interest in my business, Ivory Homes, which builds and develops new family homes. We became instant friends, realizing we shared similar backstories. Both of us had come from moderate backgrounds and built our own businesses. But even more than that, both of us felt a strong sense of stewardship toward the community.

Larry clearly wasn't interested in the Jazz as a revenue stream. The team didn't turn a profit for the first several years of his ownership. While I'm sure he was proud of his eventual financial accomplishments with that entity, I could always tell from our first meeting together that he viewed the Jazz as a community builder. It was during my first few minutes of speaking to him that his modern pioneer spirit began to come into focus. It didn't take long for us to reach an agreement for a sponsorship.

For an entire season, we would select fans from the audience each game to come down and attempt a single shot from the half-court line and from the three-quarter-court mark. If a fan sank a shot from half court, he or she would receive a thousand dollars. If a lucky fan was able to make a shot from three-quarter court, Ivory Homes would build him or her a new house. Several fans made shots from the half-court line, but no one ever made the shot that would net a new home.

My relationship with Larry stayed consistent throughout the years. Larry would often invite me to sit with him at a Jazz game. But our relationship took new form when I became chairman of the board over This Is the Place Heritage Park in Salt Lake City. The park honors the history of the Mormon pioneers who settled the Salt Lake Valley in the mid-1800s.

It was a difficult challenge to tackle. The park wasn't self-sustaining and required the support of outside funding. The nature of fundraising is that donors generally don't get excited about making contributions simply for maintenance purposes. I went to Larry to see if he could help.

When I spoke with him, I was pleasantly surprised to learn of his passion for history and preservation. He had a special place in his heart for Mormon history and the story of their settlement in the West. He pulled out his checkbook and immediately wrote a check for fifty thousand dollars.

Larry and Gail were always proud sponsors of this project, just as I have always been a proud sponsor of their organization. Their gifts to the park include the construction of Ottinger Hall (in memory of Larry's ancestor who was the first fire chief in SLC), the magnificent Mormon Battalion monument, the Miller Youth Camp, and many thousands of dollars to help with the operational deficits during those tough years. Every time we met to discuss the challenges and progress of the Heritage Park, Larry would tell me of his concern that we never forget the stories and principles of our pioneer forbearers.

One time, Larry called me on the phone. "Would you like to go for a drive?" he asked.

I went with him, and we drove out to some warehouses west of Salt Lake City. It was here that he showed me all the props he'd used for his pioneer-themed Work and the Glory movie franchise. Sadly, he'd lost a lot of money on the project and had nothing to do with these thousands of props, losing money in renting the space to store them. "Could you use them at the park?" he asked me.

Absolutely we could. The costumes and historically accurate items have been on display in one way or another ever since.

To further carry on this pioneer spirit of community preservation, a group of downtown businessmen and property owners, including Larry and myself, began to hold monthly dinner meetings that we dubbed the "Downtown Dinner Group." Here, we would meet and discuss the question, "What is good for the city as a community?" Through these dinners, I learned further that Larry simply felt he was a lucky man who'd been blessed by his surroundings, and he wanted to give back in every way that he could to the people who had helped make it possible. I don't think anyone else could have done what Larry did for Utah. His vision and his courage to adhere to that vision were unparalleled.

At This Is the Place Heritage Park, there has only been one time we have ever honored an individual with a monument, and that honoree is Larry H. Miller. He will always be a modern pioneer to me, and a man who loved our history. In the years to come, when new generations learn the stories of the Mormon pioneers, I have no doubt that Larry's will be included in that legacy.

THE MODEL CITIZEN

Rabbi Benny Zippel

I had the good fortune of meeting Larry Miller—one of the greatest American citizens—on the same day I became an American citizen myself.

In 1992, I was given the privilege to move to Utah with my wife, Sharonne, and our eldest son, Avremi, as an ordained rabbi on behalf of Chabad Lubavitch, the world's largest Jewish outreach organization. At that point, I had no specific plans as to where life would take me, but I always knew I wanted to be a teacher, mentor, and educator. Now, it was my opportunity to represent "The Rebbe" throughout the state of Utah and to share his teachings to enhance people's lives.

As an Italian immigrant married to a Canadian citizen, gaining legal status as a "resident alien" was somewhat of a logistical nightmare. But with the help of many kind and loving people and much determination, the endeavor was done. In 1993, I was granted a green card that enabled my family and me to permanently reside in the United States. We settled down in Utah.

On December 27, 1999, I became a naturalized citizen. That day is one of few days in my life that I will remember forever. The trepidation and the excitement leading to that occasion were immense. Shortly before the event, I was informed that due to the unusually large size of the group undergoing the naturalization ceremony, the venue was changing to the Delta Center. We were to be guests of owner Larry H. Miller and his beloved wife, Gail.

Not only was it touching that Larry and Gail allowed for the Delta Center to host the event, but Larry also partook in the event himself. It was very moving to hear Larry address us with his remarkable words of encouragement. He told us, in no uncertain terms, that he wanted each and every one of us to pursue the American Dream and experience great success in all areas of our lives. It was easy to hear the passion behind his voice, knowing he meant every word he spoke.

I can still hear Larry's impassioned words, "Be a student. Be a teacher. Be a leader," reverberate in my own mind. Larry spoke with love and true admiration. He stood there that day as an example to all of us to be responsible citizens of this country.

After the formal part of the event, I was so moved by his words that I decided to connect with him personally and asked him to pose for a picture with me. He graciously agreed and asked me with genuine interest what had brought me to Utah. I briefly shared with him the scope of my outreach work, specifically geared to reaching out to at-risk teens. He then told me how much he valued this work and how he wanted to be a partner in it.

This was the beginning of a long friendship that I have cherished and many memories that will stay with me every day of my life. Larry's devotion to helping those less fortunate than he impacted me greatly. Once, in 2008, he called me on a Friday afternoon and told me that he was looking forward to getting together with me to discuss the progress and the needs of Project HEART, my at-risk organization, once the NBA Playoffs concluded and his schedule would be lighter.

Sadly, this meeting never took place. Shortly thereafter, Larry suffered a heart attack, and his physical health rapidly deteriorated. Nevertheless, countless men and women throughout Utah have benefited and continue to benefit from Larry H. Miller and his family's larger-than-life generosity and love for a fellow person.

Larry H. Miller may have passed on physically, but his legacy and his deep love for fellow humans lives on forever. He was a proud American and still serves as a constant reminder to me to serve my fellow citizens as a student, as a teacher, and as a leader.

A DIFFERENCE MAKER

Judge Andrew Valdez

I thought my son was joking when he told me Larry Miller had called earlier and left a message. I knew who Larry was, but I didn't know him personally, and I didn't think he knew me. "Yeah, right," I said.

"No, really," he repeated. "Larry Miller."

"The Utah Jazz Larry Miller?" I questioned, still thinking my son was having some fun with me.

"Yes," he slowly confirmed. "Larry . . . Miller."

That was in 2001. Larry had heard me speak a few months earlier at a Salt Lake Community College awards ceremony. I received a doctor of humane letters award, and Karl Malone was also being honored at the same function. Larry was there accepting the award on Karl's behalf.

In my speech, I talked about my journey from being born in a poor New Mexico town to migrating to Utah and later attending law school at the University of Utah. I spoke on how I didn't make it alone, about how so many people had reached out and helped me, both when I was young and also when I was going to college, trying to find my way.

In retrospect, I think what Larry may have felt in my words was a connection we shared through our high school. He was a few years older than I was, but we both graduated from West High, and there was definitely something in that student body that I would call a "West High mentality." West High kids are scrappers—they want to feel like they scraped and scrapped and earned everything that they received in life. But when I was growing up, kids at West High often weren't successful because they didn't have available opportunities.

I was fortunate in that key individuals took an interest in me, and I was able to thrive and become a juvenile court judge for Utah's third district because they set the conditions in which I could achieve this type of success. Because he'd come from the same place, Larry knew and understood the environment of my youth and what I had overcome. My story resonated with him, but I had no idea at the time what a ripple effect my words would have in co-creating a difference in the lives of young people in our community.

I don't know if it was my speech or if Larry was feeling moved by Karl's award, but he was teary eyed when we shook hands at the end of the ceremony. He gave me a hug and said, "Geez, that was so nice. Your remarks were beautiful." A few months later, Larry phoned me at home.

When I returned his call, he got right to the point. "I want to create more Andy Valdezes," he said. "Your talk inspired me, and I want to give more. I want to establish a Gail and Larry Miller Enrichment Scholarship Fund at the University of Utah."

He asked for my input on what kind of student I thought should receive the scholarship, emphasizing that he didn't want to target the "usual kids." "The high achievers always get awards," he asserted. "I want to recognize the middle-of-the-road, blue-collar kids, first-generation college attendees."

I shared my college experience with Larry and told him that one of the elements that I had greatly benefited from was a weekly ten-dollar stipend. I knew that he heard and understood how much that meant to me because in the scholarship that Larry created he included a monthly stipend for the recipients.

The scholarship wasn't fully developed until months later when Larry spoke with Stayner Landward, who was serving as University of Utah's dean of students. Stayner knew me because he had been a student counselor when I was a student at the U, so he knew who Larry was talking about when Larry shared the story of what had inspired him to form the scholarship.

Stayner helped Larry facilitate the Larry H. and Gail Miller Enrichment Scholarship, which has been active since 2002 and has benefited hundreds of young minorities who come from under-privileged, hardworking families—adolescents who don't have the accomplishments or achievements that are recognized through the conventional academic awards system.

Since then, I've had many encounters with parents who approach me and say, "My daughter received that scholarship that you helped put together at the university." Apparently, in the letter that awards the scholarship, I am recognized as someone who helped initiate it. I'm humbled by the recognition and also deeply appreciative of the tribute. I tell them that not I, but Larry Miller, a friend of mine, established it. I might have planted a seed, but Larry was the generous benefactor.

When Larry heard me talk about my experience, about how I stood on the shoulders of so many people and how sometimes hope happens and opens doors for us, it resonated with him.

Larry was a difference maker. He saw that as a kid I got a boost in life when I really needed it, and because of that kind of support, I was then able to help others. He didn't make a difference at just high corporate levels. He made a difference in individual lives of those he had never met. He gave the gift of education and possibility, and many of those young students are now leaders in our community. And all of this came from just one phone call. Larry's one phone call initiated generations of positive change.

THE DINNER

George B. Cook

Valene and I were having an enjoyable dinner at Carver's restaurant with Larry and Gail Miller one evening in March of 1994. We talked mostly about the recent marriage of our daughter, Jennifer, and their son, Stephen. Toward the end of the meal, a fun exchange over who would pick up the tab unfolded between Larry and a nearby table of ten diners. What was different about this check-grabbing incident was that Larry did not know the people at the other table. The unknown benefactor knew Larry, however, and asked the waiter for Larry's tab. Larry wouldn't hear of it and instructed the waiter to bring both checks to him. This went on for a few minutes before the stranger won the tussle.

But the real reason the Millers had invited my wife and me to dinner was that it was a particularly challenging moment in our lives. At fifty-four, I had just been laid off from the downsized division of my company, and the Utah economy was far from robust. We had eight children and a mortgage payment. As the table was cleared, Larry asked how the job hunt was going. I said that it was going okay, given the current economic conditions, and that I had several prospects.

Larry removed an envelope from his pocket and handed it to me, saying that it might help us until the situation improved and requested we not open it until we got home. Although Valene and

96

I had a modest—but steadily shrinking—"rainy-day" fund, one of our financial concerns was the hefty monthly cash outlay required to support our son who had just begun his LDS mission. Inside the envelope was a substantial amount of money and a note from Larry and Gail, underscoring that the money was not a loan but a gift to us.

Taken aback by this genuine act of concern, we decided to put the funds to good use: our son's missionary endeavors. But the story of the Millers' generosity doesn't end there.

A few weeks later, still searching for employment, I was driving to Provo for another interview. Those who have been unemployed for some time will recognize the fear that was taking hold of me. It reflects in your attitude and ability to interview effectively. I was nearing desperation. This particular employment possibility in Provo seemed like a dream job with the organization run by the late author and management adviser Stephen Covey.

While driving to that noon interview, I received a call on the old "brick" cell phone my previous employer had allowed me to use until I found new employment. It was Larry. I took the next freeway exit and stopped to talk. As usual, he got right to the point: he had recently started an auto finance company, which was in need of my expertise. Considering my previous business and banking experience, he said that I could be an integral part of this venture.

Typical of Larry's approach, he already had scheduled interviews for me later that day with individuals associated with his new company. Larry asked only that I be there at the time appointed. (That's Larry-speak for "Be there or I will be very put out.") I said I would, and I continued on to my Covey appointment, which went well, but it turned out the company desired someone for their Canadian office who spoke fluent French. I did not. But I did get to the afternoon interview that Larry had arranged, and that was successful.

I began working for Larry within a week and continued to do so until I retired fourteen years later. Larry's additional gift, that important final push in my career, restored my dignity, self-confidence, and financial stability.

THE TEXAS OPTION

David Nielson

Technically, Larry Miller was my competitor. But that didn't stop him from becoming a trusted advisor, potential business partner, and life-changing mentor. And that was all in the course of a single afternoon in Larry's office.

I owned a fifty percent stake in an independent used car dealership in Utah, so it's not an exaggeration to say that Larry and I were rivals when I picked up the phone to seek out his advice. I did it anyway, and I'm extremely glad that I did.

My business partner and I had jointly owned Low Book Sales since 1996. The company had been growing, but our partnership was struggling by 2007, and we both knew it was time to part ways. Each of us wanted to purchase the other's interest in order to become full owner, and the situation grew more stressful as time went on.

I needed advice from someone with undeniable business expertise to help me strategize my next move. After much prayer and personal thought, I got the impression I needed to reach out to Larry—at this point an automobile giant and well-known businessman—even if he was my competition. I had never spoken personally to Larry and had no reason to believe he'd take my call.

I called the corporate headquarters of the Miller companies and was transferred by an operator to Larry's assistant. She asked what the purpose of the call was so that she could pass along a message, and all I could think to say was that the call was personal in nature. She took the message and I hung up, not sure if he would even find the time to return the call amid all it takes to run a multi-billion dollar enterprise.

The very next day, my phone rang and I was surprised to hear the voice on the other end say, "This is Larry Miller returning your call. How can I help?"

I expressed my appreciation for the call and began to explain why I was seeking his counsel. He listened intently as I described my desires to buy out my business partner, and finally he suggested we meet in person. He said he could set aside some time the next day for me to come to his office, where we could discuss a strategy.

The next day, my CFO, Chas Felt, and I waited in the lobby of the Larry H. Miller corporate office. I was humbled that he would take the time and nervous about the ensuing meeting, but I was mostly excited to finally meet the man.

He came out and personally greeted us, escorting us to his large corner office that doubled as a conference room with a large table and panoramic views of the Salt Lake Valley. He sat down at the head of that large table and said, "I have about forty-five minutes."

I began to delve into more detail about the struggling partnership, and the conversation naturally flowed into a discussion about the state of our company. I told him about the growth of our company since we had started nearly a decade earlier, literally selling cars from the parking strips next to our parents' driveways. I recited the sales numbers that I had committed to memory over the course of ten years, and as I shared the facts and figures, I could see Larry's eyes go into a trance as he followed along like some kind of human calculator.

He asked me what I wanted of him. I told him I wasn't exactly sure, but that I had felt a strong prompting that I should discuss the situation with him and seek his advice.

We were discussing our business model—a unique one—along with other details of the company. He asked about our sales numbers, our margins, how our finance company worked, and a number of other very detailed questions. Larry did the math in his head along the way and complimented the results we had achieved in building the business from scratch. Larry caught me off guard with his next move as he suddenly posed the hypothetical: what if *he* bought my partner out?

I could tell he was a quick thinker and a dealmaker. But I hadn't even considered the possibility of seeking a new partner. I asked if he would consider backing me with a $7.5 million loan so I could buy out my partner but retain full control. He politely indicated that was not something he was interested in, and we went back to the task of mapping out my next strategic move.

I asked Larry what he would do if he were in my shoes. He then asked, "Have you heard of the Texas option?"

The Texas option, he explained, was a binding and effective way to settle things. It is essentially like splitting a cookie in half—one person decides how to split the cookie and the other gets to pick which half he wants. Basically, I would present my partner with an offer for his half of the business. If he felt it was a fair price, he would accept. If he felt it was too low, I would have to sell my half to him at that price. This was how Larry had purchased the second half of the Utah Jazz from Sam Battistone in 1986.

But Larry wasn't done providing great counsel. He gave me advice on starting my own insurance company and my own management company. He told me how he would structure the debt and the repayment calendar of the buyout money, provided my partner accepted. Chas and I furiously took notes, hoping to capture as much as we could.

I looked down at my watch and realized that our forty-five-minute meeting had now gone over three hours. I politely expressed my gratitude for his time and attention but more importantly for his willingness to coach a competitor and to be so open with his advice and experience. It was obvious that Larry enjoyed this type of strategy session.

The three-hour meeting changed my life. The Texas option

worked perfectly, and I followed Larry's advice to raise money from private lenders to execute the transaction. Many of his other ideas and pieces of advice are still evident in how we run our company today.

A few months after the meeting, Larry recognized me at a Jazz game and came to follow up with me. He asked how the transaction had gone and how business was going, and it was obvious in his tone and his body language that he was genuinely interested. This was no ordinary man, and certainly not an ordinary competitor.

I could have easily ignored the impression to try reaching out to the business giant Larry Miller, but I'm glad I didn't. I'm grateful I got the chance to learn from him what I did, and both my company and family are better off for it.

An Unexpected Guest

Charles W. Dahlquist II

As the Honorary Consul of Germany, I saw a wonderful side of Larry Miller in December 2001. During this time, Utah and the sporting world were gearing up for the 2002 Winter Olympic Games—to be held in Utah. Prior to this time, the European press had been primarily focused on scandals surrounding the 2002 Winter Olympic Games, as well as providing inaccurate, incomplete, and inappropriate articles about The Church of Jesus Christ of Latter-day Saints and its connection with the Salt Lake Games.

In November, I received a telephone call from Peter Sartorius, a well-known, respected, and seasoned German editorial writer for the *Süddeutsche Zeitung*, a regional newspaper with significant power and impact in southern Germany. Peter indicated he would like to come to Salt Lake City and look at the relationship of the LDS Church with the 2002 Winter Olympic Games.

To get the full story, Peter preferred to come on location, experience the culture, and interview people in person. This had been his hallmark style in the past. For example, on one occasion, Peter flew to Texas for a week, suited up, and practiced with the Dallas Cowboys prior to writing his story on the team. That's his level of dedication to the story. For this investigation, Peter specifically asked to meet with a number of LDS Church leaders and members of the Church who were influential in the community during his ten-day visit. I happily offered to make arrangements.

Peter arrived in Salt Lake City on a cold December day. He rented a car and checked into the Little America Hotel, where I'd agreed to pick up him the next morning. By the time I arrived at 11:00 a.m., Peter already had an amazing story to tell.

After waking up early, Peter had decided to drive around and check out the city.

"I looked up on the mountain and saw this huge building that appeared to be a hotel or a museum. I thought it would be nice to go up there, get a cup of coffee, and look over the valley," Peter recalled. "When I got there, it was apparent that it was not a hotel. However, because of the statuary in the front yard, I thought it was a museum."

Curious, Peter parked his car and approached the front door. He knocked but nobody answered. He then tried the door. It wasn't locked, so he walked in and was immediately smitten with the beautiful open area replete with paintings and statues. Things got interesting when a housekeeper walked into the room while he observed the décor.

"What are you doing here?" the woman asked Peter.

"I thought this was a museum," he replied. "I was enjoying the art."

She promptly informed him that it was not a museum; it was a private home. Peter was extremely embarrassed and started to leave. On the way out, he asked who owned the house.

"Larry Miller," she replied.

"Who is Larry Miller?" he asked.

She gave him a look of consternation, much like one would give a kindergarten student.

"He owns the Utah Jazz!" she exclaimed.

As Peter told the story, we both had a good laugh at his experience. Then a thought popped into my mind.

"Would you like to meet with Larry Miller?" I asked Peter, who indicated he would.

At that time, I had never met Larry personally, so I called Elder M. Russell Ballard, a leader in the LDS Church's Quorum of the Twelve Apostles, to inquire about arranging an interview with the prominent businessman and Jazz owner. Elder Ballard said he would make a couple of calls, and then he called me back with a cell number. Within a few minutes, I was on the phone with Larry.

I explained to Larry that Peter would like to talk about the community, the Church, his business, and the Olympics.

"My time is yours," he said. "How can I be helpful?"

I had already procured Jazz tickets, so I asked if Larry could meet with Peter for a few minutes before that night's game. He agreed to it. We were told to meet in the arena parking lot at 4:00 p.m., three hours before the game started.

"That will give us a good couple of hours together," Larry said. "I'll then be glad to host you for dinner prior to the Jazz game and then we'll look at your tickets and see if I can improve them a little bit."

We met Larry at the appointed location and time. He drove up in an older, well-maintained Toyota Land Cruiser—very unpretentious for the owner of one of the largest car dealership groups in the country. He warmly welcomed Peter and me, and we spent the next two hours in a conference room talking.

Larry was very open and willing to respond to any question Peter asked. He was more than gracious and gave a marvelous impression of one who really cared about his faith, his family, his Church, and the fact that the world was looking at Salt Lake City and the LDS Church during the 2002 Winter Olympic Games. Larry was the perfect ambassador. He impressed me with his openness, humility, enthusiasm, competence, and kindness. After the interview and a nice dinner, our tickets were upgraded, and we enjoyed a wonderful evening watching the Utah Jazz play.

During his visit, Peter also met with numerous Utah residents, including Alan Ashton of WordPerfect and local and general leaders of the LDS Church. Because of his experience with Larry and others, Peter returned to Munich and wrote two marvelous full-page articles on Salt Lake City, The Church of Jesus Christ of Latter-day Saints, and the 2002 Winter Olympic Games. His positive articles changed the entire tone and focus of the German press with regard to the Salt Lake Games. He recounted his experience with Larry throughout the article, including the inadvertent visit to Larry's home and the time spent prior to the Jazz game. In his articles, he also detailed Larry's success and the impact he made from a business standpoint and in building the community.

As I have pondered that experience in the years that followed, not only have I been impressed with Larry's willingness to assist Peter in getting the information he needed, but also with his openness and his humble approach to the great impact that he and his family have had on those around them in large and small ways. It reminded me of when Larry spoke to the Salt Lake Rotary Club years before and openly wept while talking about this community and his strong feelings for those in need.

In light of how Larry's interview had had a profound impact on Peter's article, I was most impressed to be a firsthand witness of a great servant-leader in action—one who really cared about others. Former TV anchor Tom Brokaw once said, "In this country, it's easy to make a living, but it's tough to make a difference." Larry Miller was one who truly made a profound difference wherever he went, and his impact was felt even further than that—in this case, in far-away Europe.

THE BEST TIP
I EVER GOT

Brent Morley

L arry Miller is a bad tipper!"

I heard that more than once from teenage servers who worked at Joe Morley's BBQ, the family-owned restaurant my dad had started decades ago. Larry Miller had been a customer from the very beginning, and I was always surprised and a little amused when I heard a server accuse him of being a bad tipper.

I would usually follow up with the offended server by asking, "He really left you a bad tip?"

"Yeah," one might reply. "He left me $3.00 on a $20.00 check!"

"Well that's fifteen percent, isn't it?"

"Yeah, but that guy's loaded. He owns the Jazz!"

"Does that make him a bad tipper?"

This wasn't the only way I'd notice how Larry's public image contrasted with my own personal experiences with him and Gail. I would see some press coverage about a major investment costing millions of dollars, and then I'd see them at one of our tables, just two normal people out for a bite. No fancy clothes, no flashy watch. Just a Sprite, a pulled pork platter, and some baked beans on the side.

Over the years, I remember several interesting incidents that resulted in unfavorable attention for Larry: a well-documented blow up with a Denver Nuggets fan at the arena, a controversial decision not to screen a certain movie at a movie theater, or a heated contract negotiation with Karl Malone. I imagine that those were surreal moments for the Millers, examples of life in a fishbowl. In many of those situations I would have guessed they would have disappeared from public view for a while, stayed under the radar. At the very least, I expected to see them more often accompanied by a personal assistant or maybe a security guard. But almost like clockwork, Larry and Gail would show up for dinner a day or so later, Larry in his golf shirt and tennis shoes.

Occasionally I'd attempt to offer some feeble condolences or empathy for their situation, as if I had any way to relate to what they were going through. They would express their gratitude and go back to having dinner.

After several years of my trying to make small talk regarding the Jazz or the latest big project they were working on, I got up the nerve to ask Larry if it would be okay if I asked him a business question. "Sure," he said, and I launched into my story. I'd been working in my dad's restaurant my entire life and wanted to figure out a way I could either take things over or get out of the business.

"You sound just like one of our kids," Gail said.

Then Larry chimed in. "Why don't you and your dad come and meet with me in my office? Call my secretary and set up an appointment. Here's my card."

I was excited, stunned, and flattered all at the same time. Larry Miller was inviting me to his office to talk about business? I had been serving lunch to governors, business moguls, and power players for years. I had never actually sat down and talked with any of them.

My dad and I took Larry up on his offer. We went to his tenth-floor office in Sandy, viewed one of the NBA Western Conference championship trophies on display, and spent a couple of hours listening to Larry recount his experiences. He told us that he was planning for his sons to take over the business. He told us of family meetings they'd had to discuss the transition and shared some of his health concerns before they were widely known. He was completely open with us and gave us several pieces of advice and suggestions on how we might manage our own transition.

There was nothing held back, no fluff and no agenda. Larry was giving us the same advice for a smooth transition of our little family barbecue business that he was following himself to transfer his multibillion dollar company. And he did it in a way that made us feel as though our business was just as important.

The meeting changed how I viewed my own role in the family business. It changed how I treated the employees who worked for us, and it strengthened a desire I had to grow my dad's business and extend his legacy, much the same way Larry was hoping his family would do with the Miller family businesses.

After that meeting I saw Larry in a different light. I watched as his health declined and when he named Greg his CEO and followed through on the transition plans he had outlined for us that day in his office.

After Larry became wheelchair bound, he made one last visit to our barbecue restaurant. I was happy to see him, and we were both still optimistic that he would recover, but he was different. He asked me about how things were going with the business, and I expressed some mild frustration that our process wasn't going as smoothly as his appeared to be.

"Come up to my house tomorrow and we can talk," he offered graciously.

At his house that Sunday afternoon, we again sat for a couple of hours as we talked more about the really important things in life: family, friends, and charity. I watched as Gail patted him gently on the back and got him a blanket. It was a view of Larry and Gail that I wished everyone else could see. And it was the last time I would ever see Larry.

After Larry passed away, Gail invited my wife and me to attend a Jazz game with her. For us, this was a once-in-a-lifetime opportunity. We parked in the Millers' private parking lot. We enjoyed a very nice meal. We sat on the front row. Gail sat in Larry's chair, and I sat in hers. I could feel the players bounce the ball on the hardwood as they ran by. At one point the ball bounced out of bounds and into my hands. It was an amazing night—having a front-row perspective, looking from my feet on the hardwood floor to the top of the rafters and seeing what Larry had built.

The very next home game, still with a strong case of Jazz fever, I drove down to the arena again. This time, I made my way to the very top and sat on the top row of the upper bowl. From the hardwood to the rafters, I gleaned another perspective of Larry's influence.

When I asked Larry Miller a question that deserved a ten-second answer, I instead received life lessons, a mentor, and a friendship.

It was the best tip I ever got.

Returning the Favor

Jack Frost

On a February afternoon in 1984, I was moving into my new office in the Salt Lake City International Airport after the then-Western Airlines had transferred me from its San Francisco operations. I was noticing how much less hectic this hub airport was compared to my previous Bay Area location.

That's when the phone rang.

A somewhat demanding voice asked who I was and what sort of authority I had. Sitting up in my chair, I gave him my name and job description and asked what I might do for him. Before I could finish, he blurted: "This is Larry Miller. My wife just arrived in Hong Kong with a group and discovered she has my passport instead of hers."

Hong Kong authorities, he said, had given her twenty-four hours to come up with her passport or they would deport her. He related how everyone so far had told him to call FedEx or DHL and have it shipped. None of those services could get the passport to her in time, he said, and he was looking for an alternative arrangement.

I had never heard of Larry Miller, but I told him he was talking to the right person. I had connections in the airline business who could work with me to solve his wife's dilemma. Western (which merged with Delta in 1987) had a flight from Salt Lake City to San Francisco leaving within the hour. Once the passport arrived in San Francisco, I could arrange to have it transferred to a flight bound for Hong Kong. How quickly could he get Gail's passport to me, I asked?

He said to consider it on its way.

I told this Miller guy I would be waiting outside the terminal. I took down his phone number and said I would keep him updated. I barely reached curbside when screeching tires in the distance told me the handoff was imminent. I snatched the envelope from the driver and rushed it to a Western flight attendant who would take it to San Francisco. I had a friend at Japan Airlines who would be at the arrival gate to take the passport handoff when the attendant opened the cabin door.

JAL had a nonstop flight to Hong Kong leaving shortly after the Western flight landed. I received a call from the courier, who relayed that everything had worked to perfection; the passport was winging its way to Hong Kong. Hoping he had calmed down by then, I called this Miller guy back with the news that the passport would arrive in time.

This was the type of stuff I frequently was called upon to do in my position. It was no big deal. And that's the last I heard of Larry Miller until a letter from a local Toyota dealership arrived several weeks later thanking me for my help. I soon forgot about the incident.

What I couldn't brush off as easily was that the Honda I drove lacked air conditioning. A car with A/C was not required in the Bay Area, but after a couple of Utah summers, the temperatures were starting to get to me. Since I commuted to the cooler Bay Area for the better part of three years to be back with my family on weekends, I survived.

One sizzling summer night in Salt Lake City, however, I was driving down State Street when I spotted a Larry H. Miller Toyota sign. The name sounded familiar, so I pulled in. I was expecting a guy in a checkered jacket and a bowtie to come out and attempt to persuade me to drive off in a new car. Somebody met me, but not in that sort of uniform. He and I drove around in a small Toyota—complete with A/C—until I cooled down. On the return to the dealership, I told the salesman I thought I had done a favor a few years back for someone named Larry Miller. He gave me the keys to another small Toyota and told me to try it out.

When I returned, there was a nice-looking, middle-aged couple standing on the curb waving at me. It was Larry and Gail Miller. We had never met, but when the salesman called to see if there was any validity to my connection, they jumped in their Toyota and drove down to meet me. It was like a family reunion. They were friendly but incredulous that my car was not equipped with air-conditioning.

Larry said that if I could wait a few weeks he would have the demo Toyota he was driving cleaned up and would make me a good deal should I want it. I did wait, I did want it, and it was a great deal. Larry also told me that if I ever desired to attend a Jazz game he could provide me tickets if I called his secretary.

I didn't know much about the Jazz or what Larry Miller had to do with the team, but I called his secretary a couple of months later and got a "let me check into it" feeling. She soon called back telling me that my wife and I had seats behind the bench for my first NBA game.

Larry and Gail would usually give me a shout when they flew on Western, and we would visit. I casually mentioned in one of those airport meetings that if the Jazz were ever to play an exhibition game in Japan, as was rumored, we would be interested in tickets. Sometime later, it was announced the Jazz and the Suns would play two games in Tokyo at the beginning of the 1990 season, but it was also noted that only twenty tickets would be given to each team. I put the idea of attending out of my mind.

A short time later, I received a call from Larry's secretary saying she was putting aside two of those twenty tickets for the Frosts. Working for an airline, it would be no problem getting to Tokyo, and I graciously accepted. The tickets would be held for us at the Intercontinental Hotel in Tokyo, where Larry and the NBA staff from New York would be staying. We presented ourselves at the hotel the afternoon before the first game to request the tickets. The hotel staff remembered putting them somewhere, but no one could find them. After a time, Larry came into the lobby and saw us. Everyone was embarrassed. Larry reached into his pocket and pulled out four tickets for seats near the floor.

"Here, take mine," he said. "They are better tickets than yours were anyway."

We rode to the arena on the NBA bus with Larry, Commissioner David Stern, and a few others. I am not sure where Larry ended up sitting, but those two games were an unforgettable experience.

LOYALTY

STUBBORN

Karl Malone

Larry Miller and I had the same problem: we always wanted the best for the organization and for everybody. Sometimes we'd disagree about what that meant or how to go about it. But no matter what was said or done, we were always able to work it out.

There's not a day that goes by that I don't remember something Larry Miller said or find myself using one of his favorite phrases. Sometimes you don't understand the magnitude of what somebody says to you until after he's gone, and I have had plenty of those moments, going clear back to the day I met Larry.

I had just been drafted as the thirteenth overall pick in the 1985 NBA Draft. I flew to Salt Lake City, where general manager Dave Checketts picked me up at the airport and took me to meet Larry Miller for the first time. Twelve teams had passed on me, and I got a big vote of confidence when I first shook hands with the man who had just become full owner of the team. That resonated with me. Whether I was good enough to play at that point or not, I knew that if I worked hard and did the right things, I could be special.

"So I guess we're going to start this thing together," Larry said to me. I didn't know him, and he barely knew me, but his attitude right from the start immediately told me what he said was true.

To say I'm grateful to have arrived in a situation where Larry was the franchise owner is an understatement. Part of that was because of the unique relationship we had and the trust he had in me. We never looked at it as though he was my boss; we worked together. *If I'm doing my job and you're doing yours, we both figured, it's going to turn out pretty good.*

Many times Larry was offered big money to move the team, and every time the answer was no. It was his commitment and passion that affected me most. When someone gains that level of my respect, I will die before I'll let them down.

Larry always understood this. One day we were talking about our roles on the team and our relationship with one another, and he said, "You do realize, by the time you realize I'm your boss, all the damage will have been done."

I just sat there for a moment, unsure what he meant.

"I'm not your boss," he went on. "When I become your boss, it's over and done with."

More than a boss, Larry was a leader and a teacher. There aren't enough teachers out there, people that don't just tell you you're wrong but go on to say, "Here's how we should have done it."

Besides my own mother, Larry was the first person to take that approach with me. That teaching influence of Larry helped mold me as a young man and allowed me to grow. It's a big part of who I am. Yes, I played with an edge, and yes, I sometimes said the wrong things. Larry could have just ripped me up and down over some of those things. He never did that. He would always say, "Look, when we walk out that door, we're together on this, but this is how we should have done it."

In the end, I never took it personally. We always agreed that no matter what was said and done, Larry and I would come together and work things out.

"Okay," Larry would say, "I'm going to do my job, Karl. Now do yours. Let's do them very well."

I believe we did just that.

As much as Larry loved teaching, he also loved building bridges for people. He believed in giving people chances, putting people in positions to be successful, making connections. One day he told me, "You'd be good in the car business, and I got a guy you need to meet."

He told me about a young general manager he had working for him, Andy Madsen. Soon after, Andy, Larry, and I were looking into options. Before long, Larry had news for me. I'll never forget how he delivered that news.

On the team, we had this thing we did in the locker room after games. We'd fill a bucket or a big Gatorade cooler with ice water, and when a teammate was getting out of the shower, we'd get him with the water. I was always getting people. Every now and then John Stockton or Bryon Russell would get me, but I got somebody every night. You know when you do that, your day is coming.

One night after a big win, everybody was in a good mood, so Larry came by and told me he needed to talk to me about a dealership possibility. I told him I'd get ready and come see him. Most of the guys had left, so I figured it was safe to take my shower while Larry was out talking to some people. Suddenly, I felt a blast of ice water hit me. I cursed loudly and then heard a voice behind me.

"Hey, you eat with that mouth?"

Larry was standing there with the bucket. He had gotten me.

Then he added, "Hey, and by the way, that business deal is going to happen. I need a check from you."

That's probably not the way most new business deals are celebrated, but that was Larry.

But, as many people know, it wasn't always fun and games. We also had our little disagreements. We were both stubborn, although I'll admit for the record that I was probably the more stubborn of the two. Either way, we had some tense moments in our relationship.

Toward the end of Larry's life, we had a chance to replay some of those moments. It was warm, refreshing, and unrehearsed.

It started with a call from Andy. "Hey, have you talked to Larry?" he asked. "You need to give him a call."

"Okay," I said. "Is everything all right?"

"I hear that he's not doing too well."

We were planning our normal yearly trip to Alaska, but I told my wife, Kay, that I wanted to go see Larry. Without asking any questions, she said that would be great.

We flew to Salt Lake City and I went to the hospital to see Larry. I walked into the room and saw Larry connected to machines. I don't know what I was expecting, but the scene affected me. Larry was talking to a nurse and hadn't noticed me. I had to step back out of the room.

I got myself together and got ready to go back in and lighten the mood. Larry and I had a way of greeting each other with some trash talk, like, "I'm just going to kick your butt." The other would respond with something like, "It ain't gonna be easy," and then we'd start laughing.

I stepped back into the room and said, "You know what? What if I just come kick your butt over there? Get up."

The nurse looked shocked. Nobody talked to Larry Miller that way. Larry looked back at me and said, "You better bring your lunch."

I spent the next few days in Larry's hospital room with him. I barely left, except when Gail was there and I'd step away to give them the room. Larry would take a nap, and when he'd wake up, I'd be there.

"Really?" he'd ask when he noticed I was still there. "Do I have to see your face when I go to sleep *and* see it when I wake up?"

Over the course of those three days, we relived my eighteen-year career through warp-speed conversations. I helped him through his attempted rehabilitation. We talked about all the disagreements, all the great moments, all the bumpy contract negotiations. Throughout it all, he was a fighter. I haven't seen many professional athletes with healthy bodies work that hard.

We talked about his regrets and how he wished he had spent more time with his family. Larry never shied from his faults, and that was one of them. If my biggest fault is being guilty of working my butt off, I'll take that, but it came at a cost. We're all better off for the hours Larry spent doing what he did, but that required some sacrifices, and he wished he had been there more for Gail and his kids.

After a few days of talking and reminiscing at Larry's bedside, I went back to my family and gave Larry back to his. Only a few months later I got the call: Larry had passed away.

But what a legacy he left. Utah is better because of Larry Miller. The NBA is better because of Larry Miller. Every town that the Larry H. Miller companies are in is a better town because of it.

And me? I just miss him. I miss him every day.

TWO RIVERBOAT GAMBLERS

Jon Huntsman Sr.

Larry Miller and I had a lot in common. We both came from very little, and we both bet the entire farm several times over. If either one of us had lost, we would have been cleaned out. We both sacrificed and built. By the time we met in 1985, we were both on our way to forming what would become successful business empires, but at that time we were just two riverboat gamblers.

Largely because of that connection, Larry and I became fast friends. Our relationship was always behind the scenes and never publicized. When people saw us exchange a big hug in public, they weren't quite sure what our relationship was or what support we had already given each other. But it all started in that 1985 meeting.

I was asked to meet with Larry that spring about an investment opportunity. I had just expanded a successful plastic container company into Hunstman Chemical Corporation, manufacturing a number of petrochemical products around the world—things like computer components, tennis shoes, golf balls, carpets, automotive supplies, and so much more. It's a $2.5 trillion industry in the U.S. alone, and we were a relatively new player in the market. For his part, Larry had bought his first few car dealerships and was starting to experience success himself due to his hard work and vision.

Larry approached me about an opportunity to jointly purchase the Utah Jazz from Sam Battistone. We had entertained the idea of getting involved with professional sports before, but never felt like it was a fit. We were industrialists, used to running businesses that don't shut down, that we could have control over. The idea of having a business where success was dependent on a few key players was contrary to our philosophy. But Larry wanted to keep the Jazz in Utah. He knew that Sam had to sell all or part of the franchise, and he worried that many prospective buyers would take the team elsewhere. "I think we could have an opportunity to buy the Jazz together," Larry told me. It was our first meeting, but hardly a formal discussion; we simply had an early conversation about whether or not it was something we could do together.

But later, he called me back. "I've met with Sam," he told me. "I have a deal with him where I can buy half the business this year. Would you be interested in the other half?"

"Larry," I ultimately responded, "let me make a deal with you. Whatever you do, whatever amount you invest with respect to the Jazz, I will be your safety net. I will guarantee you that I will always be there to loan you the money if something goes wrong."

Larry almost started to cry over the phone. "That's the nicest thing anybody has ever said to me."

A year later, he came to me again. "I've got an opportunity to buy the other half," he said. "Do you want to do it?"

Although a year had passed, my feelings hadn't changed. I told him I'd rather keep my promise of guaranteeing his investment. "You're taking a huge risk," I told him, "and it may or may not succeed. It would be an honor to be your backstop if I have the money, and I think I will."

Larry wasn't done. When he started work on the Delta Center, he came over and showed me the plans. "Jon, I'd like you to go in with me fifty-fifty on the building."

By that time the chemical business had taken off and I was on the Forbes 400 list. At that point I felt even more confident in my ability to stand behind Larry, so we had the same discussion again.

"Larry, listen," I said. "I'll be your financial backstop. Don't you worry about it. Don't tell anybody about it. Just know that if something goes wrong, I've got your back."

We had a similar conversation when the opportunity arose to buy KXIV in 1993 and turn it into KJZZ. "You're the finest man I've ever met," I told Larry then. "I trust you. You're doing a great job with the Jazz, and your other businesses are doing well. You're the only guy I know who has the drive, the determination, the mentality, the intelligence, and most important, the toughness to get these things done. I'll give you my last penny if you need it, but go for it yourself."

I meant every word. There are several things that made Larry successful, but at the core are three. Risk-taking is number one. He understood his risks. He calculated them carefully, and then he made a huge plunge. Number two is a no-nonsense approach to a very tough and difficult industry. Larry was very serious about it, and he didn't play games. He wasn't in it for the money or the status; he wanted the Jazz to be a community asset that brought people together and made them happy. And third is focus. He was very focused on whatever he was doing and did it extremely well.

Later, I had the chance to turn the tables on Larry and ask him for his partnership, but not in business—in the fight against cancer. We were building the Huntsman Cancer Institute, and I went to see Larry. I was going to ask him for $5 million. Nobody had ever given me that much.

"Larry, I was wondering if you'd be interested in helping us," I started. "It's costing me a lot of money, but we've got to solve this. This is the worst disease in the history of mankind, killing millions of people each year. We need to bring an end to it." Larry asked how much I was asking for. I had gone in thinking $5 million, but I decided in that moment to ask for $10 million.

"Whew!" Larry said, wiping his brow. "I thought you were going to ask me for some real money!" He and I joked about that moment ever since, but within two days, he had given me a check for $10 million.

When Larry became sick, I visited him and invited him to stay at the Huntsman Cancer Institute that he had so generously contributed to. Even though he didn't have cancer, I knew that he would enjoy the beautiful rooms and views and that the four large family suites we had there would be able to accommodate family and others visiting. He told me he'd love that, so I arranged for him to stay in one of those suites. He was our only patient up there who never had cancer, and I made sure he had the run of the place. "Anything you want, Larry," I told him, "you just tell us. We'll make you cakes. We'll make you pizza. We'll bring you in milkshakes. Any time of day or night, whatever you want."

Eventually, complications from Larry's diabetes necessitated amputation of both of his legs. The night before the operation, I received a call from Elder M. Russell Ballard, an Apostle in the LDS Church and another close friend of Larry and Gail. "Larry would like a priesthood blessing," Elder Ballard said, "and he asked if you and I could come up and give him one." I was so honored that I was one of the two men Larry wanted to have administer him a blessing. Elder Ballard gave Larry a powerful blessing with me assisting, and then I gave a priesthood blessing to sweet Gail, whom I've always loved as a dear friend.

It was a very emotional time. We all knew the consequences of Larry losing his legs; it was going to be a tough twenty-four hours for Larry, but the aftereffects could be devastating. We all knew it might be the beginning of the end, but Larry remained upbeat and cheerful. We talked about the early days, how we started out. We both cried. When it was time to go, we were both still very emotional. He pulled me down and gave me a big hug and a kiss on the cheek.

That was the last time I saw him. Less than a month later, he passed on.

Larry was a wonderful friend, a brilliant man, and a tenacious worker. He had a tremendously generous heart, and his philanthropy and generosity will have a lasting impact. He had a very deep faith that many people didn't see. All these things made him special, a common man who could do very uncommon things.

A riverboat gambler, and my dear friend.

A Team Player

Marc Amicone

Not long after Larry Miller and I became fast friends through softball, our Engh Floral team was playing at the Cottonwood Softball Complex—now the Larry H. Miller Softball Complex—in Murray, Utah. That night, Larry gave a stark example of how he felt about his team and showed his competitiveness and loyalty.

One of our teammates, a player Larry didn't get along with that well, got into it with an opponent during the game. Their jawing went on most of the night. It didn't amount to much until after the game, when it became a much different story. Neither player wanted to let it go. It turned into a near riot in one of the ballpark's warm-up areas.

As the situation escalated, Larry got in the middle of it. He pulled our teammate out of the fracas and told him to leave it alone. He insisted the bickering wasn't worth it and urged him to go home. Larry's words worked—on our teammate, at least. As soon as Larry calmed our player down and got him out of the mix, Larry himself turned on the other team's player. The arguing started all over again. Other players then needed to calm Larry down and move everyone out of the situation to avoid a brawl.

The moral to this story from the early 1980s is simple: despite personal feelings, Larry would go to battle to protect his team. If he was your teammate, that's all that mattered. This was just one of many instances in which Larry showed his extreme competitiveness and loyalty.

My friendship with Larry dates back to 1979. I was working for the Salt Lake Golden Eagles minor league hockey team when Larry and Gail moved from Colorado to Utah after purchasing their first dealership. Larry H. Miller Toyota became a sponsor with the Golden Eagles, giving me an opportunity to work with Larry and his staff. With that connection and being softball teammates, our mutual interest in the operations of pro sports teams became a frequent topic of conversation.

Larry expressed his interest in purchasing the Triple-A baseball team in Salt Lake City if the opportunity ever presented itself. "Marc, when I buy the baseball team, I want you to be my general manager," he told me.

Over the next several years, we would have that informal conversation now and then. Larry's message was always the same: we are going to work together running the baseball team one day.

Larry surprised me during one such conversation. "If we haven't spoken to each other for eight years and I buy the team, you will be my first call about being the GM," he said.

As time went by, Larry's business interests began to grow. He purchased the Utah Jazz outright, built the Delta Center, and continued to expand car dealerships. I moved on to work at the University of Utah, Larry's dealerships, and KJZZ-TV, which he had purchased. He became partners with us at the university, so our relationship was still one of friends doing business together.

In the spring of 2004, Larry called and asked me to come visit him at his tenth-floor office in Jordan Commons. The conversation began about our families and where I was in my career. After a while, Larry got down to business.

"I've made a deal to buy the Stingers," Larry said, referring to the minor league team he later renamed the Salt Lake Bees. "I've told you for a long time that I want you as my GM. Do you still want to do it?"

It took about a half a second before we were shaking hands.

Twenty-five years after Larry first promised me the job, I accepted my dream career opportunity, becoming the general manager of a Triple-A minor league baseball team. It's been an even bigger blessing to be in this position to work with Larry and the Miller family as owners. It is my pleasure and goal to always have an operation that would make Larry proud.

I often recall Larry's loyalty to me. He promised we were going to do this together if it ever presented itself, and he followed through. That is one of the great aspects of Larry that I will always aspire to emulate—be loyal to your friends and to your word. A handshake was always good enough for Larry. When he looked you in the eye and made a deal, it was a deal.

Mr. Larry

Mark McKown

My first encounter with Larry was thrust upon me prior to a preseason game at the Delta Center. I was there a little after four o'clock because Karl Malone was always the first player at the arena, and we had a pregame routine on the court and in the weight room.

Karl sat at his locker lacing up his shoes, and I was talking to him when Larry walked by to say hello.

I had had a couple of opportunities to meet Larry after being hired a couple of months earlier, but I'd always chosen to step to the back of the room or to stand behind big players like Greg Ostertag in hopes that he wouldn't see me. I figured the best thing for my survival was to stay below the radar.

"There goes the boss of all of us," Karl said. "Boy, you better be on your best behavior."

Karl then asked if I had met Larry yet.

"No, it's all good," I replied. "I can meet him at another time."

Karl stood up. "Come on."

I silently prayed we were headed out to do his shooting routine, but instead of turning toward the court, Karl veered in the direction Larry had walked. I followed, hoping he was gone. We hadn't taken two steps when the Jazz owner came back into the hall. My heart began beating rapidly. Larry and Karl greeted each other like buddies, not so much like boss and employee.

Karl then asked Larry if he'd met me. He replied no with an expression that didn't seem overly friendly. I was thinking that this guy had hundreds of employees, and the last thing he wanted to do was meet some worker bee like me. Karl told him my name.

"Oh, you're the new weight guy," Larry responded.

Strength coaches tend to not like that title. It's like calling physical education teachers the "gym teacher," even though they don't teach gyms. Likewise, my job entailed more than just weight training. But to be honest, I was so flattered he knew who I was, he could have called me the new court jester and I would have been happy.

"It's nice to meet you, Mr. Miller."

He looked at me for a long second. "Do you have a first name, Mr. McKown?"

Being from South Carolina, I answered as most southern boys would. "Yes, sir. It's Mark."

"So do I. It's Larry," he responded. "You call me Larry, and I'll call you Mark. Okay?"

In the South, we often attach the title of Mr. or Mrs. before a person's first name as a matter of respect. So I responded the way I'd been brought up to do. "Okay, Mr. Larry."

Second life lesson of that day: it ain't done that way in Utah.

"Just Larry, Mark. Okay?"

At this point, Karl was laughing—a bit too much—at my discomfort. "Yes, sir," I said.

Larry looked at me, shook his head, glanced at Karl, and walked out of the locker room, laughing.

I saw him at every game and at Jazz functions, so it got easier to greet him by saying, "Hey, Larry." I always appreciated that he remembered and called me by my name, especially considering the number of employees he had. I witnessed the unique relationships he cultivated with the folks surrounding our team, which I feel for certain stemmed from his character. He was loyal to his players, and that loyalty went both ways. Karl's relationship with Larry, for example, was uncommon in professional sports. Karl and Larry had a mutual respect and love for one another.

One time, when a seasoned player didn't show what Karl considered to be proper respect to Larry—by snubbing Larry after their post-game handshake—Karl scolded this player like a child. That player always greeted Larry with a verbal response from that point forward.

The team's loyalty to its owner was tried and true. Before one of our home games, a colleague from another NBA team told me he had heard that Larry once had to be restrained from going after an opposing fan. I'd heard the story, and I didn't feel like discussing it with this guy.

"Well, if that's true, then that fan was a lucky man," I said.

"He doesn't look so tough," my colleague joked. "I think I could take him."

This guy wasn't my friend, and his joke wasn't funny. I told him bluntly, "You'd never get a chance to find out. Nobody on our team would let you get near him, and the first two guys you'd have to deal with are right there," I said, pointing to Jerry Sloan and Karl Malone.

Coach Sloan made it perfectly clear to our players at our first meeting every season that Larry was the boss. Larry was fair and loyal, and his organization—from himself to his family to coaches—expected players to represent the club like gentlemen. Coach's respect for and loyalty to Larry was evident in every word he said.

I'm glad that Karl finally forced me to meet this unique owner. He's a man who earned the respect of others not only through a title but also through his actions. It's the kind of respect a great, loyal man like Larry deserved.

MAY I TAKE YOUR ORDER?

Mark Iwasaki

I'm not sure exactly when Larry and Gail Miller became regulars at the Pagoda Restaurant, but I'm glad they did, because it gave my family and me an opportunity to know them on a uniquely personal level.

My parents started the restaurant in 1946, just two years after Larry was born, right in the heart of his native Salt Lake City. For the first several years, the restaurant was downtown, in the basement of the Colonial Hotel, where the Salt Palace Convention Center now sits. In 1961, my dad moved the restaurant up into the Salt Lake neighborhood known as the Avenues, the neighborhood where Larry and Gail spent their youth. At some point, the couple discovered Pagoda and became familiar faces.

They became good friends with my parents over the years. When my parents retired and my wife and I took over the day-to-day operations of the restaurant, we got to inherit a friendship several years in the making.

It was fun to get to know the Millers in this casual setting and to get to see just how down-to-earth they both were. They came in to eat and were just like any other loyal customers. When we weren't too busy, we were able to stop by and check in. I'd ask how things were going, and we'd talk about his latest projects, or how the Utah Jazz were doing, or we'd talk cars. I remember one time when Larry excitedly filled me in on the details of the new racetrack, including precise facts about the project as it was nearing completion.

One time during a conversation, I told him I had gone to see a movie and he asked me what theater I went to. For some reason or another, I didn't go to the Megaplex. He teased me a little over this: "Why didn't you go to my theater?" We just made small talk and enjoyed each other's company. Shortly after that, Larry and Gail dropped off theater tickets for us.

My wife, Jodi, had even more interaction with Larry. I was usually in the kitchen, but my wife was out front, so she developed a barometer of sorts for understanding what he was feeling. There were days he would walk in and she could tell, from knowing him over the course of all those years, that he was preoccupied with concerns and details of all his businesses spinning around in his head. On those days, she'd tell our employees to give him some space. "Leave him alone tonight," she'd say. "Don't go over there too much."

Most other times, when he wasn't preoccupied, he would get deep into conversation with her. Jodi also taught at nearby East High School, and since education was one of Larry and Gail's passions, he always had questions for her.

Through their generosity, Larry and Gail would often express their appreciation by inviting us to attend Jazz games. We'd go as the Millers' guests and sit there with them next to the arena floor. It's always special to sit so close and see the game from that perspective. They took such great care of us, and it was a privilege to have the opportunity and memories.

But one of my favorite memories of Larry, which has a lot of meaning to me, is the day he went to work for us, if only for a few moments.

On this particular evening, Larry and Gail had come to eat on a very busy night. A busy kitchen can be hectic: servers coming and going, people calling out orders, the piercing sound of dishes being washed and stacked, exhaust fans on full blast, cooks communicating to servers and to each other, the phone ringing. It's all very stressful and frenzied, yet somewhere in this chaos there is purpose and order.

That was the type of night we were having when Larry decided to stop by the kitchen and say hello. Amid all this commotion, as Larry and I tried to make small talk in the kitchen, the phone rang. Apparently the hostesses were too busy with guests to answer the phone, so it kept ringing, adding a noticeable din to the already raucous kitchen.

Larry paused, looked at me, and said, probably only half seriously, "You want me to get that?"

"Sure," I said, a bit surprised. But he did just that. He picked up the phone and answered with the same greeting that everyone at our restaurant was trained to say. The customer wanted to place an order, so Larry listened and began jotting down what they wanted. Once, they asked a question he had to consult me on, but by the end of the call, like a seasoned professional, Larry had taken the order without the person on the other end having any idea who had just helped him.

It was a very humorous moment, but the reason this story means so much to me is that it showed how one of the most influential men in the state would grab the phone to help out in a busy kitchen. He was an automotive magnate, an NBA team owner, an entrepreneur, and a philanthropist—but for those few minutes, he was just there to help. It was a huge compliment to all of us, especially to me, that Larry felt comfortable enough to take the liberty as a family member would. It was funny and unbelievable, but also very meaningful.

That's just who Larry was. He was so genuine and unassuming, never one to act like a big shot. He was a regular guy, so much so that he wasn't above lending a quick hand to a friend on a busy night. It was precisely because Larry and Gail were both so humble and approachable that we developed the friendship we had.

I believe it was a credit to Larry to know that he was so down-to-earth, a humble person who, half amused and wanting to get everything precisely right, answered the phone for a customer. To this day, I often wonder what the caller would have said if he knew that Larry H. Miller was taking his order.

THE FIRST MEETING
TO THE LAST

Matt Harpring

Meeting an NBA owner for the first time can feel like a big deal. You expect the owner to come in with a suit and an ego, and the anxiety can run a bit high.

My first meeting with Larry Miller was nothing like that.

I had already been in the NBA for four years when I came into Utah on a free-agent visit. I had met at the arena with general manager Kevin O'Connor and team president Denny Haslam, and then it was time to meet Larry. I was immediately blown away.

"Hey, Matt," he said when I walked through the door. He had on a polo shirt and tennis shoes, and there was zero pretense to him. My anxiety dropped by about a thousand percent, and it was clear that he just wanted to get to know me. Our conversation went on, and Larry mentioned the first time I had made an impression on him. It was a couple of years earlier, when I played my first game against the Jazz in Utah, and I had played well, with nineteen points and ten rebounds.

"I first saw you play when you played against us here in this building," Larry recalled. He mentioned a specific play in that game and said, "From that moment, I knew that we wanted you." He talked about what he saw in me and what I could bring to Utah, which was a great confidence boost.

I was still a bit nervous because I would be replacing Donyell

Marshall, who had been pretty popular with the fans during his two years with the Jazz. "They liked Donyell," Larry assured me, "but they're going to like you more."

That vote of confidence was good enough for me. I signed a contract and became a member of Larry's Jazz, where I'd see even more evidence that this was no ordinary NBA franchise owner.

A lot of team owners sort of butterfly around the team. They'll make an appearance every now and then with a handful of other people from their posse, and that's about it. Larry was around all the time. He'd be in the pregame huddle, listening along with the rest of us as coach Jerry Sloan got us ready to go. His hand would be in there with the rest of ours when we went in for the final cheer. Before games, he'd get on the court and rebound for us while we warmed up with a few shots.

"Matthew," he'd say before sending a rebounded ball back out to me at the three-point line. "Here you go: three!"

He was a part of the team and really cared about us doing our best, and that made a difference for us as players. We were playing for a guy who genuinely cared.

Of course, his competitive desire to win had another feel entirely when we weren't playing well. The players knew right where he sat, across from the scorer's table on the first row. On the nights I didn't play well, or the team didn't play well, I'd glance over at Larry, and his facial expression always let us know exactly what he was feeling.

One time, he actually came over to our bench area and just stood over us. We weren't playing to the best of our ability, and he was fed up with the effort. He didn't mind the nights that we played hard and shots didn't fall, but he couldn't stomach the nights when we weren't working hard enough. The tone was always, *You guys are better than you're showing right now.*

I was always the last one to leave the locker room because I always iced my knees. That gave me a lot of opportunities to talk to Larry outside of a basketball game. We talked about his "batting average," a numbers system he had come up with to discern who had played well. Then we'd go into stories. I'd ask him a question and he'd go into anecdotes about the past, about Jazz history.

Soon, our friendship grew outside the locker room and the court. He'd take me to lunch, or he'd call me in the summer just to check in with me and the family. Toward the end of my career, we were quite close, and that meant a lot to me. Before I negotiated my last contract, Larry told me, "I don't want to lose you, so let's get this done. Please don't go anywhere else."

Going into a free-agent negotiation knowing that the owner didn't want you to go elsewhere was really a comfort. I told my agent, "If you can work it out, work it out." When the deal was finalized, Larry personally called me to make sure I was happy. "Yeah, I'm happy," I said.

"Well, we're ecstatic," he replied.

I never played another NBA game in a jersey other than the Jazz's.

Larry was a loyal guy, and he showed me over and over again that I could trust him. One time, a rumor surfaced while we were in Oklahoma City getting ready for a game. Reporters approached me for comment, saying, "We hear you've been traded to Miami."

A little stunned, I went to Coach Sloan and asked him if he knew anything. He responded, "I haven't heard about this. We're playing tonight, so get your uniform on." The media people were convinced I was getting traded, so I played that whole game wondering if the shoe was about to drop.

As soon as we got back to Salt Lake City, Larry came to practice and met with me. "I just want to let you know that you're not being traded," he said. "I'm never going to trade you. I don't care what the deal is. There are a few players on this team I might consider trading. You are untouchable in my eyes."

For the rest of my career, I'd always hear my name in trade rumors, but I could tune it out and play because I had Larry's word.

It was a special relationship, and that's why it was hard to say goodbye. I was driving with my wife, Mandy, in Salt Lake City in early 2009 when team executive Randy Rigby called me. "Matt, I know you and Larry are close," he said. "You need to get over there. They're telling me he doesn't have long."

When I arrived, Larry and I shared just a few minutes together.

He said, "I just want to let you know: you've meant so much to this franchise. You're one of my favorite players."

From that summer day in 2002 to the moments I spent at Larry's bedside, I know that he cared about me and appreciated me, on and off the court. As a player and as a person, that meant a lot to me. And it still does. I told him, "Larry, you don't know what you've meant to me and my family."

One last time he gave me the confidence and appreciation he always had, all the way back to that first meeting when I came in as a free agent.

JOB INTERVIEW

Jim Derrick

Larry Miller was an unusual manager.

While leading thousands of employees across a diverse range of businesses, he did things differently. He managed his time differently, he solved problems differently, and he most certainly hired differently, as was the case when I joined the Miller family of businesses in 2001.

At the time, I had been working as a consulting engineer on an energy department project in Monticello, Utah, several hours from my Salt Lake City home. Larry, a neighbor and fellow member of our church ward, took an interest in my situation, and would often stop by on Sunday evenings to talk about the work I was doing in the opposite corner of the state, about my family, and about our respective business philosophies. Sometimes we would chat in my living room. On other occasions we would go for a ride, like the Sunday he picked me up in one of his Cobras and we made a quick round-trip to the top of Emigration Canyon. With the high speeds and roaring engine, we didn't talk too much, so I just held tight to the roll bar.

During one of our Sunday conversations, we were discussing ideas about leading people. I shared with him my view: I thought we should all be in the business of building up individuals. Larry agreed with me, and maybe that's what triggered the invitation that followed soon after.

I was invited to meet with Larry at his office at Jordan Commons. We spoke for a few minutes, and then he made me a job offer unlike any I'd ever received. There was no official title, no job description, and no clear idea of what I would be doing. Before I left his office, I asked him what he would have me do.

"Well," he began, smiling, "we can call it special projects."

He went on to add a promise to this unusual job offer: never a dull day. With that, he handed me a piece of paper and told me to give it to the payroll clerk to start my employment as the newest member of the Larry H. Miller organization.

On the way to the clerk's office, I noticed that someone else had the title of "special projects." Over time I realized that he frequently gave this title to those he hired when he had no particular position in mind for them. It was a unique way to join an organization; usually you have a round hole and you look for a round peg to put in it. Larry didn't want to limit himself that way.

As instructed, I delivered the paper to the payroll clerk, expecting to learn the terms of my employment. But the note only told the clerk that I was being hired, so I was asked how much I was to be paid. So there I was, a new employee without a clear job description, negotiating my salary with the payroll clerk! I'm sure Larry signed off on our discussion behind the scenes, but it was another unusual step in an already very unusual process.

Larry gave me an office next to his, but I didn't have anything to do. So for the first three or four weeks, Larry invited me into his office to sit in on his meetings and listen in on his telephone calls. This "fly-on-the-wall" exposure to Larry's hour-by-hour agenda gave me a unique view of the Larry H. Miller businesses, and also of Larry himself. I learned a lot—and have since learned much more—about the singular way Larry operated.

I learned that Larry didn't like contracts; he preferred handshakes. He understood that he lived in a world where contracts were necessary, and he begrudgingly conformed. But he liked to shake hands and know he could count on a person's integrity.

He also spent a lot of time making sure his managers knew what was happening with the empire. That was important to him. About once a month he would walk through the department and gather fifteen or twenty of us for an impromptu lunch meeting. He would tell us what was happening across the Miller Group of Companies.

Larry liked to have people think his door was always open, but it wasn't. You had to get past Marilyn Smith to see him, and that was no small thing. As such, people learned not to waste an interaction on just one item; most of us carried around a "Larry List" so that we could capitalize on our time when a few minutes materialized. Once you had an audience with Larry, he was attentive and talkative—always teaching.

Larry had a temper, too. People who were familiar with that side of his personality knew that once he lost his temper, everybody lost, so nobody wanted to tip him over. We often banded together to make sure he was happy and properly informed, handling problems and bad news early.

These are lessons I learned over the course of the next decade, but those first intensive weeks alongside Larry helped immensely. He liked to take calls on speakerphone, so I would listen while he checked in with the governor or discussed player issues with the NBA commissioner. After several weeks, I was ready for my first special project.

A car salesman who had been with Larry since the very beginning had suffered an allergic reaction to bee stings while vacationing at his family cabin. The long-time employee passed away, and Larry put me to work to make sure that the man's family was taken care of. My first assignment was to contact the widow and find out her emotional and financial status and offer any kind of help we could. We helped her iron out disputes with the insurance company, got her a vehicle at a good price, and otherwise helped her through a difficult time.

One by one, other projects began to materialize. It was about five months before I had my first proper title: property manager at the Jordan Commons complex. Since then, I have managed construction projects, performed community service, worked with TV producers on the *Joseph Smith Papers* program, met with lawmakers and public officials, and much more. All of those experiences have enriched my life.

My friend and boss is gone, and I'm journeying into retirement, but there's no question that Larry's promise was fulfilled: there never has been a dull day working with the Larry H. Miller Group and with the unusual, incomparable Larry.

LARRY MILLER, BOOKS, AND ME

Curt Bench

In late 1997, I received a phone call at my bookstore, Benchmark Books. The caller identified himself as Larry Miller. Yes, it was *that* Larry Miller. I could not imagine why the owner of the Utah Jazz would be calling me. He revealed that a friend had recommended me as the person to talk to about a rare book that someone wanted to sell to him, politely inquiring if I might be able to spare some time to answer a few questions about it. Like most people in Utah, I knew only of the public image of Larry Miller—successful and famous owner of multiple car dealerships, the Jazz, and the Delta Center, and one of the busiest men in the state.

Larry soon proved how humble, considerate, and down-to-earth he was.

It turned out that someone wanted to sell Larry an 1830, first-edition copy of the Book of Mormon, a scarce and very valuable book. Since he knew little about it, he wondered if I would be able to help him determine its authenticity and fair-market value. I assumed he would ask if I could come to his office to look at it, but instead he offered to come to my store, at my convenience, to show me the book and discuss it. We set up an appointment, at which time I examined and evaluated the book for him. I assumed he would want to find out the basics and leave quickly so he could resume his busy schedule. Even though Larry had been very polite on the phone, I tried to prepare myself to meet and talk only briefly with a very important, if not intimidating, person. When he came into my office, any such preconceptions vanished as he put out his hand and introduced himself simply as "Larry Miller."

After some pleasantries, Larry showed me the Book of Mormon. It was soon obvious that Larry (not "Mr. Miller") had come to learn and not to teach. He wanted to know all about the book, its physical makeup, history, and value. He asked intelligent and pertinent questions. Mainly, he listened carefully as I tutored him about this book that he looked at not only as a rare item for possible purchase, but also as a sacred object. It was soon apparent that this edition of the Book of Mormon meant more to him as scripture than as a collectible book.

I was pleasantly surprised—and more than a little amazed—when our conversation turned to other publications. We spent a good two hours talking about Larry's love of books and reading. Imagine that! One of Utah's most famous and important businessmen was also a bibliophile. Who knew? As a fellow book lover (and bookseller), I was thrilled.

As we concluded our stimulating discussion, Larry graciously thanked me and offered to pay for my time. I said I wouldn't accept money but wouldn't mind if I could get a couple of complimentary tickets to a Jazz game. He told me to consider it done, to pick a game and contact his secretary. After deciding on a game, I called her and then somewhat tentatively asked whether the seats for me and my wife, Pat, would be in the lower or upper bowl, thinking I would be happy with any location at all.

I was floored by her answer.

"You will be Mr. Miller's guests and will sit with him in his seats on the floor," she said.

If that weren't enough to dazzle me, she had one more surprise.

"He'd also like you two to be his personal guests for dinner at the Jazz 100 Club before the game."

When the much-anticipated night came, we showed up at the Jazz 100 Club at the Delta Center and had a delightful and delicious meal with Larry, his charming wife, Gail, and a couple of other invited guests. They treated us as if we were just as important as the other VIPs who came to dine in this exclusive setting before taking their seats on the arena floor. There was no pretension or ostentation on the Millers' part; they were as humble, kind, and thoughtful as one could ever imagine. We had a spectacular night sitting next to the Millers, watching an exciting game on the court level. The players seemed ten feet tall, and you could hear almost every word they uttered and sound they made. We were in basketball heaven!

That would have been quite enough for a lifetime for me, but Larry turned out to be a steady customer for years to come. He was willing to trade Jazz tickets for books. He frequently made purchases from me for his personal enjoyment, but, even more often, to give as gifts to friends and members of the LDS Sunday school class he taught. He racked up quite a bill at times, but we quickly whittled it down by getting tickets for my family, employees, and friends.

In a January 1998 letter to Larry's secretary, Vickie, I wrote: "Please thank Larry for trading and for doing business with us. He has always been gracious and generous by inviting my wife and me to games as his guests, by allowing us to use his seats in his absence this week, by trading tickets for books at very fair prices (the printed ticket price and what Larry asked for them in trade were two very different figures), and by his thoughtfulness in general. We really appreciate him."

We mourned the premature death of Larry Miller, as did thousands of others throughout Utah, the sports world, and elsewhere. Some had the privilege of knowing him, but more did not. I am so grateful that my path intersected with Larry Miller's for an all-too-brief but wonderful period of years and that we shared a profound love of the printed word. My life is richer for having known Larry H. Miller.

FRIENDSHIP

THE PERSONAL TOUCH

Gerald Lund

I met Larry Miller for the first time over the telephone. I wish I had made a record of exactly when that was. I'm guessing the summer of 1994.

"Hello. Is this Gerald Lund?"

"Yes?" I answered very tentatively, not sure yet who I was talking to.

"The one who wrote The Work and the Glory?"

"Yes."

"Well, it's good to meet you. This is Larry Miller. Love what you're doing. I've got a bunch of questions about that series you're writing. I'd love to talk to you about it. Would you have lunch with me sometime?"

My first thought was, "Is this *the* Larry Miller?" But I didn't say that. By this time I had recognized his voice, and I stammered out something about being delighted to join him for lunch.

"Good. How about tomorrow? 11:30? You like Mexican food?"

"Yes."

"Good. Let's meet at the Restaurant Morelia, northwest corner of 6100 South and State Street." He said goodbye and hung up.

When I drove up to the restaurant ten minutes early, I was surprised. It wasn't that large. The parking lot held only ten or twelve cars. I guess I had expected something pretty lavish. As I got out, I saw that Larry was already there. He was on the phone in his Lexus. He waved to me and motioned he would be just another minute.

As we entered the restaurant, Larry was recognized instantly, but it was more than that. The man at the reception counter broke out in a broad smile and approached him. They gave one another a big *abrazo* as Larry called him by name. Then two of the cooks saw him and came out to greet him. He called each of them by name. A waitress and a couple of other employees smiled and waved. Everyone in the restaurant had turned to watch.

Ahh, I thought, *so this is what it's like to be famous*.

As we were escorted to a table, several patrons smiled, waved, or called out a hello. We were handed menus, and a man came over and introduced himself. He wanted to thank Larry for what he was doing with the Jazz, adding that he was driving a car from one of his dealerships. Larry thanked him and they shook hands.

As that was going on, my eyes were drawn to the center of one page of the menu. I had to smile. I couldn't help it. I saw:

LARRY MILLER'S COMBO

(2) CHEESE ENCHILADAS, (2) GROUND BEEF TACOS, BEAN TOSTADA

"You eat here often enough that you have your own entree?" I asked.

He laughed and explained that some time before, he had learned the Restaurant Morelia owners were in financial trouble and were going to be forced to close. "I helped them out a little," he added. "Now I have my own menu item."

He ordered it, and so did I. I probably would have done so anyway—cheese enchiladas actually are my favorite Mexican dish. As advertised, Larry wanted to know all about the book series, especially the development of characters. No business talk, just personal. We ate lunch together several times at Restaurant Morelia over the next few years. Each time, the welcome from the staff was the same. Each time, the response from those in the restaurant was the same. Each time, the conversation was about my writings and his love of the arts. And each time, Larry and I ordered the same entree.

I didn't get much chance at those lunches to ask him questions about himself. He always was genuinely interested in what I was doing. Each time my wife, Lynn, and I dined with Larry and Gail at their home, they would pepper us with questions—about the books, about what I had learned about Joseph Smith in writing them, about Lynn's music, about our family, and a myriad of other things.

Larry and Gail also invited us to attend home Jazz games, sitting with them in the front row of what was then called the Delta Center. On most occasions when Lynn and I joined the Millers for a Jazz game, Larry would meet us at the security booth on the arena's bottom level, where the teams entered, and escort us to the incredible buffet in the top-floor dining room. Walking along the corridors of the arena to the dining room elevators, we encountered various employees rushing about doing their jobs. I can't remember the exact number of employees he told us it took to run the center during a night of professional basketball, but it was in the hundreds. It didn't happen in every single case, but it did occur over and over and over: employees would call out to Larry or stop to briefly shake hands.

Two things impressed me about that.

Not once do I remember anyone referring to him as "Mr. Miller." It was always "Larry." No surprise there. He was just "Larry" to strangers as well as friends. Just like at Restaurant Morelia. (Later, Larry appeared in some of his auto dealership commercials. The tag line was, "After all, you know this guy." When I saw that for the first time, I thought, *Yes, we all like to think we know Larry personally.*)

The second thing was that I couldn't get over how often he greeted employees by name, stopping long enough to inquire about their lives and families. He asked the elevator operator how his granddaughter's high school graduation speech had gone. The man gave Larry a quick report, adding, "And she asked me to thank you for the gift you sent." He asked a concession clerk how her mother was feeling after recent surgery. He talked to the chefs at the buffet, to the waitresses who served us, to the referees on the floor, and to the mascot, the Bear.

On one occasion, Larry invited me, my son, and his best friend to a game. They were fifteen or sixteen at the time. Larry always left as the game ended to be in the locker room with the players, and on this night he turned to ask if the three of us would like to accompany him into the locker room. As if we would turn down such an offer! The boys will never forget the experience. They were so hyped on the way home they couldn't stop talking about it. And while they went on and on about meeting Stockton and Malone, the thing that amazed them most was captured in something they kept repeating: "I can't believe Larry did that for us."

When I read Larry's autobiography, *Driven*, I was astonished at his accomplishments, amazed at his gifts and abilities, and awed by his business acumen and prodigious ability to keep complex numbers in his head. I learned much about the man from that book, but when the invitation came to contribute to this book, it was not those things that came to mind. My first thought was, *Yes! He was an incredibly gifted and brilliant businessman, but he was so much more. He also was a remarkable person, always so beyond just being driven.*

BREAKDOWN

Steve Van de Veere

My car breaking down outside of Denver in 1971 might have been the best thing that ever happened to me.

I had just completed two years of military service and was on my way to start a new job with the parks and recreation department in South Lake Tahoe, California. I had just gotten my degree in parks and recreation management and was excited to start my career when, just outside Denver, my car stopped working.

An old roommate of mine, somebody I played baseball with in college, lived in Denver, so I gave him a call. My friend, Butch, said, "Sure, come stay at my place until you get your car fixed. I'm busy this weekend, though. I have a softball tournament."

Over the next few days, it became clear that the car wasn't getting fixed, and I was going to lose the job in Tahoe. I decided to apply for a parks and recreation job in the Denver area, since it looked like I was going to be there for a while. With nothing else to do that weekend, I told Butch I'd like to come watch his tournament. That's where I met Larry Miller for the first time.

Larry was the starting pitcher on Butch's team, and I watched each of the six games he pitched that weekend, winning all six of them. They won the tournament, and after the award ceremony I approached the team manager. "Can I try out for your team?" I ventured. The manager told me they didn't have any room on the team, but I could try out next year. But I didn't give up. "I'm probably better than anybody you've got on your team."

Larry overheard this and stepped into our conversation. "You're pretty cocky, aren't you?" he interjected.

"Yeah, but I'm really good, too."

They let me try out at their practices over the next two weeks, and finally I made the team. I played alongside Larry, our ace starting pitcher, for the next nine years, and in that span we played in eight national tournaments.

Larry was a great teammate to have because he was so intense, for better or worse. If somebody got a hit or drove a run in, Larry was the first guy to come out and give him a bear hug and lift him off the ground. "Great job!"

One time, I saw the other side of that intense desire to win. He was letting a teammate have it for a mistake in the outfield. "You don't know what you're doing!" Larry yelled.

The outfielder peppered back, "Hey, I didn't throw that pitch that the guy hit off the fence!" It was getting heated, so I decided to step in and break them up. When I did, Larry grabbed me to move me out of his way, and when he lifted me up, he inadvertently hit my head against the roof of the dugout, knocking me out. I woke up a few minutes later with a cold towel to my forehead and Larry saying, "Veere, Veere! Are you okay?" Bumped heads aside, I had a great time playing softball with Larry for all those years.

During that time, Larry was promoted to the role of general manager at Stevinson Toyota, and he gave me a call. "Hey, Veere," he said, "quit your job. Come and sell cars for me."

I had never sold a car in my life and had no idea how to do so. "Don't worry about it," Larry reassured me. "We can teach you how to sell cars." I think Larry had seen my intense desire to win and to be the best that I could be on the softball field, so he figured that same will would help me succeed elsewhere. I made the huge decision to leave parks and recreation and join Larry selling cars.

It was an incredible experience. I learned a lot about cars but also about life. Even back then, he loved to teach us about steward-ship and accountability.

I worked for Larry until 1979, when he moved back to Utah to operate his own dealership. But I rejoined the Group in 1987 when Larry bought a dealership back in the Denver area, starting with Boulder Hyundai. For the next seven years, I worked for Larry at dealerships in the Denver area, Salt Lake City, and Phoenix. In 1994 I took another short break from working for the company, un-til Larry called me that fall. "Veere," he said, "I got a plane ticket for you. Fly to Utah." So I did.

He showed me his plans to build several new dealerships at the Southtowne Auto Mall and told me about Prestige Financial Services, a new company that would provide consumer finance solu-tions to dealerships across the country. "Wow, this is cool," I said as Larry shared with me his plans. "I want to be a part of this." I moved back to Salt Lake City in January 1995 to work at Prestige, and I've been there ever since.

We'd meet every Friday, and then if he had time we'd go out to lunch and talk about our families, sports, and other topics. I even had a few opportunities to sit on the front row at Utah Jazz games with Larry and his wife, Gail. Those were special times.

Larry was a very encouraging and positive leader. He frequently talked about being willing to take risks, and he would put it in terms he knew I would understand. "Think about it, Veere, if you're a baseball or softball player and you hit three out of ten times, you're a .300 hitter and you're going to the hall of fame! And that means you failed seven times out of ten. You can't let those failures bother you. Learn from them and get better." That's why it didn't scare me to take on any new challenge to follow Larry, including mov-ing state to state, trying new businesses, and working with different people. I would have followed Larry through a brick wall.

In January 2009, I received a call on my mobile phone from Larry's home number. I picked it up, and Gail Miller was on the other end of the line. "Larry wants to talk to you," she said.

Larry came on the line. "Veere," he said, as he always did to start our phone conversations. "I just wanted to call you and tell you how much I love you and how much your friendship has meant to me over the years. I'm honored to call you my friend."

A bit taken aback, I said, "Please, I'm the one who's honored. I love you, too." I didn't know what else to say. I was shocked.

The next morning, Larry passed away. I am so touched that he would call me in his final hours and tell me how honored he was to be my friend. I will never forget it.

Like I told Larry, I'm the one who is honored. I have been blessed by our twenty-eight years of friendship and association. And I owe it all to a job offer, a softball tournament, and a broken-down car on the side of the Colorado highway.

A KID FROM
THE AVENUES

Governor Norm Bangerter

Larry Miller was a highflier, and as governor of the state of Utah, I got to see just how singular he was in his ability to barrel through challenges and get things done.

Larry was someone who made decisions and took risks to create great things. But he was still Larry Miller, a kid who grew up in the Avenues area of Salt Lake City. He was still a real guy. Even with all the money he made and the success he had, I think the thing that made him special was that he never thought of himself as anything other than Larry Miller.

I had an up-close view of some of those early big moves of Larry's. I was sworn in as Utah's thirteenth governor in January 1985, just weeks before Larry Miller became part-owner of the Utah Jazz. During my eight-year tenure at the statehouse, I saw Larry tackle a number of trials. Those were the early days of the Miller enterprise we know today, and it was interesting to have a view into those moments and how they affected people in the state of Utah.

When Larry bought half of the Jazz, everybody scratched their heads and wondered what he was doing. He was still relatively unknown, and he had to take great financial risk to buy in. A year later, he bought the other half, and at that point I never would have guessed that Larry would yet be taking more big gambles to keep the Jazz in Utah.

I was still the governor in 1989 when Larry began to seek financing for a new arena. Team salary and other expenses were on the rise, and he knew that for the team to remain financially viable, he had to build a new venue with more capacity. But funding the multimillion-dollar project was not easy.

One day he came into my office, and I could tell it was a difficult time for him. He said, "I don't know what I'm doing," making it clear he was feeling both humble and overwhelmed.

After sensing that Larry just needed somebody to talk to, I switched gears and said, "Can I give you my opinion on things?"

"Yeah," he replied, "I'd appreciate it if you would."

"Look, we all love the Jazz and want to keep them in Salt Lake. You're working hard to try to do that and do it in the right way. But make sure you do what's right for you." I knew he was already in debt due to his dealership investments and the two transactions that had made him sole owner of the Jazz. I wanted to make sure he had thought through whether this was the best decision.

Of course, Larry had already made his decision, and it was just about finding a way to get it done. So, about a year later, I stood next to Larry with my hard hat and shovel at the ceremonial groundbreaking for the Delta Center. Larry had determined not to fail, so he found a way.

One of Larry's characteristics that lent to his success was that he knew how to make a decision. I'm sure all of his decisions didn't work out to the same degree, but it's important to know how to make decisions, how to move. Larry knew how to analyze and how to look at things, but he knew that no matter how much research you do, you can never be sure of an outcome. He was comfortable taking that risk. Larry probably worried about the risks the same way anyone would, but he didn't let that keep him from charting a course and taking action.

Part of his determination came from the fact that Larry didn't like losing. That was obvious in a number of settings, but nowhere more than on the softball or baseball diamond, where Larry had been an accomplished softball player. One time, we had a fun little exhibition game up at the University of Utah. The teams were made up of different people from throughout the state, and then there were two major-league pitchers, one for each team.

Larry and I were on the same team, and Tom Seaver, a former pro who had spent most of his career with the New York Mets and the Cincinnati Reds, was pitching against us. Seaver was bearing down, throwing hard pitches. He was retired and older but could still throw, and he wasn't holding back. Our team's pitcher was just lobbing pitches in so the other team could get some hits, but not Seaver.

Nobody was getting a hit off of Seaver, but Larry was not going to be denied. He dug in, fought him off, and got a clean hit off of him. Seaver was a little irritated, but that reflected Larry's competitive nature.

He used that same drive to will several efforts to success. He came from no advantage, perhaps even a disadvantage, but he applied himself and went to work. There are so many opportunities that Larry Miller seized in order to make an impact. It's amazing to think of all the good he did, including various endeavors that don't get the same broad attention as the big-ticket items. People in the LDS Church will certainly remember his contributions to projects like the Joseph Smith Papers. People in the academic field will recognize all he did for local colleges and the education system. But he did it all in the most unpretentious way.

Based on our few conversations on the subject, I don't think Larry was worried about building a legacy, but he certainly did so. I think he simply wanted to do the right things, and that became the legacy he left for us.

He was a personality. He wasn't just a run-of-the-mill, suede-shoe-black-tie guy. He was down-to-earth, and what set him apart was that he didn't set himself apart. He wasn't putting on anything false. I think that probably made a difference for a lot of people.

He was just Larry Miller, a kid that was born up in the avenues. He had his tough days and his good days, but he lived his life with energy and dedication and service. I don't know of anybody that I would rank higher in terms of impact on our community.

LOYAL LARRY

James Grant

My uncle and aunt, Reed and Lou Ashton, lived across the street from the Millers when Larry and I were kids. I didn't live in Utah, but I struck up a friendship with Larry while visiting family in Salt Lake City. My two cousins, David and Denny, were a year older and younger than Larry, but I was just his age.

I moved to Salt Lake City in 1960, and Larry and I bonded while going through trying times. He did not get along with his parents, and my father had been killed in an airplane crash in Alaska. My family lived with the Ashtons for a year while my mother was recuperating from a nervous breakdown. We then moved two houses down from Larry.

I survived West High because Larry basically put his arm around me and accepted me as his friend. I was the new kid. He was the only one I knew in the high school. But he made me part of the group, and I will be forever grateful.

One of the things that impressed me so much about Larry was his competitive spirit in all he did. This was evidenced in everything from marbles in grade school to metro softball championships. We played darts and softball, and neither one of us was a good loser. Once, we decided to play canasta to a million points. When either of us would lose a game, we'd both lose our tempers. Cards would go flying in the air and the table would be upended. After we had broken several tables and lamps, his mother forbid us to play anymore; we had to quit at 530,000 points.

One of the things I appreciated more than anything about Larry was his loyalty. After making my transition to high school a relatively smooth one, he remained my loyal friend for the next forty-nine years. It didn't matter what your occupation was or your standing in the community—once Larry was your friend, he was your friend forever.

Larry, who was best man at my wedding in 1967, called my wife, Karla, when her father passed away. Larry had only met my father-in-law twice—once at our wedding reception and another time at a Utah Jazz game—but he wanted to do something to help Karla's grieving family.

Larry told Karla that he wasn't good at situations like these, but he made an offer. He volunteered to make the hundred-mile drive to Logan, Utah, to shine her family's shoes. This would have been a large task, considering Karla has ten brothers and sisters and a huge extended family.

"He insisted that he could drive up in an hour and a half," Karla remembers. "He was so humble in this request that it brought tears to my eyes and endeared him in my heart forever. I knew how busy he was, and I turned down the offer. But I knew he meant it! He would have dropped everything to perform this service."

It was no surprise that people from throughout the community attended the twenty-fifth business anniversary party for Larry and Gail. Members of the Jazz, the Golden Eagles hockey club, politicians, church leaders, neighbors, coworkers, and childhood friends rubbed shoulders and were all on an equal basis. And this was nothing new. That community camaraderie happened at every party or event hosted by Larry and Gail.

Larry had great integrity. He didn't just talk the talk; he walked the walk. He was a great influence on my life, and I am a better man because of my association with him. Larry was the best friend I have ever had. I loved him as much as any of my brothers. I appreciated the opportunity to visit with him just before he died. We expressed our love for each other and said our goodbyes. Gail was so gracious to allow friends as well as family that privilege.

Someday, I hope to get the chance to finish that game of canasta with him.

WRESTLING MATCHES

Al Rounds

Larry had the remarkable knack for always showing up out of nowhere, always at the right time. He'd suddenly appear at my house and say, "Can you go for a ride?" As a local artist, he often gave me inspiration and encouragement just when I needed it the most.

Actually, that's precisely how Larry first walked into my life. I was out front washing cars when Larry and Gail Miller pulled up in their convertible. I knew who Larry was, but I didn't know him at that point. He had come to see me about some commission work, and that's how our friendship began.

Most of the interactions Larry and I had started that way. He was so busy with all of his different businesses and projects that I wouldn't hear from him for a while, and then he'd simply show up on my doorstep unannounced.

I often get really strong feelings about a painting I should work on, but I don't know exactly what it should look like or what should appear. I often go searching, literally and figuratively, for images to match the feeling I'm trying to convey. Larry became a facilitator for that process. We'd go on drives or walks, and he would help me find clarity and inspiration.

I had big dreams and was a hard worker, and Larry loved facilitating for those types of people. He gave me father-like advice: he was always very honest and straight with me, but also so positive about how to move forward in my work. His belief in me provided the validation I needed and helped me to believe in myself as an artist.

One day, Larry characteristically showed up on my doorstep and asked if we could go for a ride. He wanted me to do a painting for his office that would remind him of growing up in Salt Lake City, but he wasn't sure exactly what he wanted the painting to look like, and he wanted to give me freedom to create the perfect painting. To provide inspiration, we drove and walked around Larry's old neighborhood. Larry grew nostalgic as we walked, and he told me about his youth.

"Over there," he'd tell me, "we used to play army and have dirt-clod wars. And on that corner, there used to be a drugstore where we'd buy Lime Crushes, and if you froze them and drank them fast you got a brain freeze." Larry went on like that, showing me the exact places that were part of his youth.

Ultimately, an idea struck me. What began as a painting of Larry's old neighborhood became a view of the valley from that same spot in 1885. The very spot where the cart stands in the painting is the spot where Larry and his friends would have their dirt-clod wars. The first house to the left is where the drugstore would later stand and Larry would later buy his Lime Crush.

When it came to negotiating the business part of the transaction, I saw another side of Larry. Larry liked my idea, so I began drafting it to be 36" x 50". But as I drew it out, I realized it needed to be bigger. "How much bigger?" he asked, knowing that the price was dependent on the size. We then began what can only be described as a wrestling match. The wrestle over the price was all verbal and Larry would figure the numbers in his head. A few weeks later, I called him and told him it needed to be even bigger—three times bigger. Based on the scale of the painting, it needed to be nine to ten feet long. Larry sounded displeased and said, "How much?!"

I told him and we wrestled again.

When we finished the negotiation, Larry joked with me about the price. "So, are you planning some big trip, like to England?" From then on, whenever he talked about the painting or showed it to people, the story of how the painting got so big was that I wanted to go on a big trip.

Wrestling with Larry was not one of the things at the top of my fun list. It was down somewhere close to where I list getting scraped elbows and bloody noses. Frankly, I'd rather have a dirt clod thrown in my face. He liked to win, and although we were friends, that side of our relationship was temporarily suspended for the sake of negotiating. Once you finally agreed on a price, that number was set in stone. He never forgot, right down to the cent.

The painting, originally commissioned for Larry's office, ended up being placed in the Millers' home. Their new home in the Avenues was finished right when the painting was finished, and Larry decided that would be a fitting place for it.

On a different occasion, he similarly showed up out of nowhere and asked if he could take me to the Delta Center, which was then under construction. He wanted me to do a painting of the arena and he knew that I needed to see it for myself to get the touch and feel of the place. As we were cruising through the construction zone in a golf cart, many times we came upon groups of workers and Larry stopped to greet them. He shook everybody's hands and thanked them for their work. "I'm Larry H. Miller," he'd start, never assuming that they knew who he was, although by their stunned silence and stares it seemed they all did. Larry was always teaching me—he showed me how to treat people and how to help people share your vision.

I grew to love all the sides of Larry. He was such a support to me and helped me find inspiration and belief in myself. Over the years, our conversation became more and more spiritual, and the last few years before Larry passed are when he helped me the most. He was a huge friend to me.

It was always quite a surprise to have Larry H. Miller show up at my front door and want to take me for a ride, always just when I needed inspiration and support. How could he possibly have known? Each time it would start the same. "I've been thinking, let me show you something." For a few seconds I might hesitate, remembering the wrestling matches. Then I'd jump in the car and off we would go.

ONE PHONE CALL, FORTY YEARS

John Knaphus

M y friendship with Larry Miller spanned more than forty years and started with a single phone call.

In early 1968, Larry and I were working in the parts departments of two competing Toyota dealerships in the Salt Lake Valley. We were both running our respective departments, and occasionally it was necessary to call around and see if another shop in town had the part you needed. Larry placed such a call to me, and it wasn't long before we were well acquainted.

That spring, Larry asked if I would consider coming to work for him. In May 1968, I left Wagstaff's Toyota to join Larry across town, and over the next few years we worked together at three different dealerships. At that point I thought I knew a lot about the parts business, but I quickly realized that, compared to Larry's encyclopedic knowledge, mine was limited. More important, I began to learn about Larry's intense work ethic, impeccable follow-through, and legendary philosophy of service.

Twice during those early years, two different colleagues were struggling with debt and consequential personal challenges. Larry spoke to his wife, Gail, and they agreed to use their own personal savings to help these coworkers resolve their issues. This was long before Larry and Gail were owners of a successful business empire; in fact, they didn't even have their own home at the time. But such was their desire to help those around them that they made a point to help, and in both cases lives were touched and examples set. This was an important precursor to the type of generosity the Millers have offered ever since, but for them it was just the right thing to do.

Soon our career paths would diverge, if only for a while. Larry was being recruited to pitch for a softball team in Denver, and he lined up employment there to facilitate the move, ultimately landing at Stevinson Toyota. I returned to Wagstaff's, but Larry and I stayed in touch almost daily, frequently reaching out in search of parts the other might be able to help track down.

One time, Larry called me in need of a condenser, a very small part. We had what he needed, so Larry asked me to have it shipped to him freight collect at his Denver dealership. In the spirit of fun, we found the largest box we could find—a windshield box—and taped the small part inside the wall of the box, filling the rest of the box with packing filler. When Larry received it and found his tiny part enveloped in giant packaging, he was amused and called to share a laugh. But he wasn't done laughing yet.

It wasn't long before I had a similar request, and Larry had the small part I needed. The next day, I received a very large box, but this one wasn't filled with packing peanuts and filler; Larry had filled the box with buttered popcorn. Larry was a great ally and always got things done, but he found ways to make them fun.

In early 1972, I contacted Larry with a much larger need. My dealership needed a Toyota Hilux pickup truck for commercial parts delivery, but they were in such high demand that I called to see if Larry could sell us one from his Denver store. One turned into two when my boss sold the initial truck, but again Larry was able to arrange it. When I reported back that two trucks were waiting for us in Denver, my boss surprised me by announcing that we were going to fly to Denver right away and drive the trucks back. We were in such a hurry that I forgot to call my wife, Peggy, and let her know that I wouldn't be home that night.

Larry met us at the airport and insisted I stay the night in his extra bedroom and then drive home in the morning. Both my boss and my wife—who by now was in the loop as to my whereabouts—were fine with it, so I spent the evening visiting with my old friend and the next day made the trip back along Interstate 80. Only I didn't make it all the way back to Salt Lake City.

Just outside Rock Springs, Wyoming, I became distracted by a large herd of antelope and the truck drifted to the right. When I noticed what I was doing I corrected, but way too abruptly. This caused the rear wheels to slide in the loose gravel on the side of the road. The truck slid, snapped off the nearby mile marker, and headed straight for the deep median separating me from oncoming traffic. A small car would have bottomed out and come to an abrupt stop in the bottom of the median, but because it was a light truck, I continued up the other side, went airborne, and cleared the oncoming freeway lanes, even flying over a state road crew truck.

I was fortunate to survive the accident, but not without multiple surgeries, months in the hospital, and even a full-body cast. It was nearly a year—ten months, to be exact—until I could return to work, and I spent much of 1972 in hospital beds. Throughout that year, Larry and Gail made several trips to Salt Lake to visit. On one of those trips, Larry called my wife and arranged to "kidnap" me for the day. The second of our six children had just been born, so Peggy was probably exhausted from having to take care of a newborn baby and an equally needy husband in a hundred-pound body cast, so she welcomed the invitation.

Larry showed up in his station wagon, packed me outside, and slid me in the back cargo area of the wagon. Larry took me for a hamburger, and then we went to the Utah State Capitol grounds, Larry's childhood playground. He literally leaned me against a tree, in my full cast, and tossed a Frisbee to me on and off for about four hours while we talked. It was great therapy for me, and Larry even took a picture to capture what must have looked like an odd game of Frisbee toss. A couple of years later, on one of their frequent visits to Utah, the Millers brought me a framed picture from that day, a gift that still provides me with solace as I reflect on the trials I've made it through with the help of loved ones.

When I did return to work, I joined my father's tile and stone business. Years later, Larry moved back to Salt Lake City, and he became a frequent customer. I tiled many of Larry's dealerships, but more important, we remained close friends. In fact, Larry's guidance was the pivotal force behind my next big career move: in 1986, I started my own contracting business. Before all of my paperwork was even complete, Larry announced that he'd become the first paying project of my new business. He had just purchased the rights to a Hyundai dealership and asked me to do all of the tile and stone for the new store. Starting with that job, we were contracted to do tile and stone work for many other Miller projects. The biggest job came in 1991, when he asked me to do the tile work at a new project he was working on: the Delta Center, home of the Utah Jazz.

Larry Miller has been a very large part of my life since that first phone call, changing how I go about businesses and relationships. I love Larry and Gail Miller, and I owe much of what I have and enjoy today to the profound influence of my best friend, confidant, and mentor.

CAPITOL HILL KIDS

Dennis Haslam

It's hard to say exactly when my experience working for Larry Miller began. I was president of the Utah Jazz and Miller Sports and Entertainment for ten years, starting in 1997. Before that, I began offering legal counsel to Larry and his companies in the early 1980s. But long before then, clear back in the 1950s, I began plying my services at Larry's side as his paperboy understudy, bottle collector, and delivery assistant.

Larry and I knew each other since he was six years old and I was two. His family's backyard abutted mine, and our families were close. There were probably twenty or thirty families in our neighborhood, a little society of baby boomers, each with four to seven kids. There were a lot of different ages, but everybody knew everybody, so kids of all ages played together. We were the "Capitol Hill Kids."

We came together and played tag, kick the can, football, and baseball. Find a ball of any size and we'd find a way to create a game with it—and sometimes we didn't even need that. We made up a game called "Pomp," which was football without the ball. Kids tried to get over the goal line while their friends tried to tackle them. That's how my friendship with Larry started.

Later, Larry would employ me and others in what might be seen as an early display of his entrepreneurship and leadership. He had a paper route delivering the *Deseret News* when he was about twelve—probably thirty to forty papers a day. Like Tom Sawyer with his friend Huck Finn, Larry cleverly pressed me into service by making a game of delivering papers: "See how close you can get to the front door without breaking a window."

That wasn't the only Tom Sawyer moment in our friendship. He had figured out where employees at the Capitol would discard their bottles after eating. We'd go around filling up crates with soda bottles and then take them down the hill, where we could exchange them for three cents per bottle plus twenty-five cents for the crate. We'd walk back home with a Coke or a Nehi soda. Later on, after Larry got his driver's license, he had a job with a coverall service, driving a van around to service stations to pick up greasy, dirty coveralls and taking them to be laundered and redelivered. He would often say to me, "Why don't you come with me? We'll have fun." Like Huck, I was along for the ride again.

Already he understood hard work and reward. I don't think he had at that point any inkling of the businessman he would become, but he was willing to work hard and often shared the reward with me by taking me out after we spent a day tossing papers, collecting bottles, or picking up dirty coveralls and replacing them with clean ones.

When Larry was nineteen, he had a falling out with his parents and needed a place to stay. I didn't know exactly what had happened, but he had a problem, and he came to our house. My dad let him move into our home for several months, and at that point, Larry became pretty much a brother to me.

Eventually, Larry went off to Denver to play semi-professional softball and continue a career in automotive parts. During those years, I was involved in military service and then college and law school, but I always stayed in touch with Larry and Gail, who by then were married. By the time the Millers moved back to Salt Lake City, I had graduated law school and was a practicing attorney. And that's how the next chapter in my relationship with Larry Miller started.

Larry needed counsel on some legal issues, and I began

representing him. His uncle, who had helped him purchase his first dealership and was a fifty/fifty partner with him up to that point, was asking to be bought out, and it was important to Larry that it be done right. Because of the family relationship and Larry's sincere gratitude for Uncle Reid's help, he wanted to make sure that Reid was dealt with fairly, but Larry didn't have the funds on hand to pay the near $700,000 they had agreed on. That meant putting everything he had on the line and borrowing the money. This wouldn't be the last time.

As his lawyer, I advised Larry to be cautious. "Larry," I said, "this loan document has you tied up three ways to Sunday. If you don't perform on this loan agreement, and you are in default, you're going to lose everything that you have."

But he knew what he was doing. He looked at the fifty-page loan document and said, "I have to do this." He accepted the responsibility, signed the papers, and was now on his own. He took similar risks many times. When he first purchased half of the Jazz franchise, it was a complex transaction involving multiple lenders and some six or seven promissory notes. Building the arena was another "all-in" moment for Larry, when he put not just his finances on the table but his whole self as he threw himself completely into a complicated design-and-build project.

Working for Larry was both remarkably fun and incredibly demanding. My wife began to accept the notion that I was always on call, and "It's Larry" was a common phrase in our home. My wife and I are scuba divers, and once we were diving in the Caribbean. Of course, at the bottom of the ocean with a regulator in your mouth, you can't talk, so we often dive with little white boards we can write on to communicate. We were below the surface, some 100 feet down, when Deborah tapped me on the shoulder and pointed to her board. "It's Larry," the board said. I started laughing through my regulator.

During my many years working officially for Larry, people frequently asked me what Larry's defining characteristic was. I would always say two things. First: what you see is what you get. Larry doesn't hold very much back, if anything. He's as real as they come. Second: the other reason for his success is that he is incredibly driven.

Starting in 1985, Larry held annual management meetings with leaders from throughout the Group, and I usually took copious notes. To look over the notes from those yearly meetings is to recapture the Larry Miller story piece by piece, sort of a time capsule of what was important to him.

There are so many fantastic insights and Larryisms in the notes from the more than twenty management meetings that I attended. Things like, "It's okay to *be* big, but don't *act* big." He talked a lot about how investing time in training employees would make their lives better through education and also enrich our company. He told us, "I want to be a builder of things and ideas, and we as a group should be bridge builders." He talked about upholding our integrity, being ready for change, never forgetting the basics, and so many other important lessons.

But perhaps the most important thing that came from those meetings was when Larry reminded us why he was in business in the first place: to improve the lives of others.

I know that's what Larry would be most proud of: the family of employees and millions of touch points with people in the community. Through the dealerships, the sports franchises, the theaters, the entertainment properties, and everything else, a staggering number of people became interconnected. That's the legacy of Larry Miller: the Capitol Hill Kid, my friend and brother, and creator of a massive network that brought people together and improved lives.

Taking Dr. J
to Church

Tim Howells

I'm one of the few people who can say that *I took Larry Miller* to a Utah Jazz game, and not the other way around.

Larry and Gail Miller had just moved from Denver to Utah after he purchased his first Toyota dealership, and they happened to move in right behind our house. My wife, Patty, and I had second row seats at the time, so we decided to get to know Larry and Gail by inviting them to join us for dinner and a game. It may have been the first time he ever attended a Jazz game.

But it would take more than one evening out to understand the complexity of Larry. He was a complex person by nature, a bit of an enigma. He had a combination of qualities that, when you pour them all together, don't create a simple product. I probably still haven't fully come to understand and appreciate that, though I certainly saw those qualities as his neighbor, friend, and eventually his employee.

For one, he had an incredible power of will. He could just will things to happen with his great energy and drive. The results of that drive and willpower are all around us, especially in and around the state of Utah. Second, he had great intellect. Larry was a genius. There's no doubt about that. His ability to grasp and understand complicated things is a testament to his extraordinary mind. The third quality Larry demonstrated regularly was his vision. He could see things others couldn't. He was always several steps ahead of most people, and when others were wondering, *What is this guy doing?* Larry was building an empire with his willpower, intellect, and vision.

I gradually began to grasp the nature of Larry Miller, and in 1988 we actually had the opportunity to serve together in the presidency of the Young Men organization in our LDS ward. One week that summer, Larry came to inform me that he wouldn't be able to attend church that Sunday because he was picking up Julius "Dr. J" Erving from the airport to host a visit with the superstar free agent and try to convince him to consider joining the Jazz. Larry actually hosted Dr. J at his house, barbecuing hamburgers while they discussed the possibility of a signing.

Larry indicated that he would try to persuade the eventual Hall of Famer to come to church during the time the young men were together for their priesthood meeting. We arranged to have the fourteen- through eighteen-year-old boys together in case it would work out, but we kept our plan a secret so that nobody was disappointed in the event that Dr. J was unreceptive to the idea.

I honestly didn't expect to see them, so I was as surprised as anyone when I heard a knock on the door during our meeting. I stepped into the hallway to see Larry next to "The Doctor," eager to introduce his surprise guest. When I stepped back into the room with Larry and the NBA superstar, jaws dropped and eyes doubled in size. For the first minute of this encounter the young men were speechless, which was quite rare for this group. Dr. J shook each young man's hand and was extremely gracious in providing an experience they would long remember. Larry's efforts to bring Dr. J to the Jazz proved to be unsuccessful, but I'll always remember how excited Larry was to share Dr. J and the experience with a roomful of young men.

About a year after the Dr. J visit, Jazz general manager David Checketts stepped down from his position. Patty came home a few weeks later and said, "I passed Larry and Gail down on the bike path, and they were talking about you. I think he's going to hire you." This was the craziest thing I had ever heard. I was in commercial real estate, not professional sports.

But a couple of days later, I was walking down the ramp at the Salt Palace with Larry when he said, "Why don't you come and see me in my office at about 2:30?"

I had no idea why I was there. We talked about his automotive business for two hours, and the thought ran through my head, *He's going to offer me a job in the car business*, which made no sense. Then he switched gears, and we started to talk about the Jazz. Finally, out of nowhere, he said, "How would you like to be the general manager?" I was blown away. I had been a major NBA fan since I was eight years old, so it was an easy answer.

It was a dynamic world to be in with Larry. He always had something cooking, so I had to be on my toes. I joined the Jazz in 1989, and soon after that there was the new arena, then the other business opportunities, then Jordan Commons. It was an exciting time to work for Larry.

I took my responsibility to Larry very personally. As GM, I spent his money in a very real way, so I was very cautious. His interests were always first and foremost on my mind. I tried to anticipate what Larry would want. I didn't always guess right, but I tried to scrutinize how I spent his resources even more closely than if they were my own.

Again, Larry was an enigma. I can tell stories of Larry being a generous, warm, kind, loving person. There are also stories of Larry being tough and emotionally charged. But his heart was big and in the right place.

He left behind such a powerful legacy, especially as a great community benefactor, both for the people who worked for him and for the community at large. He also had tremendous integrity in his dealings with people. He always wanted to do the right things for the right reasons, and I would trust Larry with any material possessions I had. And certainly his financial generosity is well documented, but he has done some wonderful things that perhaps nobody else knows about, even in terms of giving of himself and his time. For nineteen years, he volunteered at BYU, giving post-graduate business students the type of insights that you just can't find in textbooks. He invested time in sharing his experiences and his strong belief in our country and our free enterprise system and in sharing his faith and religious convictions with others.

But perhaps more than anything else, Larry's legacy to me is in that special combination of willpower, intellect, and vision. The ability he had for marrying those special gifts is something I saw throughout the eleven years I worked for Larry, and I don't think there's another period in my life that can compete with those years in terms of producing amazing experiences and unique memories.

ONE IN A MILLION

Hilary Drammis

I don't know anybody else like Larry Miller.

Larry was a visionary, an exemplary man, and my friend. To tell the story of our friendship, I need to start with the friendship between Larry and my dad.

My father, Joe Buzas, was a former New York Yankee who later in life owned and operated over forty minor league baseball teams. In 1994, I was living in Chicago when my dad decided to move his franchise from Portland to Salt Lake City. NBA franchise owner Larry Miller was instrumental in encouraging this process.

Larry loved baseball and had spent much of his adulthood as a Hall of Fame fastpitch softball player. My dad felt camaraderie with fellow athletes, so he and Larry got along well right from the start. Larry was instrumental in getting a new baseball stadium built, and he even contributed financially to its construction. Soon, the Portland Beavers franchise became the Salt Lake Buzz, now known as the Salt Lake Bees.

Days before opening day, my dad was anxious with anticipation, pacing around and worrying whether the stadium would be ready. Larry calmed him down and assured him that everything would be ready in time. My dad admired him on all levels and considered him a close friend. Occasionally, Larry would visit with my dad at the baseball park, where they would talk sports for hours at a time. My dad commented to me how he loved those conversations with Larry and loved to attend the Jazz games, in his four second-row season tickets. These two sports franchise owners and former athletes were instant friends.

A couple of years after the team had settled into Salt Lake City, my dad became very ill. I relocated from Chicago to Salt Lake to take care of him and learn the sports business. I felt that could be good security for my own children, so I began to help run the team and learn everything I could about Triple-A baseball.

My father's health continued to deteriorate, but even then he enjoyed attending Jazz games whenever he could. Larry insisted on allowing my dad to use his parking area at the arena, the section reserved for Larry, his family, and the players. That way, my dad was close to the door and there was always an attendant there to help wheel him in and transfer him to his seat. This was such a great act of kindness exhibited by Larry. I felt immense gratitude for his compassion and caring. This type of extraordinary goodness was second nature to Larry. He was a giant among men by doing simple acts that most neglect to think about. He never made a big deal about it; he just took care of it.

Soon after, my father was completely bedridden, and I was running the team. I asked several local successful businessmen to serve on an advisory board for the team, which at this point was named the Stingers. The day of our first meeting, these successful people started to trickle into the owner's suite at the ballpark. The last to come in was my dad's friend Larry. When he walked in, the ambiance of the room changed. He exuded such command and presence that all eyes were on him. People paid attention, and all acknowledged him.

After mingling for a few minutes, we got down to business. I asked how we could improve our operations to make attending a baseball game more enjoyable for the fans. The initial answers were discouraging. One gentleman said he found baseball boring so we needed additional entertainment of some sort. Another member of the board stated he simply didn't enjoy baseball. At that point I was feeling a bit dismayed.

Then Larry spoke.

"I can watch baseball for hours," he said, "just to see one great play."

The room changed again—Larry had altered the tone of the conversation from critical to positive. I was thrilled by his comment and knew that he was a true baseball fan, plus it was obvious he was concerned about my feelings. His statement was definitely appreciated, and the other members then focused on providing productive suggestions.

The difference between my dad and me is that he's a baseball purist. I didn't play, as he did, so I was more interested in family entertainment. My dad knew everything about the game. I focused on fans having a great time.

Larry understood the family fun and entertainment aspects of the business, but he also was a baseball purist who loved the game. His support was much appreciated.

In 2003, my father went to heaven after losing his courageous battle with cancer. I was asked if I wanted to sell the team, and at first I refused, but after some time and consideration, I set a price for the family franchise. Larry stepped forward as one of the prospective buyers, and I remember vividly the discussion we had in his office.

"My dad highly respected you as a friend and businessman," I told him. "But there's no negotiating about the price."

We went on to discuss other details: team affiliation, sponsorship agreements, the lease, and other factors that would influence the sale and the ongoing operation of the team. On each topic, I would share my opinions, sometimes in a rather dogmatic way. He would listen and consider my ideas and point of view.

At one point, he stopped and said, "Hilary, you may not take this as a compliment, but I think you are a lot like me."

I was a bit taken aback. It impressed me how humble he was in prefacing his remark, but of course I took it as a compliment.

I responded, "That is one of the greatest compliments I have ever received. Thank you." I think it was my honest, straightforward way of conducting the conversation that prompted the remark. There was no haggling or trying to move anybody around. That's how we both operated.

In the end, Larry was comfortable meeting the terms I had set forth, and we agreed on a deal. I was pleased to leave the team in the hands of a great friend like Larry, someone my dad had admired.

I am so happy to have known Larry and to be able to say he was my friend. I have such affection for Larry and deep gratitude for the friendship and care he showed my father. He is an example of what we all should strive to be.

He was one in a million, and the world is definitely a better place because he lived in it.

My Greatest Friend Ever

Donald A. Dyson

There was just one light on in the whole dealership. Everybody had gone home for the night—except for Larry Miller.

Early in the fall of 1968, I bought a new truck from a dealer in town, and it was to be delivered to me with a trailer kit installed. I called the dealership to find out what time I should drop by to pick it up, only to learn that they had not even started the installation. I was disappointed because I had plans to go horseback riding the next day with some friends in the Uintah Mountains, and I needed the truck. They told me they would work on it and that I could pick it up later that evening.

I went by to collect the truck that night as instructed and discovered that the dealership was closed. I was frustrated as I saw the empty dealership with all its lights turned off, but then I noticed one light in the back of the service department. My spirits picked up. I wouldn't know it until later, but that is when I first met my greatest friend ever.

I walked to the back and found a guy underneath my truck, alone at the dealership, installing my trailer kit. Such was his work ethic and dedication that he was the only person left to make sure they had met their commitment to a customer. We briefly visited as he told me what he was doing, without saying one begrudging word about having to stay late to finish the job. I drove away in the truck that night.

I didn't learn until later that I had just met Larry. Since I was in the insurance business and worked with a lot of car dealerships, I had heard stories of this parts guy with an unbelievable memory. But it was that night under the solitary light in the service department that I finally met this man people raved about.

Several years later, my office received a call from Larry, just after he had purchased the Toyota dealership in Murray. Looking back, this call was possibly the most significant call in my business and personal life. Larry requested a meeting with me to discuss his coverage and liabilities, to which my officer manager responded with an enthusiastic, "Absolutely!"

I cleared my calendar and met with Larry that week. He handed me a binder with the policies and coverage details of his current plan. "Will you look at these and tell me if I'm covered correctly or if I should do something different?"

I made a few suggestions, and he agreed with me and asked me to go ahead with those recommended changes.

Even though I worked with Larry, I hadn't just yet realized how brilliant he was. The next year, I came back to talk about the renewal of my policy, and we sat down once again to review his coverage. As we did so, he remembered every number, every coverage detail, and everything I had said a year earlier, as though it were typed out in front of him. It's a good thing I had my notes or I would have been unable to keep up with Larry.

Our relationship continued, and I had the opportunity to learn more about Larry Miller the man. We began to build a solid friendship, and this was long before he began to receive recognition for his incredible business talent and vision. At that point, probably only Gail and a handful of others realized what an incredibly talented and driven businessman he would become.

For almost thirty years after that first phone call, I had the opportunity to work with Larry and some of his key people. I watched as, by his own sheer force, he built his business empire. His presence, generosity, kindness, and love were truly exceptional.

Each year there were other companies that were looking to take my place as Larry's insurance agent. Each year Larry would request that I review the competition and report my thoughts back to his people. That's how much he trusted me. In about the eighth year of our association, I was shocked when one of these companies submitted a proposal that was significantly better than ours. Naturally, I was concerned about the possibility of losing my relationship with Larry and the Group, but I nonetheless offered my honest opinion. I told one of his principal people, "This is much better than what we can do. The coverage is appropriate, the limits are adequate, and the price is better. You should take it." I knew I had lost.

I was told they'd take a few days to review it and then let me know their decision. As promised, I was asked to meet a few days later, and I went in fully expecting the guillotine to fall. But to my surprise, the conversation went very differently.

"Don, what does your company make on commission for our policies?" Larry asked.

I shared the number, which was not insignificant.

"What if we just paid you that amount, and had you as a consultant?" Larry went on. "You'll be available to us to share your recommendations as a consultant, and we'll just pay you directly."

The answer was an easy yes. From that point forward, I sat in on all the meetings, reviewed all the quotes, and then helped select the best proposal.

Our trust and friendship had grown beyond what I ever thought possible. As the years went on, we became even closer. Larry and Gail became close with my wife, Tess, and me, and we would go to dinner, to Utah Jazz games, and otherwise enjoy each other's company. One time, my wife mentioned to Larry that she really liked Adam Keefe, a hardworking reserve on the Jazz. She said she really respected his approach as a player and that he seemed to be a really nice person on top of it all.

The next time we attended a game with Larry, Adam came over

to Tess and personally thanked her. "I appreciate the support," he told her, making it obvious that her remarks had been relayed. Larry just winked at us.

One of the prouder moments of my life happened at one of Larry's annual Christmas gatherings with managers from the Group. He stood to address the large audience and said, "I'm very happy that five of my very best friends in the world are here with us tonight, and I'd like to introduce them to you." It meant so much to me to be introduced as one of Larry's best friends, and the feeling was mutual. I just loved him.

Several years later, a manager at the Group felt our involvement with the company was no longer necessary and subsequently came to my office to tell me they no longer required our services. I was heartbroken. I wrote Larry a letter telling him I would miss working with him but hoped that we could remain close friends.

When Larry got my letter, he called our home immediately. He told my wife, "Tess, I knew nothing of this decision. Tell Don that as long as I am involved with the Group, he will be, too."

Larry did so much for me and for other people. He did so many things that people don't even know about. He helped me and my family with things and showed me a brand of loyalty that is extremely rare. He was more than a successful businessman. He was a kind, gentle man who never forgot the importance of loyalty, honesty, and friendship. He was a man who would stay late to install a truck hitch to ensure a customer was happy. I could never have predicted that a minor inconvenience would lead to one of my most cherished friendships.

Larry was born in Salt Lake City, Utah, on April 26, 1944. Here he is at a young age playing in the snow.

Larry as a young schoolboy in the Salt Lake Avenues.

Larry and his mother, Lorille. She dropped him off at a daycare every day on her way to work.

Larry with his brother and sisters
when he was twelve years old.
Top to bottom, left to right:
Judy, Larry, Charlene, and Tom.

In his youthful high school days.
Larry graduated from Salt Lake City's
West High School in 1962.

Larry and Gail met and began dating at Horace-Mann Junior High School.

Married at the Memorial House in Memory Grove on March 25, 1965.
They were married for forty-four years before Larry died in 2009.

Larry and Gail's wedding party. From left to right: Clark Silver, Myrtle Saxton
(Gail's mother), Glen Saxton (Gail's brother), Lorille Miller (Larry's mother),
Frank Miller (Larry's father), ElRay Jenkins, Larry, Lynda Saxton, Gail, Joy
Lisonbee, Diane Saxton, Margaret Medly, Grethe Larson, Charlene Miller.

Larry often toured the country as part of league softball.
Here he is with his 1978 Colorado team, sponsored by Stevinson Toyota.

In the summer of 1992, Larry was
inducted into the softball hall of fame.
Here he is featured with his wife,
Gail, and their children.

Larry was well known as a talented softball
pitcher. He ended his softball playing in 1984.

Larry standing at a 1972 Toyota regional parts managers meeting in Denver, Colorado.
Larry first moved to Denver to play softball in 1971 and worked for Burt Chevrolet Toyota.
He later went to work for Stevinson Toyota before moving back to Utah in 1979.

Larry's first Toyota dealership in 1979.
His company now owns fifty-four dealerships across the nation.

The Miller family in 1979, just after they moved back to Utah
when Larry bought half of the Murray Toyota dealership.

Larry taking his sons and grandson for a
Sunday drive in his cars. From left to right:
Larry, Steve, Greg, Roger, Zane, and Bryan.

Gail enjoying a barbecue on the
back porch of their home in 1982.

With Larry's growing business, vacations didn't happen often for the
Miller family, but here they are enjoying southern Utah in 1978.

Larry fishing at the family cabin in Idaho. Larry often referred to these fish as his pets, issuing a catch-and-release policy. Inside the cabin is a plaque that reads, "Catch and release only. Remember the fish are beings."

Larry and his grandchildren around the fire pit at the family ranch.

ElRay Jenkins and Larry were best friends and also competitors. Although Larry most often won out in athletic events, here ElRay sports his fishing victory.

Larry oversaw the construction of the Delta Center from start to finish. The 20,000-seat arena took fifteen months to build—the quickest construction for an arena of its size.

Even though he didn't purchase the Salt Lake Bees until 2003, Larry was involved from the beginning, overseeing the construction of the ballpark on behalf of the county. Here he is lying in the outfield during the construction of the ballpark in 1994.

Larry on the court with legendary basketball player "Dr. J," Julius Irving.

Karl Malone and Larry H. Miller
shared a special relationship. Here
Karl ices his legs while sharing a laugh
with Larry at Salt Lake Community
College during the summer league.

PHOTO BY NORM PERDUE, COURTESY OF NBA

While most team mascots rarely hear from the team owners, the Jazz Bear enjoyed a special bond with Larry throughout the years.

Larry speaks with shooting guard Jeff Hornacek. Hornacek and Larry worked together for fourteen years before Hornacek's retirement in 2000.

PHOTO BY DON GRAYSTON, COURTESY OF NBA

PHOTO BY KENT HORNER, COURTESY OF NBA

Ever the patriot, Larry stands
hand-over-heart during the
national anthem before a Jazz game.

Unlike many team owners, Larry was
heavily involved with the Jazz. Here he
gives NBA point guard hall-of-famer John
Stockton advice during a heated game.

PHOTO BY SCOTT CUNNINGHAM, COURTESY OF NBA

In 2008, Larry, Gail, and their son Greg helped celebrate Jerry Sloan's one thousandth win as head coach of the Utah Jazz.

Complications from diabetes rendered Larry in a wheelchair for the last year of his life. But that didn't stop him from showing his support for his team and attending all the games he could.

The first car Gail ever purchased was a red Ford Falcon. A lover of racecars, Larry made several modifications to the vehicle.

Larry and Gail riding in one of their Cobras at the Concours d'Elegance in Salt Lake City, Utah.

Larry sitting in a Shelby Cobra. Like all his Cobras, this blue model was one of Larry's most cherished possessions.

Larry, Gail, and their grandson Zane standing with Carroll Shelby, the creator of the Shelby Cobra.

PHOTO BY BRYAN J. NELSON, COURTESY OF SAXTON | HORNE

Larry's love for cars carried on throughout his entire life. This passion led him to create the Miller Motorsports Park in Tooele County, Utah, in 2006.

Roger Penske often visited with Larry at the famous Miller Motorsports Park.

Larry overseeing a race hosted at Miller Motorsports Park.

When Larry's business hit the twenty-fifth anniversary milestone in 2004, he gave his employees a memento to thank them for their dedication to building and fostering relationships. Here, Roger Racer and Larry display a large version of the commemorative sculpture.

Larry stands with Jim Brown after Jim completed the LoToJa, a 200-mile bike race from Logan, Utah, to Jackson Hole, Wyoming. Larry's son Steve also raced in the event.

Long-time Jazz commentator Hot Rod Hundley shares a friendly handshake with Larry.

Although his sense of humor was scarcely documented, Larry could let loose with the best of them. While not a born musician, Larry strums an electric guitar at one of his senior management retreats in Hawaii.

Larry attending a Slam Dunk for Diabetes event at the Delta Center in 1992. From left to right: Governor Norm Bangerter, Larry Miller, Mark Eaton, Frank Layden, and Doug Miller.

Larry with University of Utah President Chase Peterson
and Spencer Eccles at the University of Utah.

Larry knew his employees were what helped his business
to succeed, and he always wanted to make sure they were
recognized. Here, theater usher Sue Ann Larsen receives
her five-year gift alongside manager Steve Tarbet.

Larry standing with many of the key executives that helped make his
business what it is today. From left to right: Bryant Henrie, Richard Nelson,
Pat Kroneberger, Larry, Clark Whitworth, Tony Schnurr.

Larry famously avoided a suit and tie. After the purchase of the Utah Jazz, Larry figured he'd surprised everyone by showing up to a celebration dinner in tuxedo tails and a top hat.

Never a fan of formal education, Larry was awarded an honorary doctorate from the University of Utah.

Larry and Gail with British Prime Minister Margaret Thatcher when
Larry received the Distinguished Utahn Hall of Fame honor.

One of Larry's mottos was, "I don't mind getting big. I just don't want
to act big." Here he's seen shopping for groceries for his mother.

Second Counselor of the First Presidency of The Church of Jesus Christ of Latter-day Saints, Dieter F. Uchtdorf, and his wife, Harriet, standing with Larry and Gail in the Millers' home after one of President Uchtdorf's firesides.

Just before Larry's passing, he and Gail were able to attend the LDS temple sealing of long-time friends Jack and Carol Muterspaugh at the Salt Lake Temple in January 2009.

Larry modeling for Dr. Stephen Neal's statue at This Is the Place Heritage Park.
The statue was dedicated shortly after Larry's death in 2009.
Larry's face was used as "the patriot" for the *Duty Triumphs* statue.

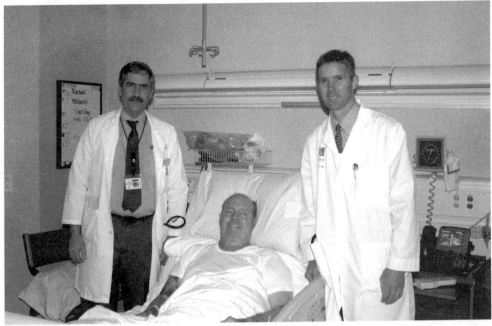

Larry's growing health problems led him to be hospitalized near the end of his life, but his spirit was never weakened. Here he is in good temperament with care providers Dr. Speed and Dr. Dunson.

The entire Jazz team visiting Larry during his hospital stay at the Huntsman Cancer Institute in Salt Lake City, Utah.

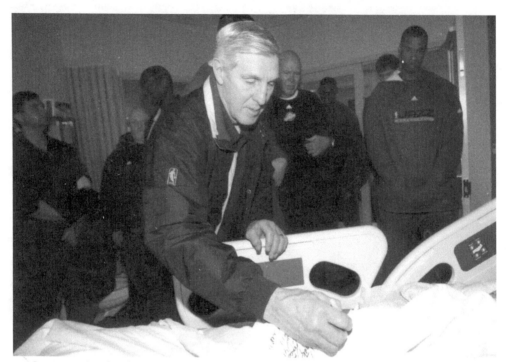

Long-time Jazz head coach Jerry Sloan signing Larry's cast after Larry's double amputation. The entire Jazz team signed his casts to show their respect and to honor Larry during his final days. Larry passed away on February 20, 2009, due to complications from diabetes.

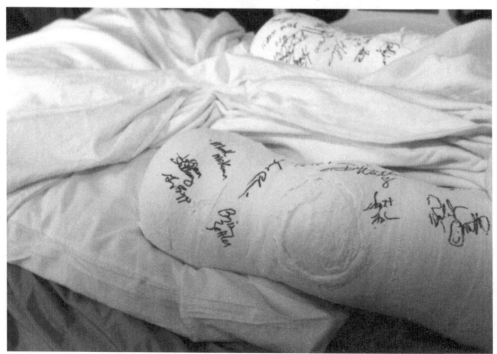

LEADERSHIP

Part of the Team

Randy Rigby

Larry Miller and I became full-time Jazzmen at almost precisely the same time. He had owned half the team for the previous year, and I had been involved as a market research consultant, but in 1986 we both became fully involved right at the same time, which means I have had the great privilege of being a part of the entire Larry Miller era of the Jazz.

Larry liked to make everybody feel like part of the team. He had a rallying ability, and a lot of that was because he made it clear that it wasn't just Larry's company; it was *our* company. He also had the ability to include people in the company vision. He spoke as though we all had roles to play in order for us to be successful, and he as the owner had his role too. He was going to do all that he could do to magnify his job, and he expected all of us to also hold up our end by doing the same thing. It was meaningful for people to be a part of that broad vision of protecting others' jobs and making the community better. He made us part of the team and instilled in us a desire to work for him and never let him down.

I worked on the broadcasting side, and we continued to build our on-air exposure as the Utah Jazz were starting out. We had a few TV games on KSL, but its station management feared that the games were cutting into BYU sports programming. TV is such an important way to build your fan base in professional sports, but we were always going to be battling against network programming. We saw all these big corporations from New York and Los Angeles buying up TV stations in Utah, and we weren't sure what that meant to the future of our broadcasts. We voiced to Larry that we needed to do something for the long-term benefit of the Jazz.

The next thing I knew, Larry said, "I've got an opportunity to buy a TV station." A small, independent TV station, KXIV, was available. Larry negotiated and bought the station, and we changed the call letters to KJZZ, signifying that the Utah Jazz now had a broadcast home.

He asked me to take on the task of running KJZZ in addition to the broadcast department and national sales. Larry always saw in people the ability to grow and do more, and apparently he saw that in me. It was a huge compliment if Larry asked you to take on more responsibilities. I took the helm, and we started to grow KJZZ. We picked up some University of Utah games, added more Jazz games, and bought other key programming. Over the next three years, the station—which had been losing $1 million a year when Larry bought it—became a profit center, netting a couple million dollars a year for the organization.

Soon, some large media companies started to knock on our door and inquire about buying KJZZ. One potential buyer from California was interested in buying the station for $100 million or more. If I had been in Larry's shoes, I would have thought about taking the deal, but Larry taught me a great lesson.

"Randy, let's say we sell it," he said. "Now what are we going to do with the money? We'd be impacting the lives of people who might lose their jobs. We'd be impacting a voice in the community when a lot of other stations represented a voice coming from the west and east coasts, not locally from Utah. We're here to protect and build this community."

He turned down the offer.

I was so impressed with Larry and his belief that money was simply the vehicle to help us accomplish something bigger. Money wasn't the end result; it was a tool. He bought the Jazz with that same community mindset. He took a major financial risk to buy the team, and he did it for the good of the community. It was not a move he had made to reap financial benefits but rather to protect an asset for the state of Utah. He wanted to make the Wasatch Front a better place to live, work, and be entertained.

One day, I walked into a meeting with team president Denny Haslam and was surprised to see that Larry had joined the meeting. Larry turned to Denny and said, "Do you want to tell him or should I do it?"

I started to worry. *Tell me what?* I wondered. Larry then told me of a problem employee he needed to fire but wasn't sure how to approach. He had asked that store's general manager if he would take care of it, but after a two-hour meeting, the manager didn't want to be the one to break the news either.

At this point, I stopped Larry. "Are you trying to tell me something?" I asked. "Is today my last day?"

Larry held his poker face for another few moments before cracking a smile and saying, "Nope. I just wanted to get your attention a little bit."

He then told me of Denny's decision to step down and extended the offer to me to succeed Denny as the president of Larry H. Miller Sports & Entertainment. "You're well qualified, and you're the person I have the trust and confidence in to take us to new heights." He couldn't help but be playful in telling me. I accepted the opportunity.

We had a very special relationship because while he was my boss we also became very close friends. He knew my family, and I could tell he cared for us. We also talked about other interests, and we both loved sports. After Jazz games, we'd have a debriefing of the game in the coach's office with the coaching staff, General Manager Kevin O'Connor, Larry, and me. Eventually the coaches would leave, but sometimes Larry wasn't quite ready to go home. So he, Kevin, and I would sit together and reminisce and talk sports.

That's when Larry would share his inner feelings about the team and particular players. It was a way to understand and gauge what strengths and qualities Larry looked for, and as we continued to build teams, that became the criteria.

He was always passing on that vision. One time he was driving out to Miller Motorsports Park with CFO Bob Hyde and me, and he said, "I might not always be here. I want you guys to understand and continue to teach the core values of this organization so that even when I'm gone, we can make sure these values continue to be carried out."

Unfortunately, Larry's words were prophetic. I'm glad he took the time to pass along what was important to him and to teach us his philosophy before he passed away. He often talked about something he called his "three-legged milk stool": have a little fun, make a little money, and take care of the customer. If we did all three of those things, we'd be all right.

One day in early 2009, Larry invited his senior management team to visit with him at the hospital. He and his wife, Gail, told us what was happening with his health due to complications from diabetes and the decision they had made to remove him from dialysis. They knew Larry would be gone shortly. I told Larry I loved him and we gave each other a big hug. And then I said goodbye to my friend of twenty-three years. It will always be an honor to have been part of Larry's team.

THE VIEW
FROM LARRY'S

Shaun Neff

From the breakfast table at Larry Miller's house, I could see across the entire Salt Lake Valley. I saw a basketball arena, car dealerships, movie theaters, and so much more. As I looked across the valley, it occurred to me that I was essentially seeing a canvas painted with a masterpiece of different accomplishments. And I was sitting right next to the artist.

I am good friends with Zane, Larry and Gail's grandson, and happened to be staying at the Miller home while visiting from out of town. I woke up that morning and Gail had prepared breakfast, so I sat down and enjoyed the incredible view, where I could see the way Larry had impacted the city.

I said to Larry, "It has to be awesome to look out from this vantage point and see all of your successful endeavors. It must be like a painter who steps backs and looks at a painting."

Larry didn't say a word in response but looked at me with a huge smile.

This was just months before Larry eventually passed away. That was my last interaction with him, but it was a special one. Through Zane, I had known Larry for a long time, but to see his pride as we pondered together the impact of all of his successes was an opportunity I'll never forget.

We also spoke that morning about his love for America. It was late 2008, and we were beginning to feel the effects of the economic downturn. It would have been easy to think that things were a bit of a mess, and I was curious to know what Larry thought.

"You know what?" Larry said. "America will be fine. America was built on hard work and the will to succeed. This country will always be strong. I'm not worried, because in the end, America will always provide opportunity for people to succeed if they work hard."

Nobody was a better example of that than Larry. Through his own hard work and determination, he had proven the American Dream was a reality. I thought of Larry as a legend, and it was always such a privilege to sit and converse with such a successful person who was so willing to share the lessons he had learned. I was all ears. As an entrepreneur working to build my own successful business, I was thrilled to get to learn firsthand from Larry's tremendous success story.

I started my company, Neff, when I was a student at Brigham Young University, about five years before this breakfast conversation at the Millers' home. Being from Southern California, I had always been interested in the surf-skate-snow culture, and I decided to chase that passion.

I printed T-shirts with my last name on them and sold hundreds of them out of my backpack. Then I met some professional snowboarders, and I knew that if I could get them wearing my apparel at competitions and in interviews, it would take off. But because of strict apparel restrictions in their agreements with different brands, they couldn't wear my shirts. I read through a typical snowboarder contract to find a niche that I could attack, and I realized that there were no restrictions about headgear.

I jumped in, at first just by writing my name in sharpie on headbands and beanies. It took off, just as I thought it would, and in the decade and a half since, we've expanded into fifty-five countries and virtually every place where youth culture accessories are sold.

Now, as my business was starting to take off, Larry had some sound advice for me. He told me to stop trying to do everything myself. "Shaun, I worked myself way harder than I should have," he said. "Don't make the same mistake. Trust your people to shine. Find good people and let them do their part to help your vision come true."

Larry went on, "When I finally learned to let the team around me go and do, things went a lot better. But I held on too long."

I could totally relate. Starting a business is a grassroots hustle. At first, it was just me, and even as things started to grow, I made sure I was involved in everything. Larry's advice helped me to grow and to trust. I still apply that wisdom today. I've since invested in other companies and tackled other businesses, and each time I'm considering a new endeavor, I reflect back on Larry's advice. *Okay, this is great,* I'll tell myself, *but who's going to do this? I'm not around from nine to five to do everything, so who's the team that's going to drive that business?*

My motto is "Move forward," and Larry's advice allows me to do that by helping me to rely on the talented people around me. Now, I absolutely see the value in allowing people around me to perform instead of trying to carry the weight of a company all on my own shoulders.

Another part of my conversation with Larry that resonated with me was when he told me that no matter how demanding owning my business came to be, I needed to find time for myself and my family. He said that business and work never shut down, and there's always something to do, so it's up to you to shut it off in order to make time for what's important. "Health and family are things I put second, and that took a toll," he admitted to me. "I was all in. Just make sure you have a balance." As I look at my life today, these two things are a constant battle. I'll be forever grateful that Larry gave me the heads-up at an early stage in order to navigate properly.

Larry also taught me the value of having fun. "Do things that you love and want to be involved in. If you're going to spend a lot of time doing something, make sure there's passion." Larry found a number of different things he felt passionate about, and I feel fortunate to be pursuing success in a culture and industry that has always excited me.

I have so much respect for Larry and for what he was able to build across so many different types of business. From basketball to real estate to restaurants to cars and so many other things, Larry's success and experience gave him instant legitimacy. I was just a young guy getting a little bit of notice in the business world, but this guy was for real. He was next level.

And if I needed proof, all I had to do was gaze out his kitchen window and look across the Salt Lake Valley, where Larry so deeply and visibly made an impact on millions.

LAY IT ALL OUT THERE

Jerry Sloan

Larry never asked us to win. He only asked that we lay it all out there and be the best we could be every day.

Larry became a part owner of the Utah Jazz the same year I joined Frank Layden's staff as an assistant coach. I became the head coach in 1988, and for more than two decades, Larry proved over and over again that he wanted to do things the right way.

Everybody wants to win, but more than that, he wanted us to play hard and to represent the organization and the state of Utah in a positive manner. He would tell us that he'd rather lose with winners than win with losers, referring to the attitudes and behaviors of the players on and off the court. That was the ultimate wish of the coaching staff. We didn't always get it done, and that's on my shoulders, but we worked like the devil to build a team Larry and the community could be proud of.

When Larry first came onto the scene in 1985, I wondered how long he was going to last. He didn't look the part of an NBA owner, so I was interested to see what would happen. That impression changed a great deal, as Larry figured things out quick.

He was a tremendous competitor, something that he probably brought with him from his days playing semi-professional softball. He quickly developed an understanding of basketball, and I was always amazed at his ability to run numbers and make sense of what was going on. I couldn't even add two and two, and there was Larry doing all these calculations in his head and breaking down the stat sheet better than anybody I'd ever seen. He frequently asked questions about why we were doing things a certain way so he could understand what was going on. He was a competitor and he wanted to learn.

Sometimes that competitive nature stirred things up a bit. At first it was intimidating for a young coach to have the owner in the locker room at halftime and after games. Larry would occasionally get upset about our performance or say something to the players, and later he'd come back to apologize and let us know we were still on the same page. Of course, he could do whatever he wanted— he owned the team. But I appreciated the way he handled things. When things got rough, he always stepped in and straightened them out.

He was also very loyal in standing behind me and the other coaches. He made it clear that the coaches were going to be staying there, and that gave us the opportunity to throw it all out there and create an identity, knowing that Larry was behind us. And then he backed up his promise by supporting us.

The earliest example that I can remember of getting Larry's support was when I was Frank's assistant. I sometimes used a little bit of foul language on the bench, and there was an influential guy nearby who had played a role in helping Larry keep the Jazz in Utah. He told Larry that he didn't like my language. Larry could have come to me and asked me to watch my language, but instead he said to the man, "Where would you like to have your seats, then?" It was a small thing, but it showed me that we were going to have his support.

He also supported us in how we dealt with the players. I once had a little problem with Karl Malone and Isaac Austin. I walked into the locker room as we were preparing to take the court for a game, and they were wearing black shoes. I had a policy that everybody was to wear the same color of shoes because I wanted us to look and act as a team. I told Karl he needed to get some white shoes.

"I don't have any white ones," Karl responded.

"Well," I said, "take your uniform off and hang it up in the locker, because you're not going to play until you get some white tennis shoes."

He stormed out just as Larry walked in, and I sarcastically said, "Larry, you want to coach this guy?"

Larry said, "No, I think you're doing all right." I was glad to once again count on Larry's support, and Karl eventually found some white shoes that night and we went to work.

The loudest message of support I got from Larry was in a playoff series against Phoenix during one of my first seasons. We were down in the series, and rumors began to circulate that if we lost the series, Larry was going to make a coaching change. Back then, once you heard your name on TV, you probably had a week or two and then you were gone. I remember riding to the arena on the team bus thinking, here is one of the most important games of the year, and now I have to worry about my job.

Larry wanted to make sure I knew it wasn't true. He had called my hotel room but had just missed me, so he called Phil Johnson, my assistant, to reach out to me. He made it clear to me that my job wasn't in jeopardy, which was unheard of. Over the years, he made it even clearer to me publicly and privately that I was the coach of the Utah Jazz until I stepped down.

He was there to support us. He always said that if there was anything he could do to help us, we should let him know. If we needed some equipment or something to help us win, he was always willing to get that for us. Of course, we worked under certain financial parameters that we understood. We knew we couldn't spend $100 million per player, so development was a big part of what we did when we went to work. It was the old lunchbox theory: come with your lunch pail, ready to work hard, and then go home knowing you laid it all out there.

In 2004, my wife Bobbye passed away after battling cancer,

and Larry and the Jazz were extremely supportive. Larry would ask me, "Is there anything we can do for you?" I couldn't have made it through that difficult time without all the support from him. Larry even volunteered to make the team plane available for the team and staff to fly to southern Illinois for the funeral. That's not something I asked of him, but it really helped my children and me get through some tough times.

Tough times soon came for Larry, too. He began to battle some of his own health problems, and we went up as a team to visit him at the hospital. He had just had his legs amputated below the knee, but he was in good spirits and wanted the visit to be a happy one. He said, "Don't come in here with a long face." He wanted to keep it pretty light and make sure everybody knew he was a fighter and a hard-nosed guy. After twenty-four years of coaching for Larry's organization, that's the last time I saw him.

When I think about what Larry started, I don't think it ever ends. The things he has done, the jobs he has given people, and the sense of community he has created are things I don't ever see ending. When I look at everything he was able to accomplish in such a short time, it's really mind boggling. He worked extremely hard to put it all together.

Just like he used to ask of us and our players, he laid it all out there.

I'LL BUY IT

Larry Baum

Larry always knew exactly what he wanted: exceptional customer service. As long as people were honest with him and followed through on his expectations, everything was fine. Though he could be stern and sometimes aggressive, his personality was such that when he spoke, you knew he could be trusted. I learned this firsthand through the relationships he built with others throughout the community.

My professional relationship with Larry goes back long before he was involved with the Utah Jazz. In the early 1980s, his first Toyota dealership bought advertising on ABC affiliate Channel 4, where I was the sales manager.

In 1983, I left the ABC station and accepted a position with the Utah Jazz as their vice president of sales. Dave Checketts was the general manager at the time, but the organization was about $10 million in debt to First Security Bank.

Dave was just twenty-eight years old, but he was very bright. He came up with a plan to pay off the debt and keep the Jazz in the Utah market. It was a simple idea—sell limited partnerships for $100,000 apiece. He asked his leaders to each list ten prominent people in the community who could afford to buy a $100,000 package. I put Larry's name right at the top of the list.

Dave went out to meet with Larry, who quickly bought half of the team, eventually buying all of it a year later. Once Larry got involved with the Jazz, things really started rolling.

"I know what you do and how you do it. Just go do it," Larry told me after he became owner. "We're going to set you goals. Hit the goals. I'll stay out of your life, and we won't have any problems."

That's exactly how it worked during the roughly twenty years I worked with the Jazz. We met our sales goals every year. Larry would keep the records, usually memorizing them. He knew every number exactly, and he never forgot them. He would proudly tell others, "Larry Baum's department did an X percent improvement over last year."

Larry offered to help me make my goals, too. Sometimes he'd even accompany me on sales calls. One such time was quite unique. I called Larry and said, "Okay. You said you want to go, so let's go."

"Where are we going to go?" he asked.

"Ivory Homes," I said.

Larry had wanted to meet the homebuilding company's owner, Ellis Ivory. I let Ellis know ahead of time that I was bringing a guest to our meeting, I but didn't let him know who. I wanted it to be a surprise.

"I'm not going to tell you," I said. "But you'll enjoy it."

Ellis was shocked to see Larry with me when we arrived at the Ivory office. They hugged and then talked for forty-five minutes straight—about every business and LDS Church topic you could imagine. We hadn't even discussed the reason why we were there when Ellis wrapped up the meeting with a surprising comment.

He looked at Larry Miller and said, "Now, I know Larry Baum well enough to know that in that folder he's holding, there's a sales package that he wants me to buy. And I know you well enough and I know what you're about, so whatever's there, I'm going to buy. I don't care how much. Whatever's there, because you're involved, I'll buy it."

It was the simplest contract I've ever done in my life.

"Don't draw it up now," Ellis added. "Just do it, and I'll get it done."

Years later, Ivory continued advertising with the Jazz. I'll never forget how we closed that deal. It just doesn't usually happen that way, with a client saying, "I'll just take whatever you've got."

It was a fun experience for me to see that because of Larry's reputation, people knew they were not going to get cheated. He held that respect from people because they knew he wouldn't over-price them. In everything we did, Larry always reminded us that honesty was the most important aspect with our clients. "Never over-promise and under-deliver," he'd say. "Always over-deliver on what you've promised you'll do. Follow through on whatever commitments you make."

Before we teamed with the Jazz, KSL-TV sold roughly $65,000 worth of advertising a year. Once the Jazz acquired broadcasting rights from Castle Television, we sold more than $1.5 million in ad sales the first year alone. When I left several years later, the Jazz were bringing in $19 to $20 million.

My job became more involved as Larry continued to buy new properties—KJZZ-TV, the hockey team, and the WNBA team, the Utah Starzz. We had extra responsibility and were expected to reach revenue goals. It was a challenge, but it was a blast.

That "never over-promise or under-deliver" philosophy is what made the Jazz organization what it is today. It's a very important fundamental concept Larry always pushed. Larry gave us the working environment that allowed us to be creative and to try new things.

Not many people earn the honest reputation he did, but he earned it through years of honest business dealings. I was sold on Larry from the first time I met him as a small business owner until the time he became a billionaire empire mogul. He had high expectations for others, but nothing more than what he expected from himself. And in the end, he always delivered.

ALL ABOUT ACTION

Mark Eaton

The first time I met Larry Miller, he was standing still on a dais. But I soon learned that standing still was not his specialty.

I was in my third season with the Utah Jazz, and Larry had just purchased a fifty percent ownership stake. There was a little ceremony held at Crossroads Mall in downtown Salt Lake with him holding up the ceremonial check to buy the team.

It's ironic that this was my first experience with him, because in reality, Larry is far more dynamic than a guy holding a novelty check and smiling for a photo opportunity. He was all about action.

Larry's legacy is that he lived his life in a large way. He was unafraid of taking risks, and his passion inspired others to follow him. He was always in motion.

Of course, I didn't know that in the spring of 1985. All I knew about him at that point was that he was a car dealer, but then he started showing up at games and coming into the locker room occasionally. Then in 1986 he bought the rest of the franchise, and we got to know him much better.

He enjoyed spending time with different players and getting to know them. I recall going to lunch with him a couple of times at Morelia, a Mexican restaurant that was a favorite of Larry's. I had interest in the automotive industry, having worked as a mechanic before I started playing competitive basketball, so he would tell me about that part of his world.

He would also spend time in the locker room, and even had his own locker stall, making it clear that he wanted to be a more involved owner. He'd throw on his uniform and throw passes to me in the low post or he'd come in to guard me during pregame warm-ups, despite a two-foot height disadvantage. He was more than an owner; he was an integral part of our team.

If it wasn't already evident that he was a different kind of owner, it became totally clear the summer after I got injured in the playoffs. I was laid up for a while, so Larry came and picked me up. He had just bought a place across the Utah–Idaho border, so we drove north to go fishing on his property. I was in a leg brace and on crutches, but I hobbled down to the edge of the lake. We spent the day fishing and talking about absolutely anything.

Now that I've been running my own businesses for a number of years, I have so much more respect for him as a businessman. There are several things I really admire about the way he conducted business.

In particular, he wasn't afraid to take risks. He made such a huge gamble when he bought the team, and then he went forward and got the financing for the arena from a Japanese bank when nobody locally would approve him. Who does that? Larry just saw a little further than everybody else, and he believed in his vision.

I also admire the fair way Larry went about negotiating. One year, my contract came up for renegotiation, so he told me, "Start negotiating with the team attorney, and if you get stuck, call me." That's exactly what happened. We negotiated for a while but couldn't get anywhere. So my agent flew into town and we had a meeting with Larry.

My agent made some good points, and Larry listened thoughtfully. Finally, he said, "That sounds fair, let's do it." In fifteen minutes, the whole thing was over.

As a team representative to the Players' Association, I also got to see Larry's negotiation skills in action in our collective bargaining conversations. He had a different way of thinking and communicating than most franchise owners. He could see clearly how we could work to a resolution and encouraged all parties to swallow their pride and get a deal done.

Another part of his business and leadership acumen that impressed me is how he was so hands-on but somehow still let people do their jobs. He hired good people, and he let management run the team. He occasionally got emotional and spoke his mind, but in the end he trusted people. He had such commitment to the coaches in terms of understanding Frank Layden's and Jerry Sloan's philosophies. I respected him for standing by them even during difficult moments. The easiest thing to do is pull the plug and fire a coach or trade a few players. Larry always kept the long-range vision in view.

But at the same time, Larry was passionate, intense, driven. That same internal mechanism that propelled him to work the ninety-hour weeks and commit parts catalogs to memory pushed him to want to be great. I think that drive and the clear vision were related: he could always see the top of the mountain when most other people couldn't. That view of what he could achieve is what kept him going.

That intensity took many different shapes, and it wasn't always fun for the players. Right after Larry had secured the arena funding, the NBA scheduled us to play two regular-season games in Japan. Larry was in the stands next to the president of Sumitomo Bank & Trust, who had just loaned Larry a large sum of money for the arena. The team came out flat after the long flight to Japan, and we laid an egg. We lost by twenty-three points.

Larry wasn't happy at all. He came down to the locker room and just leaned against the door, glaring. Then we went back to the hotel where they had a buffet set up for us. Again, Larry stood in the doorway and glared at us while we had dinner. At that point, we definitely got the message.

I can look back now and laugh—especially because we redeemed ourselves with a win on the second night of our Tokyo trip—and because Larry's softer emotions showed just as often as his temper did.

For example, when I retired, Larry rearranged his schedule to be at my press conference, and he showed up with a handwritten, heartfelt letter thanking me for my service to the team. Here's a guy with a billion-dollar empire who took the time to sit down and write me a letter by hand. He also gave me a car as a retirement gift, which was a really nice touch.

I always got the sense that Larry understood what I contributed to the team, and that was not lost on me. He had a great impact on me. The contributions that this man of action had on our community and state are tremendous. When you drive around the valley, you see the Larry H. Miller Softball Complex, or the Larry H. Miller Campus for Salt Lake Community College, and so many other things. And none of these were small projects. He didn't just write a check and say, "Here's a little donation to help your cause." He got actively involved in every single one.

Somehow, he still had time to buy and run car dealerships, build movie theaters, oversee a basketball team, and be intimately involved with dozens of other efforts. I don't know how he did it all.

But there's one thing I know now that I didn't know when I first looked up at him on that dais thirty years ago: he was all about action.

Random Acts

Scott Harding

The first time I met Larry Miller, I had no idea who he was. I also had no idea that I'd one day be working for him.

When I was about nine years old, my dad and I began driving down from Layton to attend Jazz games in Salt Lake City. In those days, you could walk up to the ticket window at game time and usually get a ticket in the cheap seats. I loved watching Adrian Dantley, Ricky Green, Karl Malone, Mark Eaton, and John Stockton. They frequently gave out life-sized posters of the players as door giveaways, and those posters became the wallpaper for my bedroom. Needless to say, I was a pretty big fan.

Many times, my dad was patient enough to let us stay after the games in hopes of meeting players and maybe getting some autographs. One night, as I was waiting for the players to come out, a man emerged from the players' area and asked me if I was waiting to see some Jazz players. I told him I was, and he asked me if I wanted to see some of the players' cars. Of course I said yes.

We walked into the parking lot. There he pointed out Karl Malone's truck, Thurl Bailey's Cadillac, and some others. Then he left and I walked over to my dad to tell him about the cars.

"Do you know who that was?" my dad asked quizzically. Obviously I had no clue. "That was the owner of the team. His name is Larry Miller."

Giving a young fan a tour of the players' parking lot is certainly above and beyond the job description of an NBA owner. This was the first random act of kindness I witnessed from Larry, but it wouldn't be the last.

I went to work for the Larry H. Miller Group in 1994, and in 2005 I was asked to oversee two downtown Ford stores as general manager. In that role I had great access to see the kindness and personal touch Larry was known for.

One day early in my tenure, Larry's assistant called me and told me that Larry wanted to talk to me. From what I had heard, that usually meant bad news, so I was a bit nervous when Larry came on the phone line. He asked if I had lunch plans, and when I said I didn't, he asked if I'd join him. I said yes, and he gave me very specific instructions. He said he would pick me up in seventeen minutes and to be out by the road in a specific spot near the north entrance. I complied, and exactly seventeen minutes later, he showed up.

That was the year the Miller Motorsports Park was nearing completion, and Larry told me we were going to an appreciation barbecue for the construction workers. We walked in and Larry immediately began making the rounds, talking individually with the workers and thanking them for their contributions. I was impressed that he would take the time to personally show that type of appreciation, and I remember the day equally well because of the great conversation we had along the drive. Larry asked about my family, my hobbies, and my opinions on different topics. It meant the world to me that Larry would take that time to get to know me on a one-on-one basis.

Of course, it was normal for Larry to take that kind of personal interest in people. One time he called and asked me to contact a tow truck company to go pick up a customer's car. He then told me that he wanted me to have the car towed to the store and to do a full evaluation of what it needed. Apparently, he had heard of an elderly lady slipping and falling on some ice while walking to church one morning. When Larry asked the church leader why the woman was walking to church in the winter in the first place, he learned that her car was broken down. Larry wanted to help, and he made it clear that he did not want the customer to have any involvement in the deal.

Once the car got to the store, we had a veteran technician take a look at it. It was an older car, and the cost to repair all the issues, even at the "Larry" rate, amounted to more than the car was worth. I let Larry know, and, undeterred, he told me to go ahead and have the work done and send him the bill. He didn't want the customer seeing the bill or knowing how extensive the issues were because he didn't want her to feel uncomfortable. We repaired the vehicle and delivered it to the customer's house.

The most incredible part happened a week later, when Larry called to ask for the name of the technician who had worked on the car. I told him it was Mike Robinson, a tenured tech who always did a great job. Larry called Mike and his manager and asked if the two of them and their wives would join Larry and Gail as their guests for dinner and a Jazz game. Mike was an avid fan, so this was one of the best nights he could have imagined.

What makes this part of the story interesting is that Mike got paid a full rate for doing the job, the store was paid, and the service manager did what he always did in fixing cars. Larry paid for the repair, and these employees did their usual great work. But Larry chose to let them be the heroes, the beneficiaries of his kindness.

Larry had a way of motivating people, and I remember one particular interaction that made me feel I'd run through fire for that man. Larry had just been released from one of his long hospital stays late in his life and held a general managers meeting at the arena to speak with us and brief us on his condition and the state of the business.

Afterward, I approached the table where Larry was sitting in order to say hello. His vision was extremely poor at the time, so even though I was close by he had a hard time seeing who I was. When I identified myself, he said, "Nice job last month."

I assumed he was just being polite or possibly had my previous month's performance mixed up with someone else's. It certainly hadn't felt like a very good month to me. My store had worked hard, but we had showed a small loss on our financial statement. I told Larry thank you, but I felt that we could have done a lot better. Then he made a statement that I learned a lot from.

"I know you lost a little money last month," he said, "but I also know that you're running a tough operation. I know the amount of work you had to put in just to get to losing a little money, and that little loss is more impressive than some of the huge profits another store might have posted."

The fact that he knew how much effort I had put in made me feel extremely valued and made me want to work harder for him. It was also an important leadership lesson for me. I learned that you can't always judge everything by the scoreboard. Sometimes circumstances are different enough that the effort behind a number means more than the number itself.

There was so much power in all these moments, these random acts of kindness, appreciation, and personal touch. I saw it as a fourth-grader at a Jazz game and again as a general manager some twenty years later, and I saw it every time Larry thanked a construction worker or repair tech. He was special not just in his ability to touch people but also in his desire to find and create those moments.

LARRY WHO?

Brent Barrett

Fresh out of college, I was in the first week of my first full-time job. It was lunch time, so my boss, Jeff Jensen, said to me, "Let's go grab some lunch and then go see Larry."

"Larry who?" I asked.

That was in 1983, and since then, I've never had to ask, "Larry who?" again.

I had just started my career in accounting, and the Larry H. Miller Group—which at that point in time was just a few dealerships—was our client. We did audit and tax work for them, so Jeff wanted me to meet Larry. I didn't realize then what a big deal meeting him was, let alone what a big deal he would later become.

In that initial meeting, Larry was excited to tell us about the final stages of the new Toyota store he was building on State Street. It was his first big construction project, and he was animated as he shared details about the square footage and features and what it meant for his burgeoning business. Having never met him before, I assumed he was putting on a show. I would later learn that this brand of excitement and intensity was pure Larry.

I could tell that Larry was different because of how driven, focused, and detailed he was. I learned that Larry expected your best, not just whatever the acceptable margin for error was.

In college courses on auditing, they teach what they call

materiality. It's basically the concept of getting to a point where you've validated something enough to move on. Depending on the size of the business and everything, you say, "Okay, it's reasonable, we're close enough; let's move to the next item." That wasn't what Larry wanted. He was willing to pay more money to make sure that things weren't just close but rather totally accurate. That was a bit of a shift for me from what I had learned in school, but it's what the client wanted, so we adjusted.

He was so focused on getting the job done right, and he had remarkable vision for what that looked like. I always thought that the difference between Larry and me was that I could look at an empty lot and see rocks and weeds. He could see a building, a business, and people. Whether at Jordan Commons or the arena or wherever else, his vision just took over. Vision, more than anything else, is what made him very unique.

A couple of years later, Larry became the owner of the Utah Jazz. My dad was in his early sixties at the time, and I thought it would be fun to take him to a game at the Salt Palace. Of course, my dad knew that one of our clients was Larry Miller, so he kept pressuring me to take him down and introduce him.

The Jazz had actually lost the game that night, so I was nervous about the mood I'd find Larry in, for starters. I also wasn't sure whether Larry would even recognize me. "Dad, I don't know him all that well," I objected. "I'm just an auditor, just one of a million people in his business life."

My dad was relentless. Just as the game ended, we made our way down toward the floor. Larry was standing in the middle, either waiting for an interview or just surveying the crowd. I loomed in tentatively, thinking about how to approach this high-profile person who, I thought, barely even knew me.

I was still figuring it all out in my head when Larry saw me. "Hi, Brent," he said. That completely broke the ice. I was surprised he knew my name, and that relaxed me.

"I'd like to introduce you to my dad, William Barrett," I said.

They chatted back and forth. Larry was cordial and attentive, and it made my dad's day. I'm sure he went back to the neighborhood and told his friends, "Yeah, I met Larry Miller," and I'm sure he convinced himself and others that I was Larry's right-hand man. It was a fun memory, and it was great of Larry to make the night special for my dad. My dad is now in his nineties and still talks about that evening.

After thirteen years as an outside accountant and auditor for the Miller Group, I officially joined the company in 1996. That gave me even more opportunities to get to know Larry and his unique style.

Every month or so—depending on his busy schedule—Larry would walk out onto the floor and grab a bunch of people. "Let's go to lunch," he'd say, and we'd pile into cars and head to Joe Morley's BBQ or Restaurant Morelia. We'd sit down and talk to him about business but also talk about the news or our families or the Jazz.

At one of those lunches, as was often the case, there was a lot of food left over. Larry had found out that I have seven children—the biggest family in the group, or at least of those at the lunch. So he said, "Let's slide everything down to Barrett, so he can take it home to his kids."

Later that afternoon, he made sure I was still on board, reminding me to retrieve the food from the fridge. "Okay," he said, "you gotta make sure you take that home to your kids." It was a little embarrassing at first, but soon it became a tradition: give Brent Barrett all the leftovers.

I had many great moments with Larry, but above all, what I think of when I remember him is that community matters. He basically gave his life for the community. He was so driven to create opportunities, keep the Jazz in Utah, and ultimately just make Utah better. He loved tradition, and there was so much of that built right into his business success. His arena was built right there near West High School, where he graduated. His theater and dining complex features Snappy's, a favorite hang-out where he and Gail would go when they were younger. He loved to reminisce, and that was evident in the way his traditions and past showed up along the way. He also loved to give back to the communities that helped his many businesses become successful. He was always in it for everybody else.

I wish I had a chance to tell him face to face a very heartfelt thank you. It's too late for that, but to Gail and the Miller family, I thank them for the great opportunities.

I'm so glad I came in contact with the Miller Group and with Larry himself, an introduction that would benefit me, my wife, and children for so many years. I'm very appreciative of that, and I certainly won't be asking "Larry who?" ever again.

BUILD SOMETHING SPECIAL

Adam Edmunds

The Larry Miller I met in 2004 was different than the one most people knew.

He was *Professor* Larry Miller.

I was set to graduate that spring with my master's in accounting from Brigham Young University, but I was filling out the rest of my elective credits for the final semester. I signed up for a course by accident and arrived to the first day of class to learn that Larry was the teacher.

Twice a week, he made the forty-minute drive from his office and spent three hours sharing stories and lessons from his business successes. It was, by far, the most impactful class I took at BYU, so much so that I often wanted to keep learning after the proverbial bell rang. I would often walk with Larry out to his car after the lectures, taking the time to pick his brain on various topics. He became a trusted mentor, and I was grateful for the opportunity to learn from him.

In one particular lecture, he was telling us the story of how he went from being a salaried employee to an entrepreneur at the age of thirty-five. He felt that was extremely rare. He explained that most people who haven't taken the leap by that point in life never do so, because thirty-five-year-olds tend to have too many family expenses to endure the risk of starting a company. Larry, though,

242

had saved enough over the course of his career to buy his first dealership. Of course, the story from there was impressive: one dealership became two, then three, and so on. Later came the Jazz, the Bees, the Miller Motorsports Park, the theater business, and dozens of other ventures. But it all started because Larry was willing to take a risk at a point in his life when many other people wouldn't.

His message to us was clear: there's no time like the present. It would be far easier to start companies right then, right out of school, he explained. Our living expenses would never be lower, and if it didn't work out, we would still have our degrees to fall back on. The conversation energized me, and I bought into the idea. I already had a job lined up with KPMG, one of the four largest auditing firms in the United States. But after hearing Larry's advice, I called them to cancel my employment.

I started my first company soon after. SilentWhistle was an ethics and compliance firm that grew quickly. We provided the first comprehensive web-based whistle-blowing system to help companies avoid illegal and unethical activities by providing for anonymous reporting. I was even named the BYU Entrepreneur of the Year in 2004. SilentWhistle was acquired in 2009, which means that five years after Larry's lecture, I had already led one successful venture and had time to seek new opportunities. Today I lead another software company called Allegiance, with 120 employees. We provide customer and employee feedback systems to global brands like Symantec, Dell, and Johnson & Johnson.

My life was forever changed because of that class with Larry. I could have taken the safe route and clocked in for what would have been a secure and gainful auditing job. But because I listened to Larry, I've had the experience of building two successful ventures from the ground up.

Now, I try to pay it forward, speaking to students and entrepreneurs to share my story much the same way Larry did for me. When I do, I like to pass along the three main things I learned from Larry in that 2004 spring semester.

First, I learned the importance of working hard. Growing a

company is hard. Running a company is hard. You have to make tough decisions every day, and some of those decisions will not make you a popular person. Larry was famous for his hard work and long hours. Although he did often talk about some regret regarding the toll his long hours took on his family and health, he definitely prepared us for the sacrifices we would need to make to be successful entrepreneurs.

Second, be generous and fair. One of my favorite quotes is, "You'll regret many things in life, but you'll never regret being too honest or too fair." I believe Larry tried to live this way as well. There are countless stories of Larry going beyond what was expected of a boss to help employees deal with family situations, health trials, and personal goals. He took joy in helping people and in cultivating a relationship of fairness and integrity.

Third, build something special. Many entrepreneurs put so much focus on the financial impact of their endeavors that they forget to enjoy what they're creating. I always felt that Larry's proudest accomplishment was not his wealth, buildings, or car lots. He spoke very fondly and proudly of the 5,000 employees that raised their families on the income created by Larry's companies. He definitely passed this on to me, as I take great joy seeing my employees and their families at Christmas parties, summer barbecues, and Halloween parades. I also try to use my company to create special moments for employees. Last Christmas, we had a software developer request a few extra days off to visit his father in Chicago, who was dying of cancer. My CTO and I decided to surprise him. We told him we wanted to pay for his flight as a Christmas bonus, but we secretly flew his dad in from Chicago so he could spend time with the whole family. The look on the faces of our employee and his kids was priceless. I try to use my company and skills to create moments like this, and I think Larry did the same.

The lessons I learned years ago from Professor Larry completely changed the trajectory of my career from that point forward. It was a fork in the road for me, and Larry's experiences gave me the courage and motivation to trust in my abilities and chart my own course.

CLASSIC LARRY

Gordon Chiesa

In March of 1997, Larry walked into my office one afternoon around four o'clock. He told me he was upset about the game the night before, a game that the Jazz had actually won. I wasn't sure what he could possibly be so distressed about.

To my surprise, it had nothing to do with the game itself. Larry told me he had counted six empty green seats in the lower bowl. This was during a period when everybody thought we were going to be champions, and the building was always packed for games. Larry wasn't a fan of empty seats at all, let alone when it was considered a big event to attend.

He was determined to find out why those six seats went unoccupied. If they were season-ticket holders, he was going to ask them personally why they had not come to the game. Larry would often look at empty seats in the arena and would calculate the lost revenue they represented on the spot.

I was an assistant coach with the Utah Jazz under Jerry Sloan from 1989 through 2005. During that time, I had many tremendous interactions with Larry Miller. About once a week he would come to my office at the Delta Center at unbelievable times for unscripted conversations, sometimes inquiring about empty seats, but mostly to talk about the game and the players.

Larry was always interested in numbers and how much a player could improve his overall shooting performance. We would have discussions about how I taught shooting mechanics to the players. I would tell him that every Jazz perimeter player needs a "float game" to improve to his scoring abilities.

One day, after an individual shooting workout with point guard Howard Eisley, Larry asked me to show him how to shoot a lane floater off of one foot.

"Please correct my mistakes, as if I were a player," Larry instructed me.

So I did.

Larry was teachable. Much to my surprise, he was a quick study and made a couple of the shots with a high arc and a soft follow-through. And, as always, he was wearing sneakers and an old-school Jazz polo shirt as he practiced his floaters. It was such a classic Larry moment that comes to mind whenever I think of him.

Even from my athletic standpoint, it was easy to tell that Larry had an unmatched memory, and not just for dollars and cents. In February of 1995, I was writing the Jazz game plan on the blackboard in the locker room for that night's opponent, the San Antonio Spurs. Larry came in and sat down at Karl Malone's locker, not saying a word. He just watched as we worked away.

After I finished writing the game plan for the Spurs, Larry asked me to explain our strategy to him, "in everyday fan language," he said.

I explained to him that one of our biggest points of emphasis for this game was defending against Hall-of-Fame center David Robinson with two of our players. Larry nodded his head in approval. That night we put the plan into action, and our double-teaming strategy won us the game.

Several months later, before a summer-league practice in July, Larry came over to me and told me that I had done a good job of preparing the team to beat the Spurs back in February. He remembered almost everything I had written on the blackboard. I wish I could say I was surprised by this amazing recall and the amount of detail he reiterated, but it was simply another classic Larry moment.

As for me, I remember that Larry was very good at expressing appreciation for little things I did. It was also exciting to get a peek into the mind of an involved NBA owner. I'm not sure whether he ever found out about those six empty seats, but his memory and business tenacity reassures me that he never forgot about them.

BACK TO BASICS

Dean Fitzpatrick

Awoman once approached Larry in the grocery store and told him that she had bought a new car from one of his dealerships and that it was having a lot of problems. She wanted him to fix everything that was wrong with it. He promised her that he would look into it. I was a general manager over the dealership, and Larry asked me to dig up the information on the purchase. What the woman hadn't told Larry was that she did indeed purchase a new vehicle from his dealership—ten years earlier! The car now had over 150,000 miles on it.

It cost three or four thousand dollars to fix everything that was wrong with the car, but Larry paid the entire bill. By that time, I didn't even have to question Larry's motive. He saw that the woman was in financial need and wanted to do what he felt was right.

The more I worked with Larry, the more I came to understand his way of thinking. I first got to know him when I joined the Larry H. Miller Group in 1988. In 1997, I was named general manager of a dealership that was, quite simply, ahead of its time.

The Chrysler/Jeep/Dodge superstore had recently opened in Sandy, Utah, but had been struggling to turn a profit. In fact, it was possibly the worst financially performing dealership of its brand in the entire country. Larry was intent on making the store profitable.

Through various interactions, I started to understand who he was and what he was about.

Larry had a vision for an entire auto mall to be built. At the time of construction, the undeveloped area was mostly an alfalfa field, but Larry knew what it could become. It was a bold decision to relocate his Chrysler/Dodge dealership, which had been doing well in Murray, to the underdeveloped area. Larry built a beautiful, state-of-the-art facility that he felt we could grow into. In spite of all the hard work that everyone had put into the operation, the store could never turn a monthly profit.

During my first year as general manager, Larry paid close attention to every aspect of the dealership's operations—sales, service, parts, everything. He wanted to make sure that they all adhered to basic guiding principles. Larry's philosophy was, "Almost always when things aren't going right, they can be corrected by going back to basics."

Contrary to what some might think, Larry didn't fly by the seat of his pants when making business decisions. Everything that he did was deliberate, by design.

While working closely with Larry proved to be a great learning experience for me, this wasn't the type of management I was used to, with the boss having so much input. I even phoned my operations manager and asked, "Is it normal for Larry to be so involved?" I never felt as though he was trying to bypass my leadership; I simply wondered how a man with so many things going on could find the time to concentrate so much effort on one facet of his organization.

After several metrics were analyzed, every indicator pointed to exactly what we were hoping against: we were overstaffed. We were doing only half the business we needed to in order to justify our payroll. The previous GM had staffed according to the size of the facility rather than the amount of business the store would generate, which was directly contrary to something that had almost become a mantra: "Manage business at the level you're doing, not the level you wish you were doing." Although Larry's vision of the auto mall was eventually realized, at that time, there just wasn't enough traffic in Sandy to support such a large facility and staff.

Larry and I both knew that we had to downsize or the dealership would continue to be significantly unprofitable. Deciding which staff members to keep is never an easy process, and the effect it had on Larry personally was very evident to me. People were an important part of the equation for his success.

"It's not just them; it's their families," he'd say to me. We both recognized that the store's financial failures weren't their fault. It was painful for Larry and me to correct this issue, but Larry made sure that we did it the right way.

We spent hours working to find other opportunities for the people we had to let go, which we were largely successful in doing. It was a great process to be able to learn that it was not only about right-sizing the business and making the business healthy, but doing it in a way that minimized the impact for those involved.

By April 1998 the store was profitable, and it has been in the black every month since. In fact, twelve years after opening, the store became the most profitable Chrysler/Jeep/Dodge dealership in the country. And it was all due to following basic business principles and doing them the right way. Larry picking up someone's repair bill might confuse a casual observer, but it became clear to me during my time as GM that he always found the time to focus on the things that mattered most. When you make the right choices for the right reasons, good things happen.

INTEGRITY

ROOKIE MISTAKE

Governor Michael Okerlund Leavitt

I was inaugurated as governor of Utah in January of 1993. One month later, the Utah Jazz hosted the NBA All-Star Game at the Delta Center. It was, of course, a very big deal.

A week or two before the All-Star break, the Bulls and the Jazz played in Salt Lake City. In the last few minutes of the game, Chicago's star player, Michael Jordan, brought the Bulls back from a double-digit deficit to beat the Jazz at the last second. Local fans were understandably upset.

The following week, as the league prepared for the All-Star break, Jordan made a public comment to the effect that he might skip the All-Star Game in Utah. He wanted to go somewhere warm and play golf. It became a major national sports story. Locally, many people were simply incensed. This added insult to injury for Jazz fans.

I was in Washington, D.C., on the day this unfolded. Someone from the St. George Chamber of Commerce concluded there might be a way to use Jordan's misstep to draw attention to the fact there were places in Utah where one could golf year round. They suggested we invite Jordan to play golf in St. George—a city in southern Utah near the Arizona border—the day before the All-Star Game. It was proposed that we call it "Michael Jordan Golf Day in Utah."

I agreed to issue a press release announcing the invitation in a quick phone call just before I climbed on the plane in D.C. By the time I landed in Utah, it was clear that our tongue-in-cheek gesture had not been interpreted as we expected.

The media and thousands of fans had misinterpreted our announcement to be the governor declaring it "Michael Jordan Day in Utah." They saw this as completely offensive.

By the next day, all the talk radio shows focused on what a foolish thing the governor had done to recognize Michael Jordan after he had made such offensive remarks about our state.

We were in full damage control mode at the governor's office. In one day, we received over 1,700 phone calls complaining about the insensitivity. I called Larry Miller to make sure he knew that we had been misunderstood.

I said, "Larry, if you get a chance, could you help us put this fire out?"

Larry couldn't have been nicer about the problem. "Don't say any more about it. Just leave it to me."

The next morning, the news media asked Larry about the governor declaring it "Michael Jordan Day."

Larry's response: "He's a new governor, and he made a rookie mistake. No big deal."

Within hours, the waters had calmed. My rookie mistake was over, and Larry Miller was in the Mike Leavitt Hall of Fame.

HONEST DEALINGS

Don Winder

I was sitting in my law office one afternoon in 1985 when Larry suddenly burst in and proclaimed, "I've just bought a half interest in the Utah Jazz. I want a simple agreement. I want it to be no more than five pages, and I want it in three days."

Larry could be demanding, but even he had to know that wasn't going to happen. The banks would generate stacks of loan documents for any financing involved. We would need an agreement from the current owner, Sam Battistone, and an approval from the NBA. This was a complicated transaction, and from a legal standpoint, the simplicity that Larry was asking for was unrealistic.

I first met Larry after he moved to Salt Lake City from Denver in the early '80s. He and his uncle had acquired a Toyota dealership in Murray, but circumstances changed, and Larry needed to buy out his uncle's share. I worked on the transactional documents with my law partner at the time, Denny Haslam.

Larry and I had a solid history working together, and he trusted that my firm would do a thorough job preparing the documents required for the acquisition of Utah's NBA team. By the time we finished—and I don't mean to sound biblical—I had worked for forty days and forty nights on that deal. Although it wasn't in three days and it was more than five pages, in the end, we gave Larry a bound volume of all the documents necessary for the transaction.

Larry was extremely intelligent, and, as always, he had analyzed the deal ahead of time. He knew the parameters. He knew what he wanted to do. He knew how this thing was going to work, and he trusted Battistone. The lawyering was just an afterthought. I bugged him often, saying, "Larry, there are things in here that I've got to talk to you about. There are things in here that you should know."

After much insistence on my end, he finally allowed me to review the documents with him after nine o'clock the evening before the closing. It took quite a while, and by the time we finished it was well after two in the morning.

He'd spent five hours with me, but I'm certain he only did this to appease the lawyer in me. He let me go page-by-page, document-by-document, explaining to him what was there and what the consequences were. He turned to me and said, "Don, I know that you've done everything you can to protect me." The next morning at eight o'clock he went into the meeting and signed. He had already figured out the transaction in his head and could probably have handwritten on five pages his outline of the deal. He really didn't need any advice or counsel, because he'd already evaluated all the factors and knew it was a successful negotiation.

Larry made a business deal that aligned with his love of sports, but inherent in that investment, he also made a commitment to strengthening the local economy. Shortly after Larry bought half of the Jazz, there was an article in the newspaper about a town that was going to lose a basketball franchise and the economic loss that community would suffer.

Larry was passionate about both sports and building a strong community, so for him, it wasn't just about a basketball game. It was also about people traveling to see it and maybe dining beforehand. It was about creating opportunity for local businesses. The Jazz wasn't just about the Miller organization, but about the infrastructure that supports a local team. It was advertisers and radio stations and the news media. It was clear to Larry that the presence of an NBA team in Utah would produce a complex and positive ripple effect on many levels of commerce and community.

Denny, my partner at the time, oversaw the transaction when Larry acquired the second half of the Jazz the following year. It went very smoothly, just as smoothly as the purchase of the first half, and when you look at it, it was truly an amazing service that Larry was doing for the community. He was not going to let that team leave Utah.

I worked with Larry for the next twenty-five years, and through our many dealings together I learned to appreciate his negotiating style even more. He would not do a deal with a person he did not trust. While he always let us prepare the necessary paperwork, it was the nature of the person with whom he was dealing and the economic sense of the deal he felt should govern. He said, "I can't take everything. If I take everything, the other person is not going to be happy, and I can't do that, so it's got to be a win-win."

I will always remember Larry as a giant in the community. We may not have given him five pages in three days, but his unique way of seeing things demonstrated that if you work hard, you're driven, and you apply yourself honestly, you can accomplish amazing feats.

THE RIVERSIDE COBRA

Steve Volk

The gavel fell, the crowd sighed, and my friend Larry turned to me with a wink.

"Integrity always wins," he said.

It was 2002 and we were at a high-powered vintage auto auction in Monterey, California, but that line could have been delivered any time or place—such was Larry Miller's commitment to doing business in an honest, straightforward way. He valued a handshake deal, put faith in people's words, and strived to ensure that his own word was ironclad.

I am very fortunate to have known Larry as a friend and to have assisted him in building his vast collection of vintage Cobras and GT40s. He loved those cars. Larry listened intently to advice on which cars to purchase and was good at moving quickly and decisively to make a deal. It was fun to work with him on these major purchases, even with all of the egos and strong personalities in play in the high-end car collector marketplace.

The purchase that had brought us to Monterey was CSX2002, the Riverside Cobra, which was the first factory competition Cobra. Famous racers like Billy Krause, Ken Miles, and Dave MacDonald drove this Cobra in the 1962 season, which was the beginning of the Cobra's racing career. Although it never won a major race due to reliability issues, CSX2002 paved the way for what was to come: a long line of Cobra victories and racing championships.

The owner of CSX2002 was a Cobra historian who had purchased the car in 1977. But his family business had entered a messy ownership struggle that involved litigation. He needed cash more than he needed the Cobra, so Larry dispatched me to negotiate a deal with him.

In all his dealings, Larry prided himself on negotiations that were tough but equitable. He wanted to secure the best deal possible, but he also liked it when both parties could come away from the table feeling good about the transaction. With that in mind, I managed the interaction with firmness and fairness. We arrived at a deal, which Larry subsequently approved.

But just before we were to close the deal and before Larry took possession of the car, the owner called me. He said that he was having second thoughts and referenced a recent sale of a lightweight Jaguar XK-E at a price that was substantially higher than our agreed deal for the Cobra. He argued that the Cobra was much more historically significant than the Jag and that he was backing out of the deal.

Upset and desperate, I pushed back. "How can you back out?" I asked. "We had a deal. You gave your word." Unmoved by my appeal, he told me he had consigned the car to an upcoming auction in Monterey. Now I had the unenviable responsibility of telling Larry—who was big on following through with commitments— about the deal unraveling.

Larry was furious at the news. Few things set him off quite like someone going back on a promise. He explained to me once again the importance of integrity in all things. In business and in life, he said, nothing matters more than a person's words being consistent with his or her actions.

Of course, I agreed with him, but that lesson did little to solve the issue of the red Cobra. I told Larry that our only chance to acquire CSX2002 was to participate in the auction. There was a strong possibility that we would pay substantially more for the vehicle at auction, especially since the Cobra was one of the featured cars in the auction advertisements. I felt a bit defeated, but Larry wasn't ready to give up: we would go to the auction and do our best to bring home CSX2002.

We traveled to Monterey, where I sat next to Larry at the auction. I felt terrible; it had been my charter to secure the red Cobra for the Miller collection, and I felt guilty that in spite of my best efforts I had been unsuccessful. Larry assured me I didn't need to feel bad about the way the deal had unraveled. He knew it was the previous owner who had reneged, and he made a powerfully symbolic gesture to show me he was appreciative of how I had handled the situation.

While we were waiting for the Cobra to come across the auction block, two vintage Le Mans posters appeared that Larry knew I wanted for my own collection. Larry purchased the posters, a thoughtful gift I'll always cherish.

Soon, the moment arrived. The crowd swelled as the Cobra was driven onto the podium. The bidding started, and emotions ran high. I held my breath as the auctioneer quickly sorted through the commotion and marshaled the bids. In a matter of minutes the gavel fell, and as the proverbial dust settled, I almost couldn't believe the outcome. Larry was the highest bidder, and his winning bid turned out to be about half the price we'd originally negotiated with the seller.

It was then that Larry winked at me and said, "Integrity always wins."

Those two Le Mans posters still hang proudly in my home in Boulder, Colorado, serving as a powerful reminder of my friend Larry and all that he stood for.

Similarly, that very same red Cobra sits today as a testament to the value of integrity and the reward for doing things the right way.

A NOBLE OWNER

Phil Johnson

In 1989, I joined the coaching staff of the Utah Jazz. Jerry Sloan had taken over as head coach after Frank Layden resigned. In spite of the turmoil, we finished the year with a decent record, winning the Midwest Division Championship. The playoffs were another story. The Golden State Warriors swept us.

The following year was another regular season success story. The Jazz compiled a 55–27 record, finishing second in the Midwest Division. We were in the playoffs against the Phoenix Suns. After winning the opening game of the best-of-five series, we lost the second one at home. With that disappointing 105–87 defeat, the home court advantage disappeared. In a short five-game series, a home loss is difficult to overcome. We dropped the next game to the Suns. That put us behind 1–2 in the series with the fourth game in Phoenix—not a position a team likes to be in.

I was in my hotel room getting ready for the game when the phone rang. Larry Miller was on the line. I was not accustomed to getting a game-day call from the owner.

"Phil," he said, "I'm trying to get in touch with Jerry and haven't been able to reach him."

"He's probably in the shower," I replied. "Call him back a little later."

There had been recent reports in the news media intimating

that if the Jazz lost the next game, the coaching staff would be fired. I knew of coaches who had been let go under similar circumstances, as coaching in the NBA is a volatile profession.

"Those reports you've been hearing are not true," said Larry. "You guys are *my* coaches. If I can't reach Jerry, tell him what I said."

After I hung up, I marveled at his commitment and loyalty to us. In the sports world, such support in times of difficulty is rare. We won the road game but returned home and lost the fifth game, and the series went to the Suns.

Larry didn't fire us. We were *his* coaches. Jerry and I continued working for the Utah Jazz for more than twenty years. Larry was a man of his word.

Penny Wise

Stayner Landward

In the early 2000s, Larry contacted me regarding the possibility of establishing a full-ride scholarship for first-generation college students who stemmed from diverse backgrounds. He'd talked about this idea with Andrew Valdez, a former juvenile court judge in Utah. Larry knew Judge Valdez had attended the University of Utah on a diversity scholarship funded by the Ford Foundation, and he and Gail wanted to establish something similar. I was Andrew's advisor during his first quarter at the University, so I was familiar with the principles and mechanics of that existing scholarship. Larry wanted to talk to me because I was in an administrative position as Utah's dean of students.

This scholarship partnership was a great fit. We already had a fluid working relationship, having worked together to set up a tuition scholarship for the dependents of the Larry H. Miller Group of Companies employees. Also, Larry and Gail had previously discussed their interest in funding a scholarship that allowed students to fully immerse themselves in a university lifestyle. It was easy to follow the Ford Foundation model, which espoused the philosophy of having students reside on campus so they could get the most out of their university experience.

Shortly after our conversation, Larry and Gail agreed to initially fund ten students with Miller Enrichment Scholarships. Each year, ten more students would be added until the total number on scholarship reached forty. From that point, the thought was that ten students would graduate and ten more scholarship recipients would begin school. This turned out to be a little optimistic. Often, there are as many as forty-three students on the scholarship at the same time.

Miller Enrichment Scholarships include full tuition and fees, room and board, and books. Freshmen can earn an additional $300 monthly stipend for volunteering ten hours of service through Student Affairs.

After the first group of students was selected and registered, the total bill came to $129,388 for the scholarships. Consequently, I sent Larry a bill for $129,400. Several days later, I received a phone call.

"Where did the extra $12 go?" Larry asked.

At first, I did not understand the question and was without an answer. Larry explained that I had sent a bill for $12 more than the projected cost of the first semester. Embarrassed that I had overbilled, I explained the $129,400 was my best estimate of the cost based on fourteen hours of credit for each student. Some students take more and some fewer credits, so I rounded up knowing that $129,388 was an estimate.

"Okay," Larry responded. "I just wanted to know why there was a difference between the two figures."

It was a good lesson to learn that Larry paid attention to detail and was careful with his financial resources. We detailed each subsequent bill to the penny.

Several years later, a Miller Enrichment Scholarship recipient broke her arm. She told me that she would have to drop out of school to work in order to pay off her $2,800 medical bill. Incidentally, I received a phone call from Larry regarding another matter two hours later. I relayed the student's concern about paying for the medical expense she had incurred. Larry inquired about the total cost of the treatment and to whom it was to be paid. After providing that information, Larry visited with Gail and they decided they did not want the student to drop out of school. They wanted to pay the medical bill. The student went on to earn a graduate degree, and I received another lesson in the thoughtfulness and generosity of Larry and Gail.

More than 150 students have received a Miller Enrichment Scholarship since its inception. Approximately eighty-five percent of the recipients graduated or were still in school during the first twelve years of the scholarship. In addition, thirty-eight percent of graduates moved on to grad school, working toward advanced degrees in education, law, business, public administration, and medicine.

We have an annual celebration dinner for the graduates, and there is a feeling of tearful elation to hear students express their appreciation to the Miller family for providing them an opportunity to receive a higher education they could not have afforded on their own.

Two Decades
of Deals

Daniel Hartmann

As a regional manager of national dealer services for Comerica Bank, I worked with Larry Miller on many financial projects over the span of two decades. Given that I am a banker and Larry was a visionary in need of financing for his never-ending growth streaks, Larry obviously affected me professionally. But his impact expanded to me personally as well. Larry was one of those rare individuals who changed the lives of others without their realizing it.

I met Larry in 1990 when I traveled to Salt Lake City from Comerica's regional offices in Denver to fashion a financing package for his dealerships in Boulder, Colorado. I liked him from the start. He was smart, loved the car business, and was open to a young banker looking to make his mark in the business. At the time, Larry informed me that "the more you look at us, the more you'll like what you see." I took him at his word—a wise call.

Clark Whitworth had recently joined the Miller Group to oversee financial matters. Clark, Larry, and I spent considerable time together. Those sessions laid the foundation of understanding and trust that allowed us to build one of Comerica's most respected bank/client relationships in the nation.

We financed many dealership acquisitions and other Miller projects, including Prestige Financial and Miller Motorsports Park. Back in the 1990s, we took a Hail Mary shot at bundling all of

Larry's debt—from the Jazz, the arena, dealerships, real estate, and acquisitions—into a consolidated loan secured by the Jazz. Such a deal would simplify servicing the debt, save money, and provide flexibility, but it didn't happen. In spite of considerable time, expense, and meetings with more New York lawyers than I care to think about, the NBA wouldn't allow a collateral lien on the Jazz franchise as large as we needed.

Think about it: I wasn't even forty. I had no previous experience with financing professional sports teams. Larry had his pick of banks and bankers, but he chose us. That was crazy! Larry gave me the nod over the big banks with their sports-lending departments because he believed in me and liked that I wasn't afraid to tackle challenges. I believed I could figure out how to make anything work.

Just like Larry.

We got another chance on a stratospheric deal a few years later when we became the financing agent for a consolidated real estate-loan facility, a financial assistance program that lends companies operating capital. It would involve all of Larry's automotive properties and some of his non-automotive entities. To my knowledge, there isn't another facility like it in the auto dealership world. Clark and I spent many hours engineering the loan structure. Some bankers said we couldn't do it or that we were the wrong choice because we were too small. But Larry believed in us and we got it done.

Comerica was also the first bank to finance one hundred percent of an acquisition—blue sky (not yet profitable resources), assets, and working capital—through a personal loan to Larry and Gail. She must have thought Larry and I were nuts. Who lends one hundred percent of the cost to acquire a business with no collateral and only five years to repay the loan? Comerica did because it was Larry H. Miller.

Trust was the foundation of our relationship. There have been few people I have trusted as much as Larry. The reason: his integrity. I have never met anyone who honored his or her word quite like Larry did. It was better than an ironclad legal contract.

That sort of integrity leaves a sizeable impression on a young, aspiring banker. Larry gave me the opportunity to do amazing things while demonstrating that honoring one's word is more valuable than all the world's riches.

Larry was a brilliant, painfully driven man whose incredible accomplishments came with equally incredible personal price tags. He screamed, he cried, he obsessed over details. He had many warts. Clark and I often commented that it would be exhausting to spend a day inside Larry's head. Larry's integrity and sense of fairness were things of beauty. I am a far better person today for having known him.

The last time I saw Larry was bittersweet. The meeting produced one of my deepest regrets. Larry was being inducted into the Utah Auto Dealers Hall of Fame in January 2009. I attended the event and spoke to him briefly. I didn't fully grasp the seriousness of his health situation; I thought I would see him again. From his wheelchair, Larry said, "Dan, I want to thank you for all you've done for me and my family."

"You're welcome," I said, and we talked a little bit longer. In the commotion of the moment, I got distracted and drifted away to talk to someone else.

I didn't realize Larry wasn't just thanking me; he was saying goodbye. He died about a month later. I hope when I see Larry in heaven he will forgive me.

If I had a do-over, I would have gotten down on one knee at that event so that I was eye level with him and would have told Larry how much *he* had meant to me and thanked *him*.

THE IMPORTANCE
OF CHARACTER

Dean Paynter

We can point to tangible reminders of Larry Miller's contributions to our community, but what I most admired about him were the intangible elements of his character. He built businesses and structures, but he also built a reputation that radiated influence throughout different aspects of his life.

I experienced firsthand the magnitude of Larry's reputation while working on an assignment for my hometown newspaper column about a residential property that had been chosen for the monthly beautification award. The spotlight piece was about to go to press and I hadn't been able to gather the homeowner's profile information, so one evening I ended up knocking on doors of nearby houses to see if a neighbor might be able to help me out.

The first two houses yielded no results, but when I earnestly rapped on the next neighbor's door, the porch light switched on. The door slowly opened about three inches, revealing the petite mouth and nose of an elderly woman.

My cheerful enthusiasm was met with a rather cool injunction to get to the point. I explained my situation, and though she revealed that she knew her neighbor well, she was reluctant to give me any information. Knowing I had maybe only one last crack at getting what I needed, I leaned in to the screen and confidently asked, "What if I told you I work for Larry H. Miller?"

To my surprise, her face lit up, and she smiled when I showed her my employee badge. The door opened wide, and she welcomed me into her home. We chatted about what it meant to work for a Larry H. Miller company, about the Jazz, and about her neighbor. With the contact info she gave me, I was able to reach the award recipient by phone.

I tell this story to every new employee who comes to work in my department. It reminds them that a good reputation, a legacy, isn't built in a day. A good reputation is valuable and is maintained through our work performance and in the way we represent ourselves to the community. Larry Miller's reputation was built, in part, through the respect people in the community had for him. I personally gained a lot of respect for Larry Miller when I had the opportunity to meet him through a project I was asked to help develop.

When I was a television news producer in the late 1980s, I thought it would be interesting to create an insider's look at the scheduled construction of Larry H. Miller's Delta Center, from groundbreaking to dedication. We would document the behind-the-scenes action of Larry's team working in a virtual pressure cooker to complete the arena in fifteen months, a construction timetable that required Herculean effort and flawless execution.

We were given access to weekly meetings for the design-build project, a planning and execution model in which all people involved in the project work together under a single contract with the project owner. Those sessions were mind-blowers, especially when I witnessed Larry's ability to ingest and later recite the most mundane details. He literally knew the size of bolts being used to screw together beams and doorways.

Shortly after construction started, I parted ways with the television station, and the Jazz organization picked up the ball and shot footage of the progress.

About one month from its completion, Jazz executives Randy Rigby and Brian Douglas asked me to produce and write the television history of the construction. I agreed, but I also had one request in relation to the production. The primary vision and inspiration behind this monumental undertaking was clearly coming from one man, and I hoped that spending a few minutes with Larry might help me understand his legendary drive.

Brian arranged for the three of us to meet one evening, and the thirty minutes I had hoped for ended up being a spellbinding three-hour brain dump from a guy who had something interesting to say on just about everything. One moment I will never forget came when I asked Larry his opinion on the status of professional athletes. Had they become too privileged, too unruly, too focused on status?

He explained why the Jazz had very few problems with player behavior on or off the court. He said personal character was one of the most important factors in determining who would come to Salt Lake to play for his team.

Then, Larry did something that caught both Brian and me totally off guard. He reached into the top drawer of his desk and pulled out a yellow legal pad.

"Let me show you what I mean."

Larry flipped through the top sheets of the pad.

"This," he explained, "is Karl Malone's contract."

Only about half the page was filled, and it was all Larry's handwriting. Larry told us part of the handwritten contract stipulated that Karl would dedicate himself as a professional to work hard on the court, to contribute heavily to the team, and to represent the Jazz and Utah as an upstanding citizen in the community. That was about it. The signatures of Larry H. Miller and Karl Malone were at the bottom of the page.

Since that evening, I have thought many times about how much better our world would be if we all could reach a level of personal integrity where contract negotiations like the one represented on that legal pad were commonplace in business, government, and families.

I feel a great deal of pride in saying, "I work for Larry H. Miller." Even though the man himself is no longer with us, his principles still reverberate throughout the walls of the structures he built and the lives of the people who knew him.

GOOD TO HIS WORD

Eric Slaymaker

Back in 2001, I had never met Larry Miller. I only knew him from the media, his ownership of the Jazz, and his auto dealerships. For some reason, I wasn't a huge Larry Miller fan. I'm not really sure why, but in my limited opinion, he always seemed to come through in the media as overemotional and overconfident. Maybe I even thought of him as a little cocky as I watched him guide the Jazz and his company. Maybe it was just my competitive businessman jealousy that colored my thinking, because he had become so successful.

Whatever the case, I fully expected to be meeting with somewhat of an egomaniac when Larry and I sat down with representatives from our companies to discuss a restaurant deal at the Jordan Commons theater complex in Sandy, Utah.

The meeting came about after I received a call from Dale Harvey, who was the general manager of Jordan Commons at the time. The complex, owned by Larry Miller, was looking for a restaurant operator for one of its vacant locations. Dale had tracked me down, as our company, the Slaymaker Restaurant Group, operated several regional restaurant brands—including Tucci's Cucina Italiana—based out of Salt Lake City.

Dale explained to me that their initial restaurant tenant, Amelia's Italian Restaurant, had recently closed its doors. Larry

Miller and his team at Jordan Commons were set on bringing in another established Italian restaurant brand.

After an initial visit to Jordan Commons with Dale, we had turned down the offer to lease a new site there. The restaurant site was absolutely beautiful, finished out with gorgeous wood and marble, but we were concerned it was too close to an existing Tucci's location in the Union Heights area of the Salt Lake Valley. We were also apprehensive because we thought lunch traffic would be soft at this site. After several additional conversations with Dale Harvey, he called and said that Larry would like to meet with us at his office, which was located on the top floor of the office building at the Jordan Commons complex.

Upon walking into Larry's office, I was immediately struck by his warm, gracious, and even humble manner. He was exactly the opposite of what I had expected. Larry, Dale, my two partners—my brother, Scott Slaymaker, and our company president, Don Morehouse—and I discussed our company and even talked about our challenges at the time. Larry told us about how he had faced similar challenges early in the development of his companies.

Considering how large of a company Larry oversaw, I was somewhat surprised that such a small deal as ours even mattered to him. Surely he had larger and more important things that he could be focusing on than a single restaurant. Nevertheless, Larry was interested in doing a deal with us and bringing the right Italian restaurant to his theater complex.

My partners and I let him know of our reservations and concerns regarding moving into Jordan Commons. We were not sure that we were ready to commit the resources and cash required to convert the restaurant into a Tucci's. We didn't know if it was a good investment, and we were very up front with Larry about this. Near the end of the meeting, Larry asked how much money it would take for the complete conversion. Our estimate was that it would require about $180,000.

Right then and there, Larry said he was willing to put up the money for the restaurant conversion. In return, he asked for a higher-than-normal percentage rent against the sales of this Tucci's restaurant. This means Larry was willing to assume a significant expense and share in the success of the restaurant.

Larry told us one final thing at the meeting: "If this isn't profitable for you, then you can back out of the lease and move on, but let's see if we can make this work."

The Tucci's restaurant opened at Jordan Commons a few months later, in November of 2001. Working with the Larry H. Miller Group was great. The restaurant turned out to be beautiful. If there is one thing I will say about Larry, it's that when this company does something, it's done right. Gorgeous marble tile work and beautiful woodwork ran throughout the dining room.

As predicted, the restaurant was bustling on those nights when the Jordan Commons movie theaters were also busy. Weekend nights did very well. Unfortunately, this Tucci's restaurant struggled to attract crowds at lunch and early in the week. For the next two years, the location operated on a profitability level that was close to break-even.

Early in 2004, we set up a meeting with Larry and the Jordan Commons executive staff for a Tucci's business review. During that meeting, we informed Larry that our restaurant was, unfortunately, not performing at the sales volume or profitability levels that we had hoped for. The restaurant struggled to break even, and our projected budgets for the upcoming year foresaw the restaurant operating at a slight loss.

We were forthright with Larry. We told him we were disappointed in the restaurant's performance and were debating whether it made sense to continue operating the restaurant when the best-case scenario was to break even. Larry was obviously disappointed and saddened to hear this. But without hesitation, he said, "I told you that if this location wasn't profitable, you could walk away. I will honor that agreement."

Both parties agreed that this Tucci's location was not meeting expectations. The decision was made to close the restaurant. Although it was a big disappointment for all of us, I was struck by

Larry's profound integrity and honesty. This deal was a very small one in his world, but it was very important to us at the time.

Despite any other legal arrangements, Larry was good to his word, even if it hurt him personally. It was one of the greatest examples of integrity I have seen over my many years in the business world. Through example, Larry showed the type of person he was. To this day, I hold Larry in the highest respect. I see him as a role model of the type of businessperson I still aspire to be. Through thick and thin, Larry H. Miller was good to his word.

PASSION & PLAYFULNESS

HUNTING SQUIRRELS

ElRay Jenkins

Whenare you popping the big question? She's your high school sweetheart!" I'd say to him. "It's about time! She's going to dump you."

I teased Larry all the time about this, but he had been dating Gail for years at this point, and he had yet to ask The Question. This was the summer of 1964. Larry had been my sidekick, hunting buddy, and constant companion for several years, and we were enjoying our weekly adventures around the state of Utah.

During this trip, I was collecting specimens for my master's thesis on parasites of ground squirrels for the University of Utah. We were in the Raft River Mountains on the Utah-Nevada-Idaho border, and I remember Larry talked nonstop about the love of his life, Gail, as we descended rapidly down a dusty, winding dirt road.

While in the vehicle, we kept our loaded guns on our laps just in case we saw a ground squirrel. Suddenly, a bobcat darted across the road directly in front of us. Larry slammed on the brakes, and we came to a screeching halt. Dust and gravel went flying. Before I could even get out of my seat, Larry was already around the front of the pickup truck. With a single shot of his .22-caliber rifle, he nailed the creature as it went over the crest of a hill.

A single shot with a .22? How did he do it?

Here's how: he was the best marksman I'd ever seen. He proved this to me time and time again.

As we headed back to the campsite that night after a great day of specimen collecting, our headlights helped us spot kangaroo rats hopping all over the wheat fields we were driving through. Kangaroo rats don't run—they hop. And they don't bite. It was a hunter's dream.

Larry slammed on the brakes once again. We both grabbed flashlights and ran around the wheat fields, trying to catch these hopping rodents. Decades later, we still hadn't stopped laughing about this experience. We had wanted to see who could catch the most. In the end, we ended up with just one each.

This type of competition between Larry and me was always fierce and could last for hours, with neither side giving in. He would challenge me to throw rocks over gullies and ravines to see who had the better arm. Larry threw underhand, and I threw whichever way I wanted. I never beat him once. Very few people could.

I accepted a lot of these challenges from Larry over the years, but there was only one challenge I wouldn't accept: you couldn't pay me enough money to catch Larry's underhand softball fast pitch.

A couple of years after our summer hunting trip, I moved away to the University of Missouri in Columbia to attend medical school. By then Larry and Gail were married, and they brought their two young sons, Greg and Roger, for a visit from Colorado.

While our wives grilled some steaks, Larry and I squared off against each other in one of our favorite pastimes: Combat Frisbee. The rules of the game were simple. The thrower had to toss the Frisbee hard enough to drive the opponent out of bounds. The catcher then had to throw back the Frisbee from where he caught it. The idea was to drive the other person farther and farther with each throw. This time, Larry was determined to drive me out of the student housing common area, and I was determined to drive him out into the neighboring woods.

The game went on and on, as they usually did. The only thing that saved us was our wives calling us to dinner. Larry was fierce, tenacious, and would never quit, except maybe for food or when our sweethearts gave us the final word.

Looking back, Larry seemed to come out ahead in most of our competitions, but I did beat him at one thing: I married my sweetheart, Uta, before he married his sweetheart, Gail. Even then, it was only by a few months—although it would have been much longer if not for Gail's insistence. She finally got tired of waiting. Instead of dumping him, as I thought she would after six years of dating, she told Larry she was going to get married and wanted to know if he was interested in joining her.

He said yes!

Maybe Gail, who'd been our accomplice on some Wild West adventures, had finally hit Larry over the head with a baseball bat, but before he could change his mind, I was standing next to him as his best man as they tied the knot. He had a big smile on his face as if he'd just caught the prize of his life. Throughout the years to come, Larry always added a description when he introduced me to friends and family: "And he was my best man when Gail and I got married."

We forged a bond in those early years that was never broken as time passed. Larry was the ultimate competitor, but more than that, he was a loyal and true friend. He was a friend to all, no matter who they were. Whether we were hunting, competing, or just hanging out, Larry was the best man I could have asked for as a friend.

I Won't Get
Traded There

Jeff Hornacek

My first professional game in Utah took place during my rookie year in 1986, when I was playing for the Phoenix Suns. I think the old Salt Palace only held about 12,000 fans, but the arena had one of the loudest crowds I had ever played in front of in my life.

In typical Utah Jazz fashion, it was a physical and intense game. Normally I didn't notice anybody in the crowd when I was playing. This time was different. A guy sitting right by coach John MacLeod was yelling and screaming at us. This man, obviously a huge Jazz fan, was really into it. His passion for the game was admirable.

When Coach took me out of the game in the middle of the second quarter, this fan was pointing at me. He started to say something, and I responded, "Sit down, you $*@%#!"

As I went down to the end of our bench, my veteran teammates were rolling around laughing. We were losing, and I was not happy.

I snapped at them. "What's so funny?"

They asked me if I knew who I had just yelled at.

"No. Just some $*@%# fan."

They then told me he was Larry Miller, the owner of the Jazz.

I'll never forget my response.

"Well, I guess I will never get traded to the Jazz."

After beginning my NBA career with Phoenix, I next played

for the Philadelphia 76ers. On the trade deadline day in 1994, my wife, Stacy, and I sat on our bed in Philadelphia, hoping to get a call. I wanted to be traded. Philly was in a rebuilding process, and I was almost thirty-one years old. I wanted to win, so I had asked to be dealt to a contending team. The first rumor I heard was that I had been traded to the New York Knicks. Then the Chicago Bulls. Then the Atlanta Hawks.

When the deadline arrived, I hadn't heard anything official. I thought we were still stuck in Philly. Fifteen minutes later, I received a call from Scott Layden, the general manager of the Jazz. He gave me the good news: I'd been traded to Utah.

A couple of days later, I was in Salt Lake City to begin that portion of my career. When Larry came up and welcomed me to the Jazz, the first thing I said was, "Thanks for trading for me."

The second thing?

"Glad you forgot about me yelling at you my rookie year."

Just kidding. I wasn't going to bring that up to him!

Over the years, I heard Larry tell that story at least twenty times. I'm glad he never held that against me.

THE PRANKSTER GETS PRANKED

Terry Stevinson

The employees at Stevinson Toyota in Lakewood, Colorado, were a hardworking, revenue-producing, close-knit team. But that didn't mean there wasn't time for a few pranks. And the chief prankster was our leader, Larry Miller.

My father, Chuck, is the guy who gave Larry his first shot at managing an auto dealership. I was working at my father's Toyota store with a great group of guys. It was forty years ago now, but I still remember each member of that group by name: Wade, John, TJ, Jack, Tom, and, of course, Larry. We had a lot of fun working together, in part because we never took ourselves too seriously. We approached our jobs and our mission seriously, though. We were the top-selling Toyota dealer in the state. We produced more revenue from all departments than any other Toyota store, largely because of some shrewd moves by Larry to secure large orders of highly profitable after-market parts.

We worked well in using each other's talents and abilities to embrace each sale and each customer. Larry was a big part of this. But he also challenged us to have fun together as we worked toward our individual and team goals.

A week never went by that someone wasn't either pulling some practical joke on someone or sitting at the receiving end of one.

284

Larry wasn't always the chief perpetrator, but he was usually somewhere close to the middle of things.

We would put shaving cream in the earpiece of someone's phone and wait for him to answer to an earful of foam. We'd staple the paper roll on the adding machines in the office so they would get stuck. Someone would put a chip of wood in the wheel of a co-worker's chair so that it wouldn't move. We would even remove a piece from the phone receiver so that you couldn't hear anything when you answered a call. None of these pranks lasted long, but we all had a great laugh and then tried to think of how to one-up each other in the spirit of great fun.

One particular spring day, Larry became the brunt of one of these pranks.

I had planned it out. First, I bought a new phone to go in his office. Then I bought a tube of super glue. Then I went into Larry's office before he came to work. I knew he had an early meeting at another store, so it was the perfect day. I glued the earpiece to the base, so that anyone who picked up the receiver would pick up the entire phone as well. Then we just waited, watched, and listened.

Larry came in and put his things down while those of us who were in on the joke waited anxiously for an incoming call to trigger the hilarity. Then it happened. The phone rang, and soon Larry's voice peppered the whole area with some salty language and plenty of emotion, which led to everyone erupting in laughter.

Later that same day, Larry and Ed Miller (no relation) went to lunch, and it was then that Larry learned who'd sabotaged his phone. When they returned from lunch, Larry had barely come through the front door when I heard a loud shout.

"STEVINSON!"

I was at the other end of the showroom when Larry approached me and playfully forearmed me into the wall. He must have lifted me off the floor by a foot or more. I fell to the floor, out of breath, but laughing all the way. I knew that I had gotten to him.

Larry stood over me, looking down at me, red with anger as he could sometimes get. I was still laughing hysterically and, as much as he would have liked to stay mad, Larry eventually started to laugh, too. After a few moments, we jumped up, shook hands, exchanged a hug, and went back to work. Then I brought the new phone into Larry's office to replace the glued phone from that morning's practical joke.

I remember Larry as hardworking, intense, and smart, but also as someone who enjoyed life. Larry liked people. He was a great mentor, and even though Larry was only six years older than I, he taught me more about myself, about work, and about family than almost anyone else. I will always remember the deep kindness he showed me and the fun we had together. I am a much better person for having Larry and his wife, Gail, in my life.

Twelve-Gauge Metal

Jazz Bear

Larry might have been the most down-to-earth NBA franchise owner in the sport's history. He proved this to me time and time again as I've served as the Jazz mascot since 1993. Sport mascots are a tight-knit bunch, and I remember one evening when four of them came into town to help me celebrate my birthday with the team. This was when they all met Larry for the first time.

After the game, the five of us had just hauled all of our equipment into the back lot of the arena. We were then just waiting for my assistant to drive the van around so we could catch a ride back to the hotel, where we would celebrate my birthday party. But as we sat there waiting, Larry walked out of the arena, making his way toward his car. He noticed me, and I introduced him to the other mascots. He observed our equipment and asked if we would like a ride to the hotel. I laughed and insisted that we had way too much to fit into his sedan. Larry shrugged and said that we could make two trips if need be.

As we spoke, the van pulled up. I thanked Larry for his generosity, and he drove away. As he did, I looked back at my mascot friends, all of them with their jaws hanging down in shock. "That was the owner of the team?!" one exclaimed. Another chimed in, "My owner sure as heck wouldn't have even stopped to talk to us, let alone offer us a ride!"

I just laughed and said, "Welcome to Utah!"

Larry was never about self-importance and pride—not even the time when I dented his new car! We were shooting a video for a Jazz promo, and I asked Larry if he wanted to be in it. He readily agreed. Part of the video featured me getting dropped from an F-16 fighter jet onto the hood of Larry's car. Although I planned on using a stunt car, Larry insisted upon using his personal, brand-new Lexus for the shoot. Naturally, I worried that I would dent the hood, but he informed me, "The hood is like twelve-gauge metal, and it would be difficult to dent."

We went ahead and shot the scene. As it happened, when I landed on the hood of his car, it created a massive dent. I was mortified and certain he would be furious. Instead, he just looked at it blankly and said, "Well, I didn't think that would happen."

I tried to apologize, but he stopped me and, with a wink, told me he knew someone that did good auto body work.

Larry always left you guessing and was as unassuming as a person could be. It was clear that he valued his people above all else, and it's been an honor to serve as his team's mascot these last two decades.

FIVE O'CLOCK

David Locke

Thursday, five o'clock in the evening—there was nothing else like it. For me as the radio host or for the listener, Thursday at five was the hour of radio when time stopped and you listened.

Thursday at five o'clock was when Larry H. Miller would join me for one hour on the radio every week. A business mogul, an NBA owner, a genius would share his thoughts with the world for an entire hour every week. Unheard of. A must-listen.

It made every Thursday game day for me. I knew I had to be sharp, but adequate preparation proved nearly impossible. Trying to guess where Larry's mind was going to go and what ideas he would share was futile.

I asked the most absurd question before every session started. "Anything you want to touch on?"

The man could talk about anything: personal stories from an NBA locker room, interactions with the largest names in the sports world, days in the parts department, stories about his family, or even the most current world issue. No matter the topic, each thought came with passion and purpose. Listeners held on to each word for wisdom.

Honestly, part of the energy was the suspense of wondering what he would say next. I'm sure nobody in the public relations department or in the league office breathed during that hour. He often crossed the imaginary line of what we thought was appropriate for an NBA owner to share, and I'd think, *You didn't really just say that, did you?*

Sometimes I wasn't sure if I was allowed to counter or disagree, but over time I grew comfortable enough to challenge and ask questions. But there was such a firmness; he was so unbending in his thoughts and beliefs. Outside of sports, I'm not sure Larry and I would agree on a lot of topics, yet we could have incredible conversations. We'd exchange ideas and he would listen, but there were certain principles that were just part of his belief system.

For one, he was an unabashed patriot. Some of Larry's final shows took place during the financial crisis that started in 2008. Our foundation had been rocked, but Larry didn't see it that way. He had an unshaken, relentless belief that America—and Americans—would overcome.

His connection with noted historian and author David McCullough was one of his favorite topics. The two connected when Larry asked McCullough to speak to managers of the Miller Group at an annual meeting, and they instantly struck up a friendship based on their mutual passion for history and teaching people to appreciate our freedoms. I'd often end our radio segments by asking him, at 5:55, what books we should be reading. We rarely got off the air before 6:15, because Larry's answers turned into a twenty-minute explanation of what a particular book meant to him. When he talked about McCullough and the importance of books like *1776* and *John Adams,* he lit up in a different way than anything else I remember.

Our relationship, though, far predated the five o'clock hour on Thursdays. I had actually started my broadcast career while working on the Jazz radio network in the '90s. I didn't know Larry well at that point, but he had a pulse on everything. As a young and rambunctious radio host, I occasionally enjoyed rocking the boat. I would share some criticisms that stirred up controversy, and more than once I found myself in some hot water.

Toward the end of my first stint on Jazz radio, I had run into one of those situations and received a reassuring call from Larry. "You're all right," he told me. "I'm in charge here. Don't forget, I'm the guy who's in charge, and you're all right." He certainly didn't need to do that, but it was a very meaningful gesture of support, and one I'd remember ten years later when the opportunity came to return to work for the Utah Jazz.

After working in Seattle for a few years, I had the chance to return to Salt Lake City, but I was nervous about coming back because of who I had been the first time. I was twenty-eight when I left the market. Now thirty-eight, I was no longer the same rambunctious young radio host looking to rock the boat, and I had to convince the decision-makers that I had grown up. Larry listened, as he always did, wanting to know how I had matured. "You're sitting here as a thirty-eight-year-old rather than a *twenty*-eight-year-old," Larry said, in so many words. "What has happened to you in ten years?"

Ultimately, I was offered the position. When Randy Rigby, then head of broadcasting, called me to let me know, I asked him, "Does Larry know, and does he want this?"

The support he had showed me ten years earlier had been so meaningful that I knew I wanted the job as long as Larry was behind me. Randy reassured me that Larry was behind the decision, and it was done.

That's when the five o'clock radio shows began, and that's when we started to develop a personal relationship. He wasn't a father figure or a mentor, per se. He was more like a sage with all this knowledge, and he was wonderfully willing to share it.

In 2013, Dropbox CEO Drew Houston gave a commencement speech at MIT, in which he compared the passion and desire of people following their dreams to that of a dog chasing a tennis ball. When you throw a dog a tennis ball, he will bound over bushes, through lakes, and wherever else he needs to go to chase that ball, and then he'll want to do it again. Houston said we should all find that "tennis ball": something we're equally obsessed with. Most people are lucky to find one tennis ball. The extremely lucky are able to find two or three.

When I heard this speech, I immediately thought of Larry. Somehow, Larry had found several tennis balls. He was passionate and obsessed about everything he did: the Jazz, the racetrack, the dealerships, the movie theaters—all these tennis balls he constantly chased.

Eventually, all that simultaneous chasing wore on Larry. We watched from up close as his health deteriorated and we could tell— even if we weren't ready to admit it—that something wasn't quite right. I remember the first time he told me he'd be in the studio for our weekly interview but wound up calling in instead. On one level, it made sense, with how busy Larry was. But he had never done that before. *Something's wrong*, I thought. And sadly, I was right.

A year after Larry passed, I became the radio voice of the Utah Jazz, taking over for Hall-of-Fame broadcaster Hot Rod Hundley. Every day I try to repay Larry Miller for the opportunity. Every day I'm trying to be innovative and to work harder than every other play-by-play announcer in the NBA. And every Thursday at five o'clock, I remember this special friend of mine who always had faith in me and offered me some of life's most memorable conversations.

VOCABULARY LESSONS

Al Fernelius

From brain damage to bras, from squirrels to cream puffs, working for Larry Miller involved a whole new vernacular.

I went to work for Larry in 1983 as a young, if naïve, CPA in my thirties. This was before Larry Miller was associated with the Utah Jazz and before he had sold a single new Ford, Chevrolet, or Chrysler. At this point he had Toyota locations in four different states, a Subaru store in Murray, Utah, and some "buy here, pay here" operations. These were the early days of the Miller empire, and we were all learning a great deal.

One of the things I had to learn early on is that Larry spoke a unique language. For the first few months working with him, I learned new words and phrases almost every day. The words could be pretty unpleasant when he was angry, and other times they were simply unique ways of explaining something that I had never heard before.

Either way, I had to learn this new language in order to keep up. Some meanings I gleaned from context, but many times I had to ask around and find someone who was familiar with the Larry jargon. But none were in the dictionary, so I started to list words and phrases I first heard from Larry that were new to me. Soon, my little "Larry Lexicon" filled up both sides of a legal sheet, about eighty or ninety words, and that was just in the first year or two of my thirty-year employment with the Miller Group.

Some of the phrases and definitions are ones I don't dare share. Here's a small sample of the ones I can:

Upside down: in a loss position (also "back of book").

Slap leather: to produce a hefty cash payment.

Put together: to be taken advantage of.

Heater: an angry or confrontational customer or person.

Brain damage: hard work, considerable effort.

Tubed: disappointed, downtrodden, deflated.

Get inside my head: to understand one's thoughts, feelings, or insights.

Sled: an old, undesirable used car.

Squirrel: a difficult-to-control customer.

Cream puff: a highly marketable used car.

Lunched: word used to describe a car that is totaled.

Load your lip: to prompt or script another person.

Skins: tires.

Turns or **ups:** opportunities to sell to a customer.

I also had to learn the lingo associated with the car business, and sometimes that meant learning a vocabulary lesson in a rather embarrassing way.

Much of my time in those early days was spent working as an internal auditor or with outside CPAs on the annual reviews and audits. Part of that process involved flipping through the books of check copies and looking for anything unusual or questionable that required further review. One day, I came upon something that concerned and puzzled me, but as a matter of integrity, I knew I had to raise it with the boss.

I was new and didn't want to make waves or get anybody in trouble, so I stewed over these suspicious purchases for a day or two before deciding to report my discovery to Larry.

Nervous but resolute, I marched into Larry's office and showed him the check copies. "The women in the accounting office are writing checks for bras," I announced.

Larry just grinned.

He respectfully explained to me that those purchases were car bras, the protective vinyl masks that attach to the front end of a car to protect it from paint chips or other damage. I'm sure he held in a chuckle the entire time he explained to me that these purchases were permissible. He thanked me for my loyalty and good intentions, and I went back to work relieved.

But the language of Larry was unique indeed. As a car dealer, a softball player, and a person with an unusual amount of assertiveness and directness, Larry communicated like nobody else I've ever known. As he entered the public eye in an era of political correctness, he did learn to tone it down and adjust to his environment, and did it quite well.

Over the twenty-five years I knew Larry up until his passing, I saw him evolve in a number of ways, not just in the way he articulated himself. I witnessed a real transformation in Larry as a person. He became an increasingly spiritual person as he served in his church callings and became acquainted with the leaders of his faith. Gail's influence had a great impact on Larry's transformation, too, especially in becoming a gentler person and a better listener—traits he observed in and learned from Gail.

And along the way, he expanded my vocabulary, for better or worse.

THE HUMAN
CALCULATOR

Brad Burrup

As part of my professional development with the Larry H. Miller organization, I once took a class during which a professor asked members of our class to name two people who made us smile every time we saw them or thought about them. Larry Miller was the first person that came to my mind.

I smile for many reasons when I think of Larry. First, he was a great friend. He was always there when I needed him. Sometimes I reached out to him, and he always got back to me, no matter how busy he was. Other times, he called me out of the blue, right when I needed him. It was uncanny. If I was having a hard time with something, he somehow knew to call. I'd ask him, "How the heck did you know I needed someone to talk to?"

I also smile when I think of the great moments and laughs we shared together. Larry had a great sense of humor, and a couple of those funny moments had to do with his gift and obsession for studying the smallest details.

In 1983, I was brought onto Larry's softball team. I wasn't an employee yet, but I got to interact with him for the first time in a competitive environment. He was dedicated to doing whatever it took to win, including studying the intricacies of the teams and players.

We were playing a game at the Cottonwood Softball

Complex—a facility that now bears Larry's name—in city-league play. Larry was standing next to me in the dugout, preparing to go up to bat. Just as he was about to leave the dugout, he leaned over to me and said, "The pitcher is going to throw me a drop ball, down and out, and I'm going to hit a line drive off his knee."

I didn't know him very well at the time, so while I chuckled outwardly, I remember thinking to myself, *Is he serious? Who is this guy who thinks he can call both the pitch and the hit?*

Larry went to the plate, glanced over at me, and waited for his chance. On the second pitch, the pitcher threw a drop ball, down and out. Larry connected, hitting a line drive off the pitcher's left foot. Unbelievable.

As Larry rounded first base, he looked back and pointed at me in the dugout, almost giddy. "I told you I was going to do it!" He could hardly contain his giggling. We both knew luck had helped, but he really did know the game so well that he knew that pitch was coming. The pitcher had used that pitch against him before, so he knew to expect it and knew how and where he'd hit it.

It was amazing how often Larry accurately made such predictions throughout the season. But, at the same time, it wasn't all that surprising, because the darn guy was so competitive that he really did spend time thinking about and studying those situations. I learned to take what Larry said seriously, even when he appeared to be joking.

I continued to play for Larry's team until I got a job with a company in Salt Lake that had its own team. I went in to tell Larry I would be changing teams and that I was sorry. He said he understood, but he wasn't done trying.

Ever the competitor, Larry started to ask, "Well what if I . . ."

I stopped him mid-sentence. "I'm not here to negotiate or to get leverage. I've made my decision; I don't want a bidding war." Finally, he accepted.

But things changed soon, largely because my new teammates and I started to do something not many people did: we started to beat Larry Miller. We got done beating his team pretty decisively one day, and it didn't sit well with Larry. He came up to me and said, "Now is not the time to talk about it; we'll wait until the year is over. But next year you'll be working for me and playing for me."

Again, I had learned that you don't take statements like that lightly. If he says something like that, he has thought about it and it is very likely going to happen. Sure enough, the next year I was working for him, having taken a role with Fanzz, Larry's chain of sports apparel and merchandise stores.

It was there that I experienced more of Larry's maniacal focus on details. One afternoon, he called me into his office. We were casually talking about business and life when Larry's phone rang. He had a quick conversation with the caller and hung up, but then wanted to ensure we wouldn't be interrupted further. He asked his secretary, Marilyn Smith, to hold his calls.

After another few minutes talking about softball and other things, Marilyn knocked on the door and poked her head in. "I know you said you didn't want any calls, but it's the mayor." Larry figured he had better take the call, so I waited patiently until he finished.

A few minutes later Marilyn knocked on the door again. She was great. She knew how to handle Larry, who could be volatile at times. She knew when she had to interrupt him, and unfortunately this was another one of those times. "I'm so sorry to do this again. It's the governor." Larry smiled at Marilyn, apologized to me, and spoke to the governor for a few minutes.

We eventually continued our conversation, but it wasn't long before we heard a knock on the door, and then Marilyn entered sheepishly. "I'm really sorry, but Sam Battistone is on the phone." Sam and Larry co-owned the Jazz at the time, so this was an important call, too. Larry put Sam on speakerphone while they talked about some of the Jazz players' contracts. Sam was wondering about incentives and bonuses and where some players' compensation would land. While Sam gave Larry the figures over the phone, Larry closed his eyes and leaned back in his chair.

Sam got done speaking, and a few seconds later, Larry produced the figure, down to the penny. "Yeah, that's the number I came up with," Sam said. They repeated this exercise two or three times, each time with the same result. Larry was calculating in his head and coming up with the same answers that Sam would confirm fifteen or twenty seconds later after calculating it himself.

At one point during the conversation, Sam told Larry, "Hold on Larry, hold on, I'm not as fast as you on the calculator." Larry just looked at me and smiled. Sam didn't know it, but Larry hadn't touched a calculator the entire time. I already knew Larry had a remarkable memory and a great capacity for numbers, but I'd never seen him do that type of complex calculation in his head before. It blew me away. It was as if we were at the Cottonwood Complex all over again, with Larry hitting line drives off the pitcher's foot.

ON CAPITOL HILL

Craig Bickmore

T he 2000 legislative session was monumental for auto dealers. Several pieces of legislation needed to be accomplished that year to make certain that the automobile industry in Utah continued to thrive. One specific statute that our association, the New Car Dealers of Utah, was attempting to put into the Utah law books was that a car dealership would not be able to be open on two consecutive weekend days. In other words, a dealership could choose to be open either Saturday or Sunday, but not both.

At first blush, it seems a little unusual for a state to regulate the hours an independent business could operate. Perhaps even more unusual, why would anyone lobby for such a rule in the first place? But Larry Miller did. Many legislators, the media, and private residents perceived this as a religious issue, one best kept away from the state legislature. Why were the auto dealers trying to pass such a restrictive law?

It was during this particular legislative session that I spent the most time with Larry Miller, as he and my organization, which promotes the general welfare of new car and truck dealers throughout the state, worked hand in hand to push this law forward. When the media got wind of such a law even being proposed, it created a firestorm of opposition and frenzy that none in the automotive industry understood or expected. The opposition didn't come from within our ranks, but from the outside. Although a couple of dealers opposed it at first, they later withdrew their concerns.

The membership of the association all did a wonderful job of contacting their legislators to help them understand our position and to help pass this critical piece of legislation. However, Larry took it on a personal level and spent days on Capitol Hill, sitting in the offices of house and senate leadership, meeting with as many legislators as he could, often multiple times.

This is where I learned a lot about the founding fathers, as Larry would share his insight on how the Constitution was drafted and how such men as John Adams played vital roles in the country we have today. Larry was very passionate about the underdog and wanting to give everyone a fair playing field, including other dealers, their customers, and their employees within the dealership. Our proposed law would do just that.

Larry was the best person imaginable to help educate the public and the legislators as to why it was so important. While most outside the auto industry saw the law as a restriction of freedom, it was actually the opposite. It was a law that would keep the industry competitive, with consideration for the employees who are part of the automotive industry.

In other markets in the West, where the Miller Group had stores that did not have a law similar to the one we were proposing, there exists a seven-day selling cycle, with little relief for a large portion of the employees. In that business model, it creates a great deal of pressure and burnout. Many times great people leave the industry as a result. This has a direct effect on the whole enterprise, including the customer.

As Larry pointed out several times in the meetings we had, the automotive pie is the same whether it has a six-day or a seven-day selling cycle, and once the market established a precedent of seven days, it would never go back.

Ironically, one of the key elements we understood was the fact that *not* passing the law would actually benefit the larger dealers over the smaller ones. Larry was well aware of this, but he still spoke

301

in defense of those smaller dealers, especially in the rural communities throughout Utah.

In the dynamics of a dealership, the bigger the dealership, the more infrastructures there are to spread the cost of the operation. However, in a rural dealership, it is geometrically weaker. There will typically be only one sales manager, one service manager, one parts manager, one advisor, etc. So realistically speaking, the smaller the dealer, the bigger the competitive disadvantage if the seven-day automotive selling cycle became statewide practice. A seven-day cycle would drive traffic to the metro areas, taking important business, revenue, and employment away from those rural districts.

From a sheer business perspective, Larry should have been arguing *against* this proposed law, but instead, he was passionately driven to pass it. He understood the concerns of the smaller dealers and wanted his employees, as well as other dealership personnel, to have a six-day selling cycle because it was a benefit to them and their families. No one lost; it was a gain for all.

As was characteristic of Larry, there were tears shed in many of those meetings that we had on Capitol Hill as he talked about why our industry was so important and how the legislative process made it possible to have a system of great laws that helped drive good business. It was not just a piece of legislation but a bill that needed to go forward for the right reasons.

As I tell this story about how the legislation put into statute this six-day selling cycle, it needs to be mentioned that Larry was part of an outstanding team of dealers throughout the state that spent unbelievable time focusing on the passage of this legislation because they knew how critical it was to have it be successful. It was important for Larry to help others to understand that our industry was not unique in this concept of putting a particular work cycle into practice and code, as it is common for banks, government, schools, etc.

Larry was as passionate as anyone I've met, and he did whatever it took to do the right thing. His legacy extends beyond passing this law; simply doing the right thing will always be his legacy to me.

THE KID AT HEART

Tom Mabey

Many stories have been told and written about Larry H. Miller the successful entrepreneur, patriot, husband, father, grandfather, philanthropist, and the guy who wore his emotions on his sleeve.

Larry was also a kid in an adult's body.

It's well known that Larry had a passion for cars, especially Ford Cobras and GT40s. He owned and drove them. More than that, Larry loved to see them race as they were intended—flat out, fender to fender, with the goal to win.

Despite Larry's constant desire to be in Utah working, he couldn't resist the draw of going to some of the world's most famous racetracks—LeMans, Spa, Goodwood, and Nürburgring—to see his cars in action.

I was fortunate enough to be with Larry; Gail, the love of his life; and his grandson, Zane, when they traveled to Europe. He actually left work behind in the summer of 2004 to visit Nürberg, Germany.

On this trip, Larry Miller the Kid came out. It was inspiring to see.

Larry donned his vintage Shelby race shirt and jumped into doing everything from putting fuel into the racecars to checking tire pressures and washing windows. His intensity was evident. I don't think the smile ever left his face.

The Nürburgring motorsports complex is located in western Germany and was built in 1929 as a dedicated road course track. The course is 12.9 miles long, features 1,000 feet of elevation separating the high point from the low, and includes an astounding 154 turns. Nürburgring also offers something no other track does (when not a race day): the chance for anyone to take their car or motorcycle onto the famous racing surface for a mere $23 per lap.

Who could turn down such an opportunity?

Not Larry.

With Gail by his side, seat belts tight, and his trusty Mercedes rental car in hand, Larry paid his money, and they were off.

I watched as Larry pulled the car onto the track and accelerated down the straightaway. I waited as the car went out of sight, imagining Larry negotiating every turn while pushing the Mercedes and his abilities to their limits.

After a respectable amount of time passed, I saw the black rental car reappear. It came down the straightaway and exited the course in front of me.

I will always carry the image in my mind of Larry as he exited the course—pure joy, pumping his fist in the air, with the smile of a little kid who had just had one of the most exhilarating experiences of his life.

Many of us try to keep the kid inside of us alive as we grow older. Remembering this side of Larry H. Miller, a vivid image I'll never forget, is a reminder to enjoy every day.

COMPETITIVE SPIRIT & COURAGE

Defending the Post

Thurl "Big T" Bailey

When I came into the NBA in 1983, the prevailing senti-
ment around the league was that team owners stayed behind the
scenes. Their job was to handle the business of the team, and they
typically left the locker-room and game-time duties to the coaching
staff.

But Larry H. Miller wasn't a typical owner.

I was in my second season when Larry became a part owner
of the Utah Jazz, literally saving the Jazz from leaving Utah. Larry
came in with a style all his own. He was much more engaged than
we were used to, and that involvement would only grow.

In fact, in my third season, Larry took full ownership of the
team, and that's when, before a game one evening in the Salt
Palace, I saw just how atypical an owner Larry was.

I don't even remember who we played that night. What I do
remember, however, is that I had come to develop the same pregame warm-up routine before every game since my rookie season.
After the usual team layup line, most teammates would then go into
their own personal preparations, each player getting some pregame
repetitions in his areas of specialty. As a post player, I would immediately start my post routine with my back to the basket. I'd take
a position on the low block and have the ball boy throw the ball

inside to me. I'd then practice my footwork and post moves but without a defender on me.

But this time, as I caught the ball during my routine, I suddenly felt a forearm in my back, trying to force me off my position in the post. Initially I didn't really pay it any mind. I figured it was probably one of my teammates trying to help me prepare for the real battle only minutes away. I was reassured in that theory when I took a quick glance behind me and could tell that my defender was in a full Utah Jazz uniform, suited up and ready for the challenge.

I started to make my signature move to the hoop, but then I realized that he had forced me out of my comfort zone, which made my normal turnaround jump-hook miss the rim by about six inches. In other words, I shot an air ball!

That's when I realized who had been defending me. On that particular game night, Utah Jazz management had added another player to the team, at least for pregame warm-ups; it was our owner himself! I was a little dumbfounded at first. I had just air balled a shot with my boss defending me. I thought, *What the heck do I do now? It's Larry H. Miller playing defense on me before the game!*

I looked at his face, and he wasn't smiling or talking. He was all business. He had a look as if to say, *You were a first round pick and you're shooting an air ball in the post on a much shorter, chunky bald guy?* It felt as though I was at a job interview and my future depended on me showing this dude how badly I wanted to keep my job. Truth be told, no opponent had ever challenged or intimidated me before or after that moment as much as he did on that night. As his message quickly became clear to me, without him saying a single word, I took on the challenge and began to make my patented moves, this time ready to battle against this serious competitor. After I had drained several in a row, Larry looked at me with his ever-so-familiar smile that meant "well done!"

That was the first time I remember Larry taking the court in his full Jazz uniform, but it certainly wasn't the last. He made a frequent habit of joining us on the court as we prepared to face our opponent. He would step in as a defender or shag rebounds for us. He even had a stall in our locker room where his #9—from his softball playing days—hung next to the rest of the team's.

Larry wasn't just a boss or an owner to me. He was my friend, mentor, teammate, and sometimes even without trying, my teacher. He was the epitome of hard work, dedication, and above all, loyalty. Almost every game night at home after the first, he was right there behind me in the post, pushing me, challenging me to be the best I could be.

Even when I was traded from the Utah Jazz in 1991, I knew Larry cared about me. He came up to me after the trade was announced. He teared up and wasn't quite sure what to say. I put my hand on his shoulder and said, "Larry, you don't need to say anything."

He was very emotional. I believe that's part of the reason I was able to come back to Utah and finish my career with the Jazz. In 1999, I signed as a free agent and played my final season for Larry and the Jazz. Even after I retired, I stayed close to the team and currently work as a studio analyst breaking down Jazz games on the team's broadcasts.

For a lot of us, especially those who played for him for a long time, Larry was larger than life. He was a very competitive man and a winner. Franchises sometimes move around and change hands, but we always knew the Jazz would be Larry's team.

There are several things I became sure of over time. One was that Larry was a better post defender than most guys I had faced in my sixteen-year professional basketball career. The other was that, without question, he loved being a part of the Utah Jazz family. He was more than an owner; he *was* the Utah Jazz.

A MIDNIGHT
PHONE CALL

Gordon Monson

The phone rang.

"Gordon, this is Larry. I just wanted to apologize."

It was midnight. And Larry Miller had something to say.

A few hours earlier, the Jazz had lost a game they had no business losing. They had held the lead for most of the game, except for the most important part—the end. A lot of mistakes cost them the lead and left them defeated by a narrow margin. I had covered the game, written a column, and, afterward, asked Larry, when I saw him deep in the bowels of EnergySolutions Arena, if I could talk with him for a minute.

My timing wasn't the best.

"No," he growled, harrumphing by as though I had jabbed him with a stick.

By the time I finished up and made it home, there were three messages on my voicemail, all from Larry, asking me to call him, leaving his personal number for me to reach him directly. Before I could punch up the return call, the phone rang again.

It was You-Know-Who.

"I'm sorry," he said. "I was a little upset about the way the game went and, well, I'm competitive, and I didn't like the way we competed tonight. You wanted to talk for a minute?"

I wanted to talk for a minute.

Larry wanted to talk for close to 180 minutes.

It was one of the most compelling, fascinating, far-flung phone conversations I've ever experienced. To begin, I asked a single question—about the prospects and challenges of Salt Lake City having more than one top-level professional sports team located here. Larry answered the question thoroughly, talking about costs and corporate dollars and population growth. He had a hundred answers for questions I didn't even think of asking.

But somewhere in that extended response, Larry opened up his brain and let all kinds of thoughts spill out. He also opened up his heart and allowed his feelings to spill out, too.

He talked about his competitiveness, about the fire that flamed within, and he wondered where it came from. He talked about his desire to win an NBA championship for the people of Utah. He talked about some of the joys and frustrations of that pursuit. He talked about his emotional ties to the community. He talked about the importance of those emotional ties. He talked about his family, about his love for his family, and about his own imperfections. He talked about some of the personal lessons he'd learned along the way, how his priorities had changed, how he had learned what was most important in life—family and faith. He talked about his state of mind. He talked about his strengths as a business leader and a team owner.

I wondered what he considered his best feature in that last regard.

"I have vision," he said. "That's what I do best. I can see things before others see them."

He mentioned his humble upbringing. And I asked him for specifics. He balked a bit at that. I remembered the story about his belongings being left on the porch when he was still young, a less-than-subtle invitation for him to move out and on. But he said he still had remnants of a poor kid in him, all these years after becoming an NBA franchise owner and building a corporate empire.

I asked, "Do you fly in your own private jet now?"

"No," he said. "I fly commercial, sometimes in coach."

He confessed that he at times badgered his wife, Gail, about buying the expensive apples at the market. "Larry," Gail rightfully reminded the near-billionaire, "I think we can afford the expensive apples."

When I later told that story to Gail, she smiled and said something about Larry's passion for expensive racecars and threw in a mention of Larry's constructing a rather costly racetrack out near Tooele.

A man owes himself a few toys, right?

As a thousand more words were exchanged, and the clock drew near three in the morning, I jokingly told Larry that the meter was running and that I'd send him my bill. He laughed, I think.

I didn't know it at the time, but the whole conversation was a precursor for what would come later in the form of a weekly radio show Larry would do with me, a radio show that to this day is probably the best sports radio ever done in Salt Lake City. Maybe that night was the night the seed for that show was planted. Larry gave such strong, varied, unique opinions. He knew everyone wouldn't agree with him on every count, but he also knew the discussion was worth having. I still remember him often rubbing his forehead and uttering the words, "I probably shouldn't say this, but . . ."

That, of course, was the exact moment everyone in a massive listening audience leaned forward to turn up the volume on their radio.

As we hung up the phones that late night/early morning, he on his end, I on mine, one overriding thought occurred to me. It was this: Larry Miller had a gift that so many other people didn't have.

He had something to say.

THE WILL TO WIN

Frank Layden

The rumors were true. I had heard talk that a new part owner was joining the Utah Jazz, some guy named Larry Miller. I didn't know who he was, but I would need to find out fast: I was in my fourth year as head coach of the team, and the talk was that this rumored local buyer would be a lot more present and hands-on than our current owner.

Finally the moment arrived, and I met Larry for the first time. When he introduced himself, the things that stood out immediately were his very aggressive handshake and his excitement to be working together on building a legitimate NBA contender.

Behind that aggressive handshake was an incredibly competitive spirit, and I learned fast that this guy wanted to win. Even in that first conversation, he said to me, "I need your help because I don't know anything about professional basketball."

Knowing Larry as I do now, I can imagine it was hard for him to admit a lack of knowledge on any subject, so he quickly added, "Give me a year, and I'll know everything."

"Mr. Miller," I answered, "[Boston Celtic coach] Red Auerbach practically invented professional basketball and has been in it for fifty or sixty years, and *he* doesn't know everything about basketball. It's a continual learning process."

Larry either ignored me or took this as a challenge, because the guy went to work. He studied everything about the game with amazing attention to detail. He learned the terminology as well as the slang the players used. He studied the other owners and how they ran their franchises. He spent time researching and thinking about ways to improve. Before a year had passed, there was no doubt in my mind that Larry knew as much about the league as any other owner.

But he didn't *act* like any other owner. He wanted to be part of the team and sometimes took it to amusing levels. During our big series with the Lakers in 1988, we were preparing for our off-day flight down to L.A. when Larry arrived in full uniform. He had a warm-up sweat suit on over his uniform, and he showed up saying, "All right, let's go. I'm ready."

We landed in L.A. and the rookies began to grab the bags. When the team traveled for more than one game, there would be around sixty pieces of luggage and equipment, and traditionally the rookies were responsible for grabbing them. Larry jumped right in the middle with the rookies and started pulling the baggage out. "Yeah, get in here," he said to a laughing group of players.

I ran over to him. "Larry, Larry, come over here," I said. "You don't have to do that. You own the team!"

"Yeah, but I'm a rookie," he said, "I got to get in there." So he kept right on going. People were watching, and I thought, *There's nobody here that would believe that guy is the owner of this team.*

Larry just wasn't your typical owner. He used to listen from behind the Jazz bench and liked learning about the plays. He would always say, "Boy, I would like to be able to call the plays just once."

In 1993, he had the chance.

That year, Salt Lake City was hosting the NBA All-Star game, and one of the preliminary events was an Old-Timers' game between former Jazz players and former Utah Stars players. I was coaching the Jazz team, and before the game I invited Larry to come sit on the bench with me. "You can be a co-coach with me," I explained.

He loved the idea. But not everybody did. An NBA executive who was there to oversee the event looked at my bench and called me over.

314

"Hey," he said, "what's going on with Larry Miller?"

"He's my assistant coach."

"No, no, no," the executive replied. "That's not allowed. You tell him he's not allowed on the bench. He's not allowed to help you coach a team."

We went back and forth for a minute before I finally said, "I'll tell you what: *you* tell him. Then, take a look around at where you are. He owns the team, the building, the town, the state. He can't sit on the bench? It's *his* bench! You tell him." When I went back to the bench, Larry asked me what the exchange was all about. I said, "I just saved your job, boss!" and we moved forward with the game.

Larry got a kick out of calling the plays, talking to the players, and motivating our team in the timeout huddle. He really got into it. We had a good time, laughing and having fun. When the game was over, we were presented with rings that had our names on them. I gave my ring to Larry. "This is yours," I said, "a memento of your NBA coaching debut."

While he liked to have fun, Larry was fiercely competitive. He had to learn that we weren't going to go 82–0. The physical demands, the travel, the schedule, and the level of competition all make it impossible to win all of the time. But Larry's will to win helped us become better faster. We would talk about different things we could do—player personnel, a new piece of equipment, adding to the scouting department. I would say, "It's going to cost us a lot of money."

His question was always the same: "Will it help us win?" If the answer was yes, he'd tell me to go ahead, and we'd never look back.

Of course, Larry's competitiveness sometimes showed up in other ways, too. In the spring of 1994, I sat at a speaking engagement back east while the Jazz were in a conference semifinal series against the Denver Nuggets. I was eating breakfast that Wednesday morning when someone said to me, "Hey, did you see the paper? Your boss went nuts last night and went after some fans in the stands."

I read the paper and saw a picture of Larry going up into the stands after some guy. Apparently a group of Nuggets fans had moved to some baseline seats during halftime while the Denver players were warming up. Larry took issue with some of the things they were yelling, and it resulted in a confrontation.

When I got back to Salt Lake City, I went in to see Larry. "My goodness," I said, "you got a little excited the other night."

Larry's response surprised me. "That was disgraceful," he said. "I embarrassed the team, and I embarrassed the league. I shouldn't have done that."

He held a press conference the next day in which he apologized to the fans, the NBA, and his family. "I screwed up," he said. Always learning, he turned the experience into a chance to become better.

On February 19, 2009, my wife, Barbara, and I went to the arena to see the Jazz host the Celtics. I saw team president Randy Rigby and told him I'd like to visit Larry, who by that time had been seriously ill for a while. I knew they were being cautious with visitors, but my son, Scott, had been in to see him, and I wanted to visit with him. I asked Randy if he could set something up in the morning, and Randy's response was serious.

"He won't be here in the morning," Randy said to me, looking me straight in the eye. "He's going to die tonight."

This shook me. Larry was such a strong individual, someone who attacked adversity and always overcame. I imagined him doing what he always did: working like nobody else. Working to learn how to handle the prosthesis from his double-leg amputation; working to beat the other effects of the illness; battling his way back into that courtside seat. But I couldn't imagine him being gone. I told Randy to keep me updated, and Barbara and I went out to the car.

The next phone call I got—the very next day—was the news that Larry had died.

When I look back on what Larry did, I see that he infused life and energy into an organization that was fragile and failing. I don't know how long we could have lasted there without Larry, but I'm glad we didn't have to find out. He had a lot do with John Stockton

316

and Karl Malone being in Utah for so long, and he made the Jazz one of the most respected teams in the league.

The hearty handshake and the excitement from that first meeting didn't lie; he had the will to create a winner, and that's just what he did.

CALL NUMBER THREE

Mayor Matthew Godfrey

It took three phone calls to meet with Larry Miller. The first two times, my administrative assistants tried to get through to him. I was the mayor of Ogden at the time, and I ran into my counterpart from Sandy, where Larry's offices were located.

"What do I need to do to get an appointment with Larry Miller?" I asked.

Mayor Tom Dolan looked at me with a puzzled face and said, "Just call him."

I decided to skip the admins and call him myself for the third try. This time I got an appointment right away.

I had asked for just twenty minutes of his time and was prepared to race through my story about why Ogden had lost its identity and become a rundown town. More important, I wanted him to understand that we had a plan that we were confident would turn the tide and help this once booming railroad town to thrive once more. His movie theaters would be the linchpin.

The failed Ogden City Mall stood as a twenty-acre monument to all that had gone wrong with Ogden. Positioned in the middle of downtown with 30,000 cars a day passing by, the situation with the mall had to be remedied for the town to be successful. We were fortunate to have the Tree House Children's Museum catch the vision early on and decide to invest in a new facility in the former mall site. We also had a "high adventure recreation center" in the works that would later be named the Salomon Center, complete with indoor surfing, skydiving, rock climbing, Fat Cat's Family Fun Center, and Gold's Gym, among many other attractions.

The partners had a basic structure put together for this project, assuming we could get the city council to approve it. A developer had committed to build out the remaining ten acres of property if we could get the Tree House, the Salomon Center attractions, and a Megaplex Theatre all to begin construction. But for that, we needed Larry to commit to building a Megaplex.

Our team was sure that if we could convince Larry, we could convince the city council to give final approval on the Salomon Center, and the entire project would move forward. We were also confident that these projects would catalyze others we were working on and create the momentum we needed to redevelop about three hundred acres of our downtown district. Everything rested on the theaters, and by extension, on this twenty-minute meeting between Larry and me.

When Larry came into the room, he was affable, deferential, and seemed to have all the time in the world for me. I was amazed by how intelligent he was. He could recall numbers and details of projects at will. I wanted to dive right into my presentation, to be respectful of his time. After all, I had told him I'd take twenty minutes. But Larry had other ideas. He wanted to talk.

We talked for about an hour about life, business, family and more. I took advantage of the opportunity and asked him what his best business advice was for me. He said, "Ninety percent of success is just showing up." He said that working hard and being diligent are far from a magic formula but they are exactly the things that most people don't do. To be honest, I was expecting something a bit more sagacious from a self-made billionaire. But over time—probably years—I came to fully appreciate the power of his advice.

Finally, I got to the business at hand. I asked him if I could talk to him about Ogden. I laid out our vision for the community—to make the town a high-adventure recreation Mecca. I explained that we had worked to put a $100 million project together but needed his Megaplex to make it happen.

He responded by saying, "We really aren't in the movie theater business." I let him know that I was aware that the two theaters he had built at that time were usually the top two best-performing theaters in the state of Utah. He brushed that off by saying, "Yes, but it really isn't what we do best," which, amazingly, is probably true.

I kept pressing, telling him that we also needed his "Midas touch." While we desperately needed his theaters, we also needed people to know that Larry Miller was betting on Ogden.

"If I were to invest in these theaters," he asked, "would I make any money?"

My heart sank as I realized this was a question I was unprepared to answer. "I don't know," I answered honestly. "I'm asking you to do this to help the people of Ogden. We need to have faith restored in our community. We need a sense of pride in our town, and I believe your theater is essential in pulling all of this together. Even if you don't make money, you will have helped turn a community around."

Larry promised me that he'd look into it. He committed to performing a market study and thanked me for coming in.

Several weeks later, he informed me that the market study said there was only a market for six screens and that they won't do less than ten. He also said that if they put in theaters it would likely close down another theater in town and that he wasn't in business to put others *out* of business.

Larry said he wasn't inclined to do the project but that he would talk again with his team and get back to us. I was on pins and needles. When the call came, he told me that they wouldn't be building the six-screen complex.

It would be thirteen screens.

To this day, I still can't describe the sense of joy and gratitude that overcame our team. The other pieces of the development came together just as we'd hoped they would, and we had a major revitalization project underway.

Larry and his wife, Gail, attended the ribbon cutting along with others from the Miller team. He was magnanimous and gave a speech professing his confidence in the city of Ogden and the direction we were heading. He remembered and fulfilled my deepest desire: to restore hope and confidence in the community. In the process, he impacted me profoundly on a very personal level. I will always consider him a dear friend, both to me and to the people of Ogden.

I'm also happy to say that the Ogden Megaplex has performed very well for the Millers. Larry's willingness to bet on the underdog paid off one more time. But just as important, this time it paid dividends beyond the balance sheet, creating real change for the 82,000 people of Ogden and the generations ahead.

I'll forever be grateful I made that third call to Larry.

COBRAS FOREVER

Dave Murray

The Cobra is not just a car; it's an *idea*, a symbol of power, speed, and agility. It took driving to the max—just like Larry Miller took life to the max.

Because only about a thousand Cobras were built from 1962 to 1967, there is a real brotherhood that exists among those few who have owned one of these rare pieces of American racing history. Such a brotherhood existed between Larry, my brother Bill, and me. We spent many years enjoying this special Cobra relationship. I've been a Cobra owner for thirty-three years, and my first one cost me everything I had. When Larry bought his first Cobra, he didn't have much either, still years from being the icon he later became. We were just regular guys, united by our passion for something very hard to obtain, keep, and maintain.

I first met Larry in 1977 through Bill, who had done some repairs for him at Murray Racing. We deepened our friendship in the 1990s when Larry became involved with the Shelby American Collection, a Cobra museum and community of enthusiasts in Boulder, Colorado, where I was curator. But the culmination of our Cobra camaraderie came in 2006, when Larry asked me to assist with the layout and design of some displays of his collection at Miller Motorsports Park.

We started by brainstorming name ideas for the museum. "Total

Performance" had been Ford's tagline in the 1960s, so I suggested that we connect his name with that phrase. Larry humbly and insistently shook his head, saying, "You don't have to put my name on it." His objection made me even more dedicated to honoring him in the naming of his one-of-a-kind collection. Sure enough, guests at the Miller Motorsports Park now have the chance to enjoy the "Larry H. Miller Total Performance" collection.

That same humility resurfaced throughout the project. While he was drawing up plans for the Utah museum, Larry brought his extensive showroom experience to bear, insisting that we could put forty-nine cars in the museum. I explained that a museum setting required more space, and that we would be able to showcase only thirty to thirty-five cars. A year later, with thirty-five cars in the newly opened space, Larry said, "Dave, you sure were right that forty-nine cars wouldn't fit in here." That's the kind of guy Larry was: even with his standing, he remembered that initial conversation and had no ego about acknowledging his miscalculation. His down-to-earth nature and high character were two of the reasons I enjoyed collaborating with him on the project.

In October of 2008, Larry wanted to discuss project ideas and general museum operations. He had recently recovered from two heart attacks, so his wife, Gail, chauffeured him to the museum. As I wheeled Larry past antique gas pumps, old automotive signs, and other nostalgic pieces, he mentioned how well the museum displays set off the cars.

Larry was on a tight schedule that day and had just thirty minutes to hear my proposals for three new museum displays. He was understandably busy, with thousands of employees in his car dealerships, the Utah Jazz, and other business interests. But Larry was never too busy to give people his full attention, even if just for a short while. Larry was very sick at the time of our quick meeting, but he listened to my proposals thoughtfully, asked questions, and thoroughly enjoyed the time spent in the presence of his favorite cars.

One of his passions was creating immersive experiences for the people who visited his businesses. He had already created a themed restaurant and movie theater, as well as retro gas stations where the attendants wore period-appropriate clothing. We sat down to discuss the diorama displays that would create a context for the museum pieces, and I kept that passion in mind with proposals that I hoped would bring the exhibits to life with vintage and experiential touches.

My first proposal was for a Daytona-style diorama of a Ford GT40 mockup. I planned to create a tilted platform that replicated the famous banking at Daytona, which at 31 degrees is almost too steep to walk on. A special rubber coating would make the platform look like the actual track. I would use old body panels to recreate the GT40 shell. While Larry listened, I could see him imagining the finished display. He was enthusiastic about the diorama and wholeheartedly agreed to its construction.

Second, I proposed a display that would celebrate Larry's background in automotive parts and his interest in what makes cars go. He had especially enjoyed the parts display we had created at the Shelby American Collection. My proposal was for a more complete parts area to show museum visitors the body and engine parts that made Cobras and Ford GT40s such spectacular racecars. Larry made some suggestions about what he'd like to see included in the parts display, and we moved on to my final—and favorite—proposal of the day.

Larry had a deep love of drag racing and in fact had been an amateur racer himself in his youth. Since he had two great dragsters—a Cobra Dragonsnake and a 1964 Ford 427 Thunderbolt—in his collection, I proposed that we videotape the two cars racing each other on a drag strip. Larry would be one of the drivers, and we'd capture video from within the car as well as from the exterior. I envisioned the museum display with the two actual cars staged in starting position behind a "Christmas Tree," the nickname for the signal lights that start races, with video of Larry's race on a big-screen TV. The look on his face as we discussed this was priceless. After all of his major health problems, Larry's excitement was obvious. He was thrilled about the prospect of being behind the wheel again and helping visitors interact with the museum via the video.

Larry gave all three proposed displays his full support. He was exuberant, and he said, "This is just the start of the museum, not the finish. We're going to have fun doing this!" The first two were accomplished and are still on display in the museum, but the third was still in the planning stages when Larry passed. It was a dream never realized.

Larry had so many admirable characteristics, but the one that stays with me and is a source of inspiration was his can-do attitude. In spite of his many challenges, he still had an abiding interest in the future of the dynamic Larry H. Miller Total Performance Museum. The last thing Larry said to me was to not get discouraged, because we had more cars and interesting things on the horizon. He hadn't given up. Larry Miller could imagine the future, and it looked good.

THE DEAL OF A LIFETIME

Curtis Kindred

I'll never forget setting up the financing package for Larry to buy his first car dealership.

Hugh Gardiner invited me to lunch in late April 1979 and explained that he was selling his dealership to Larry Miller from Colorado and that he would be coming in over that weekend to do inventory. I told him I wanted to be the first banker to meet him, but Hugh indicated Larry had been working with First Security for some time getting everything approved. But he agreed to call me when Larry got there.

On Sunday morning, Hugh called at about 10:00 a.m. and told me Larry was there, so I went down to meet him.

In my first meeting with Larry, I gathered all of the information for the Bank Loan Committee Application to put the financing package together. His uncle, Reid Horne, was going to cosign the deal and put up his two apartment houses as collateral to secure the loan. Larry had all the information together. I was very impressed with him and the fact he had everything I needed.

Larry told me he already had the deal put together with First Security Bank and that they were coming in at 10:00 a.m. the following day to close it. I told him I could do a better job for him. I then made a proposal to Larry. I asked if he would go with Zions

Bank if I could get everything approved and ready before ten o'clock the next morning.

Larry said if I could do that, he would go with us.

The next twenty-four hours were a whirlwind. I prepared the loan request that afternoon and night. I called all the members of the Zions Bank Senior Loan Committee at home and told them we had to meet at seven the next morning to get a big deal approved.

Since it was fully secured several times over, I got the approval quickly. I did go out on a limb and told them I felt Larry could become the biggest customer in the bank someday. The loan committee accused me of becoming like my car dealers in making crazy claims. My secretary prepared all the loan documents while I was with the loan committee and then met me out in front of our building with all the documents I needed signed.

I arrived at Larry's dealership at 9:00 a.m., with an hour to spare. Pleased with the arrangement, Larry and Reid Horne signed everything.

At 10:00, when Charles Crowshaw from First Security arrived, the deal was all done. Charlie wanted to know what I was doing there, and I explained that I had just signed up a new dealer. He wanted to know when I had gotten involved.

"Yesterday," I said.

Charlie left with some parting words: "I am going to report you to your bishop for working on Sunday."

This was the most exciting business deal I had ever done. Five years later, I came to work with Larry and started Larry H. Miller Leasing in Salt Lake City.

One day, Larry invited Tom Fitchett and me to an NCAA basketball tournament game at the Huntsman Center at the University of Utah. A football team from another school was sitting behind us using all types of profanity. I could see Larry getting angry. He finally stood up and told them they were offending a lot of people around us. Tom and I thought we were going to get in a fight.

When Larry finished chewing out the players, he got a standing ovation by a large number of the people sitting in our section. The football team behaved as gentlemen the rest of the game. I'm sure they did not know who Larry was, but they knew he spoke with authority after witnessing the support he had from the other fans.

Another time I witnessed such authority from him was when Larry invited me and several other managers to a Mountain West basketball playoff game between BYU and Utah at the Delta Center.

We went early because Larry was holding a press conference before the game announcing that he was selling the Salt Lake Golden Eagles hockey team.

After the press conference, we went into the game. At halftime, a number of fans started yelling at Larry, asking him why he had sold the Golden Eagles. They got louder and louder until Larry finally stood up and addressed them.

"By a show of hands, how many of you have bought tickets to a hockey game this year?" Larry asked them.

Only a couple of hands went up.

He continued.

"I rest my case," he said. "I cannot afford to continue subsidizing the hockey team several million dollars a year, and the fans do not even support it."

That ended the questions.

Larry was a master at handling these kinds of situations, and I'll always be grateful I got that first deal with him.

PROPHETIC WORDS

Doug Robinson

Capturing the story of Larry Miller is no small task.

In 2008, Larry asked me to help write his autobiography, a project we had been discussing for some seven years. Over the next several months, I spent hours next to Larry, listening and scribbling while he recounted tales and lessons from his singular life. Many of those stories have been told through the years or appear in *Driven*.

Here's one that didn't.

One morning in the spring of 1986, Larry was driving around town in his favorite Ford Falcon convertible, pondering whether to buy the second half of the Utah Jazz. He had purchased a fifty percent ownership stake a year earlier, but now he had to decide whether or not to buy out his partner to keep the team in Utah. The decision weighed heavily on his mind. He found himself in front of the LDS Church Office Building and decided to park the Falcon and place a call to Gordon B. Hinckley, a member of the Church's First Presidency (and who later would become its President and Prophet). Larry wanted his counsel.

He told President Hinckley's secretary that he was hoping to meet with him as soon as possible. "He's got a noon meeting, and you couldn't get here fast enough to talk to him before it begins," she said.

A minute later he was upstairs in President Hinckley's office.

He knew why Larry was there and began to address his concerns by asking several questions. Larry got the impression that he was up to speed on the issues. As Larry had seen in other situations, President Hinckley grasped the situation extremely well and got to the core of the issue. He listened closely to Larry's answers and then began talking and offering advice.

"Look, if you do this, it is critical that you ask yourself these questions: Can you and your family stand life in a fishbowl? Can you make it economically viable? If you can't do either or both, you should not do this."

"I want you to hear what I'm saying," he continued, and then he repeated the short list of questions two more times, asking Larry to repeat them to him. When he was satisfied that his message had come across, he said, "Now that you've got that, you need to understand that it is very, very important to the Church that the Jazz stay in Utah."

This took Larry by surprise, and he expressed as much. "Why is it important to the Church that the Jazz stay in Utah?" Larry asked.

"NBA scores are published all over the world, and when people see Utah Jazz they think Utah Mormons," President Hinckley began. "Maybe those are tiny impressions, but over the course of a basketball season and the places scores are published around the world, it results in billions of tiny impressions."

"Okay," Larry said. "I understand. What else?"

"Look, the reality is, if you do this, you'll be able to come back to me in a year or two or five or twenty and tell me all the reasons why it's important."

Eventually Larry would learn the wisdom of that statement. Hundreds of times over the years, Larry found himself thinking, *Oh, that's what President Hinckley was talking about.*

Larry attended all of the Jazz's home games and was quite visible because he sat in the same seat down on the floor. But he didn't attend the games on Sundays for religious reasons, and his absence at those games was just as noticeable. This opened many doors to questions about Larry's faith from reporters, fans, players, and other observers.

During the Jazz's great playoff run of 1997, when they went all the way to the NBA Finals, ultimately losing to Michael Jordan and the Chicago Bulls in six games, Larry found himself answering questions in a press conference in Chicago. The question was asked as to why he did not attend games on Sunday. On worldwide TV, he explained his church's beliefs about keeping the Sabbath day holy.

Later that year he was invited to BYU for a celebration of the Church's 150th anniversary. It was held in the football stadium, and Larry was invited to sit with the leaders of the Church. At some point, President James E. Faust, of the Quorum of the Twelve Apostles, said to him, "I saw your press conference in Chicago when they asked you about not attending games on Sunday. I was in London when I saw it. You did great. Do you know how many people were watching you? It was 225 million."

At this point, President Hinckley walked up and said, "See?"

This was twelve years after the meeting in his office, and President Hinckley remembered what the two had discussed—that in years to come Larry would come to understand all the reasons why the Jazz would be important in growing awareness about the Church.

That wasn't the only time President Hinckley impressed Larry with his sharpness and an awareness of situations. In the early days of the Jazz, Wendell Ashton, who was publisher of the *Deseret News*, arranged for Jazz ownership to meet with President Hinckley in his office. Frank Layden, Dave Checketts, Sam Battistone, and Larry met with President Hinckley—just a social call with a photo op. This was right after the Jazz had lost a playoff game to the Houston Rockets.

President Hinckley turned to Frank and said, "Well, Coach, you go down to Houston and you win the first game, and you can say 'mission accomplished.' But then in the second game you got blown out. Now you return to Salt Lake for game three. So here's my question: what do you say to your team to get them rejuvenated and believing in themselves again?"

Without missing a beat, Frank said, "I got that all figured out, Prez. I'm going to mass twice on Sunday and cutting through Temple Square on the way."

President Hinckley laughed.

He was right about the impact of the Jazz in so many ways, and the impact has gone well beyond religious considerations. Everything President Hinckley saw, years and years before the Jazz became the rallying point for Utah, came to pass.

GENEROSITY

THE BLUE MITSUBISHI

Chuck Horman

Our family policy was to not give our children cars when they started to drive. We made them earn the money to buy vehicles for themselves. They drove what was affordable, quickly learning that a bad ride beats a good walk.

Our youngest son, Dan, started working construction jobs when he was fifteen. When he had earned enough to buy his first car, Dan saw that the Miller dealerships were holding a used car sales extravaganza at Brasher's Auto Auction, with hundreds of vehicles priced to move. Dan wanted to check out the inventory. It was a Friday afternoon in February 1995, and we were flying out to Los Angeles that night to see the Winter National Drag Races. Brasher's was about two miles from the airport, so Dan and I decided to leave early and browse the cars before our flight.

It was dark and bitter cold by the time we arrived. We drove up and down the many rows of vehicles. Suddenly, Dan spotted a bright blue Mitsubishi sporting the color and sticker price he was seeking. I liked the fact that the vehicle had a small engine. We got the keys and drove it around the lot.

Dan was sold, and we headed for the sales tent to complete the paperwork. There were so many other buyers inside that we could barely fit. If we waited in line to complete the transaction, we would miss our flight. We left without the car, much to Dan's disappointment. He was sure it would be sold before we returned from our trip and that he would never find a replacement as enticing as the blue Mitsubishi.

I decided to do something about it. After we took off, I pulled out the "sky phone" from the seatback in front of me and swiped my credit card to activate it. I placed a call to my brother-in-law, Gordon Johnson (who had been Larry Miller's bishop), to obtain Larry's home number. I then called Larry and told him about Dan's predicament, including a description of the Mitsubishi. Larry said that the cars were priced to move, and affordable ones like Dan's wouldn't last long. On hearing that, Dan became even more dejected.

When we returned home Sunday night, the blue Mitsubishi was in our driveway, unlocked, keys in the ignition. No paperwork. Larry trusted us. I called Gordon to thank him for his assistance and told him about what had happened. He said Larry had disclosed to him at church on Sunday that he had spent nearly the entire previous day locating the car, driving it to our house, and then walking home in a snowstorm.

I returned to Brasher's the following day with the price, VIN number, and a check. A salesman wrote up the deal and gave me a temporary permit, but when he heard my story, he found it hard to believe.

Dan couldn't believe it either. He still can't fathom—nearly twenty year later—that Larry would consume so much time and effort to do a favor for a neighbor's child. Larry will always be Dan's hero.

To anyone who knew Larry Miller, it's not hard to fathom at all.

SUPPORTING THE ARTS

Michael Ballam

There's a Larry Miller on the phone."

There are a lot of Larry Millers in the world, so when I got this message from the music department secretary at Utah State University, I didn't want to presume.

"Is this *the* Larry Miller?" I asked when I picked up the phone.

"This is Larry H. Miller," came the response.

"That's *the* Larry Miller," I said.

Larry explained that he had attended a presentation I had given at Brigham Young University's Education Week and had felt prompted to reach out to help me.

"I was impressed with the way you said music can affect people's lives," he said. "I don't even know what it is you do. If I come to Logan, can you explain what it is you're doing?" I told him I'd be delighted, and we set aside a time.

When the day arrived, I took Larry to the Ellen Eccles Theatre, a beautiful and storied venue and the home to Utah Festival Opera. We sat in a balcony box while I described to him how I felt the theater could enhance the lives of people in Northern Utah and beyond. I had the vision of an international festival that would bring people from around the world to beautiful Logan for ennobling experiences. I knew Cache Valley had all the ingredients to create something magical and wonderful.

Larry got it. Larry always got it. He didn't need long explanations. He could catch the vision of something very quickly. He could see from my dreaming perspective that this company, this theater, and this community could truly bless the lives of generations to come.

That summer of 1994, Larry came to Logan to see *Madame Butterfly*. I chose the best seats in the house for Larry and his wife, Gail. I watched carefully from behind the curtain during the first act, and when intermission came, he didn't move a muscle. I was very nervous, thinking maybe he had fallen asleep. I hurried down to visit with him and found him not just awake, but stunned.

He had been so enthralled by what he had seen that there were tears on the Utah Festival Opera polo shirt I had given him. From his vantage point he could see down into the orchestra pit, onto the stage, and on a few occasions he could actually see into the wings. He saw what it took to create *Madame Butterfly*. "I couldn't keep my eyes off of what was happening down there."

He started asking about the musicians, and I explained that they were brought in from San Francisco, from Houston, and from Philadelphia. He asked about the scenery, and I explained that we hired a set designer from Virginia. There were over three hundred people involved in bringing this production to life, from handpainting the silk costumes, to the set design, to the chorus, to the orchestra. All had been sought out to make the performance extraordinary, and Larry marveled at the community behind it.

"You've brought together three hundred of the best at what they do, and everywhere you look, there is excellence." He teared up and then repeated, "Excellence. Kids need to see excellence, and they need to want to be part of excellence. Not everybody can be athletes and movie stars. But some place in this enterprise is a place where everybody can succeed and achieve."

Then he added, "I need to help you. How?"

We corresponded over the next several months, and I began to lay out to Larry what our needs were and what I could see might become our challenges in the future. First and foremost, we needed to find a permanent solution for housing the artists. At the time, we housed them in two old fraternity and sorority houses. We couldn't find enough apartments one by one, and we couldn't afford to pay a competitive rent.

Second, we needed a facility wherein sceneries could be built and stored, costumes could be perfected, and rehearsals could be held. We had been able to procure an old turn-of-the-century dance hall known as the Dansante building, but it had fallen into tremendous disrepair and was structurally unsound. It was an ideal space and could be our permanent home, but it needed a lot of work. I began to articulate these needs to Larry.

The following February, Larry asked me if I would sing at a gathering of friends he was hosting in Logan. Nearly one hundred people were gathered at the historic Bluebird restaurant, including Larry, Gail, their children, and a number of employees and friends. After dinner, we went to Ellen Eccles Theatre, where I sang a few songs and then told them what I felt the destiny of the theater and the Festival could be.

At that point, Larry stood up and said, "This evening isn't over yet, Michael. We've got a little surprise for you."

He told me that he was handing over the keys and the fully paid deed to a sixty-four-unit apartment complex. "You explained to me that housing was a challenge for you during the summertime for the artists. So, at midnight tonight, the Utah Festival Opera is going to own the University Pines Apartments." My knees almost went out from under me, but, fortunately, I was hanging on to the piano.

Then Larry began to give a speech to his friends. He thanked them for enabling his businesses to thrive so that he and Gail could have the resources to make a gift like this. He told them they were making a noble thing happen. He then thanked me for allowing him to be a part in the fulfillment of these dreams.

He thanked *me!* That's who Larry was. I was completely stunned and speechless. I didn't know what to do.

Larry and Gail had just laid the foundation that would enable the dream we shared to help lift the community to a higher place.

They had caught the vision. We had a place for our artists, and soon we'd have a new home as well.

Larry invited me to sit down with him and envision what we could do with the Dansante. We envisioned together a space with a dozen practice rooms, an area to serve dinner, the spaces to rehearse three or more operas simultaneously, a board room, executive offices, costume shop, props shop, scenery shop, storage space, and a library for musical materials. I also understood that it was important to him that we keep the core of the building intact. The Dansante is filled with history and memories, so we worked together on a design that would preserve the historic integrity. The front facade of the building and the interior beams were to be kept as they were, but we would design around that to build an ideal space for the Festival.

"Now what I'd like you to do," Larry said, "is ask every department head what their perfect space would be: costumes, props, scenery, library, development office, accounting office. I want every office to submit a design. What kind of light does it need? What kind of plumbing and equipment are needed? How much floor space?"

The resulting design would require a lot of space and a lot of money. Larry gave us both to make it happen, and the Dansante renovation moved forward with great care and skill.

He helped us not because he was an opera lover, but because he could see we would enhance lives. That's the legacy of Larry and Gail Miller, a sense of giving as an investment to bless the lives of others today and in the future.

Larry had a keen mind, the ability to work around the clock, and an extraordinary sense of adventure, but he practiced prudence at the same time. I got to see that the secret to his success was the support and empowerment from Gail. She was the stability to let Larry dream, imagine, invest, yet still have a solid foundation. Larry was like one of those great stained-glass windows of Notre Dame. Those windows can't stand on their own. They need some beautiful architectural features called flying buttresses to support them, large structures strong enough to brace the walls and hold the glass. Without them, the weight of the glass alone would bring the wall down. With the buttresses, the windows stand and can receive the light to glow from within. Gail was like those beautiful flying buttresses that hold up the stained-glass windows at Notre Dame. Larry was out in front, the light that people saw in his commercials and in front of all his enterprises. Gail gave him the support needed so he could glow.

Larry's not gone. We haven't lost him. I know exactly where he is, and this friendship of ours will continue forever. Now my job is to live a life of the kind of excellence of heart that will enable me to walk back into his presence and the presence of our Father. That's going to be a big job.

SETBACKS

Henry Garza

I began my career in the automotive industry back in 1979, when I was only eighteen. Back then, the name Larry H. Miller wasn't a recognized name in the auto industry, let alone in the state of Utah. I first worked as a salesman at another dealership in Murray, but I soon moved down the street to work at Larry's first dealership. The store was still half owned by Larry's uncle. Larry used to work the desk a lot more back then, but he quickly took over as sole proprietor.

In those days, times were hard, and it was in the late '80s that I suffered some significant career setbacks, which started when Larry's stepbrother terminated my position. Although this was an obstacle, I decided to use it as an opportunity to start fresh and open my own dealership. Roughly a year later, I faced another major setback in my auto career, as I confronted a disband with my new partnership.

As a result, I found myself unemployed for several months, when suddenly one of Larry Miller's executives called me to be the manager at their Chrysler store.

At this point almost everyone in Utah knew who Larry H. Miller was, and to be invited back to work for him was quite a welcome opportunity. Although I was happy to have employment again, two years of rough financial times on a family of six had made it difficult to catch up. As a result, our home was being foreclosed upon and we were forced to move into an apartment.

My son, Nate, who was only eight years old at the time, kept insisting that we wouldn't be moving out of our house. He truly believed in his heart that everything would be fine and promised me that things would be okay. As I backed out of the driveway to take Nate to school, he noticed the moving truck that was parked outside our home. When we pulled up to the curb outside of his school, Nate said to me, "I promise when you pick me up, Dad, we won't be moving out."

My heart sank. Housing and Urban Development had already foreclosed on the house. Nothing could be done. We had already made a deposit on the apartment that we were moving into that evening. My son would soon experience a crushing disappointment and one of his very own setbacks.

I somberly drove home to prepare for the move when the phone rang. It was Larry. "How quick can you come see me?" he asked.

He wanted me to come into his office at the Chevy store in Murray—the same store where we first met two decades earlier. At first I thought I must have done something wrong. With an even heavier heart, I went to meet with him immediately. When I arrived at his office, he asked me to sit down. I thought I was in for it.

"What's happening with your house?" he asked.

My eyebrows rose. It was astonishing to me that he even knew about the situation with my house. I told him that HUD had foreclosed on the property and that my family was moving into a small apartment that evening.

Immediately, Larry picked up the telephone and called the head HUD office in Denver, Colorado, asking to speak with the director himself, whom Larry knew personally. "Can you look up Henry Garza's file?" he politely asked.

After a moment, the director explained the situation and said it was too late for a remedy. "Give me a number for your buyout price," Larry said sternly.

The director insisted nothing could be done.

343

"Give me a number," he said again.

Once more, he was told that it was simply too late.

"Give me a number," he said, but this time he hung up the receiver. Larry knew what he was doing.

Within minutes, the director called back with an estimate: eighty-six thousand.

"Great. You will have a check in the morning," he said. "Henry will stay in the house."

I couldn't believe what I had just witnessed. Overwhelmed with gratitude, I instantly started to sob. Nate was right: we would stay in our home. But Larry's service didn't end there.

He then asked me about my deposit on the apartment. I gave him the name of the complex. He picked up the phone again, this time telling the manager of the apartments to tear up my deposit check. Larry explained the situation and mentioned that he knew the owner of that particular complex. After initial resistance, the manager agreed to return the deposit. I couldn't believe it. After a big hug and more tears, Larry told me that he would finance my loan for an entire year, and then sign it over to Zions Bank.

That same afternoon, I drove back to my son's school to pick him up. He hopped in the car with the same belief and optimism he'd had when I dropped him off that morning. He looked at me and asked, "We don't have to move, do we, Dad?"

I hugged him tight and told him that he was right. We were going to stay in our home.

That was a pivotal time in my life and the first time in a long time that there weren't any setbacks. I really loved Larry, as did my entire family. Not just because of what he had done for us, but for being my friend and the best boss I could ever ask for. I miss him more than I ever could have imagined, and I'm grateful for our time together throughout the years.

$1.5 MILLION ON A HANDSHAKE

Artoosh Hasratian

I first met Larry Miller in the late '80s, when he came to have dinner in my restaurant, El Matador. He ordered the Veracruz, and I went into the back and cooked it myself. Larry said, "I've never seen shrimp that big before. How do you do it?" Our friendship started right there, and he became a regular, always sitting in the round corner booth.

In 2005, Costco wanted to build a store on the site of my restaurant as part of a redevelopment project. My lease was expiring, and because of the Costco project, I did not have the opportunity to buy the building. I was basically going to be out on the street. I was not smart about figures and contracts, and when I told Larry about the situation, he asked to read the lease.

He said, "I want you to see something. You should have known this, but I will tell you so you don't have to get a lawyer." He showed me a clause that gave me options. He pointed out what Costco and the city needed to do in order to take over the property. Because of Larry, I was able to get $255,000 from the city. It was a quarter-million-dollar gift. I was able to buy a new property with that money.

But I still needed to build a building. One day in early November 2005, when I was still in the old restaurant, Larry was sitting in his usual spot. A guy from Wells Fargo Bank was sitting

345

at another table. He was setting up a loan for me to build the new restaurant, and he was preparing stacks and stacks of paperwork for my signature. When I turned to walk over to him, Larry stopped me.

"Artoosh, what's that guy doing?" Larry asked.

I told Larry about the loan for the new restaurant and he said, "You don't need a loan. Your loan is right here. I'll take care of it for you. Tell the guy you're sorry but you've made other arrangements. You don't need to give him an explanation. You don't need to volunteer any information." I thought that was wonderful advice: tell it the way it is and shut up.

Larry didn't need any paperwork. He said, "Your handshake to me is as good as your signature." I had never given Larry any reason to trust me or believe me, because he didn't know me financially that well. He just knew me as a restaurant owner. But he didn't hesitate. He loaned me $1.5 million on a handshake.

When a man unconditionally loans you money like that, you think about it. My family had left Armenia after the 1917 Russian Revolution, and now here I was, a kid from the old country, and this man of standing in the community was giving me a loan on a handshake. I will take that with me to my other life.

Larry always did the right thing. He taught me that if you're going to receive, you have to give. That's one thing I do in my restaurant because of Larry and Gail Miller. I get families that come in here and I can sense that they cannot afford to buy drinks and things like that for their kids. I buy it for them. Larry taught me that you can't just pick and choose people who need help. You have to give without question.

Larry also gave me a lot of business advice over the years. He would come into the restaurant to make sure we were not doing things wrong. He helped me correct a draining problem in the kitchen. At one point I was going to put in a take-out department, as a lot of other restaurants do. Larry said, "Artoosh, you want to do one thing and you want to do it better than anybody else. You are a full-service restaurant before you are a take-out department. You don't need to put in a separate door with signs and everything. Let them come in here, and you cook for them."

He said the same thing when I was building the new restaurant. I was going to build a 10,000-square-foot strip mall, use 4,000 square feet for the restaurant, and rent the rest of it. He gave me the best business advice I've ever had. He said, "Artoosh, you do not want to be a landlord. It's a very tough thing to do. You go build yourself a nice restaurant and I promise you, they will come." So I built it, and they have come.

I remember the last time I saw Larry. He came into my restaurant with Gail. They hardly touched their food. I knew he wasn't feeling well because when he walked there was kind of a limp to him. And he wasn't they type of guy to slouch around. He was a very ambitious, hardworking man. He always had projects going on. He moved. That night he just sat, and he said, "Artoosh, I don't do this too often, give me a hug."

I've sat at Larry's favorite table a thousand times, and every time I truly feel his presence. I really, really do. I will never forget that hug.

Here's Your Nickel

Jay Francis

When I first met Larry Miller, I was convinced he was someone else.

"That's not Larry Miller," I told Utah Jazz team president Dave Checketts when we walked into his office at the Toyota store in Murray, Utah.

"Yeah, it is," Dave assured me. "I've met with him."

"That's not the guy on TV!"

I hadn't met Larry at that point, but I knew the name, and I had seen the early commercials for his dealership, in which a slick talking head would say, "Come on down to Larry Miller Toyota!"

Before long, there wouldn't be any confusion as to who Larry Miller was.

I was the vice president of marketing and public relations for the Jazz at the time, and Sam Battistone was the team owner. Larry was someone who Dave, Larry Baum, and I had identified as a prospect who might be interested in a limited partnership. The Jazz organization needed major capital in order to stay in Utah. It looked as though Larry was going to buy in on the limited partnership, essentially a small ownership stake. But he called Dave Checketts that day and asked, "Can you come and meet with me? I have something else in mind."

That's when we walked into his Murray office and found out

just what he had been thinking. Larry would ultimately purchase half the team from Sam in 1985, and a year later he became the full franchise owner when he bought the other half. But my first reaction was that he was someone who had more than just a check-book ready to go. He had ideas. He was already thinking and talk-ing about things we could do to turn the struggling franchise into a successful one.

Larry and I developed a great relationship as we got to know each other. One of the first things that stood out to me was how important loyalty was to him—with employees, customers, and sponsors. After renegotiating the agreement with Coca-Cola one year, he had a lot of people telling him, "You left money on the table." They didn't think he had gotten as much as he could have. But that wasn't as important to him as thanking a sponsor who had been there since the beginning. Coca-Cola had put their faith and cash in the Jazz early on, making it possible for Larry to make some of those early investments, including building the arena. So he was extremely loyal to them.

In fact, one day he walked into a dealership and found a Pepsi machine. Apparently the general manager of that store preferred Pepsi and had placed a machine in the break room. Before Larry left that dealership, the machine was gone.

He showed a lot of that same loyalty in our relationship. In 1991, we had an interaction that was a hallmark for me as a dem-onstration of the values and loyalty I admired in Larry. We were preparing to open the Delta Center, and we were having weekly and sometimes daily meetings to plan everything. At one point, I made the comment to him, "We probably need to decide soon who's going to sell the luxury suites." He agreed, but we tabled the issue.

Later, at a separate meeting, he said, "I've decided that suites are more like ticket sales, so we're going to have you and your team manage that. I'd like to have you personally involved in the suite sales because it really requires executive contact."

Suite sales represented about $2.5 million worth of sales, but I never thought, *What's in it for me?* My father always taught me that you go to work, give them way more than what they are paying you for, and maybe you'll come out on top. I went to work, and we started selling suites before they had even poured the concrete on that level. We were basically selling based on the architectural renderings, trying to help people feel the experience and get excited about the suite without being able to stand in it. It was a new thing for our market, but by the time the Jazz played their second game in the new arena, we had signed every last contract—all fifty-six suites—on a three- or five-year basis.

Soon afterward, I was invited to lunch with Tim Howells, our general manager; Bob Hyde, the chief financial officer; and Larry. As we sat and conversed over lunch, Larry said, "I suppose you're wondering why we're here."

"What do you mean?" I asked. "I thought we were just here to have a meeting and eat lunch."

He then looked at Bob, who handed him an envelope. "Thank you for what you did in selling the suites," Larry said, handing me the envelope. "You never asked for a nickel. So here's your nickel."

Over time, we also formed a very personal relationship. Most of that centered around our families and especially around our mutual love for The Church of Jesus Christ of Latter-day Saints. Larry always used to tease me that he knew thirty minutes before I did that I was going to be called as a stake president. The area leaders had decided to issue the call to me, but one of them, Elder Jon Huntsman, who knew Larry well, wanted to make sure Larry didn't have something else planned for me that would conflict. He called Larry and told him they planned on extending the calling to me, and Larry of course supported the decision.

Before I was called as a mission president in Pittsburgh, Pennsylvania, Larry also knew from Elder M. Russell Ballard of the Church's Quorum of the Twelve Apostles that they were thinking of calling me.

Larry said, "You know, I have a little insight on you." He encouraged me to accept the calling even though I had just accepted a promotion a year earlier. He told me he'd take care of my health insurance while I served and that he'd make sure I had a job when I got back. "We'll take care of you," he said. "What else do you want to know?"

One time, Larry and I had been at a luncheon and he was dropping me off at the arena. I got out and he began to pull away. Then he honked, backed up his car, and rolled down his window. "We don't say this enough in business," he said, "but I love you." Then he rolled his window up and drove away.

I loved him, too, and I made sure I let him know that. I still remember exactly where I was when Larry called me for the last time. He told me about the decisions he and his family had made regarding his health and treatment, and that he would be going home to his Heavenly Father in a matter of days, not weeks. I told him I loved and appreciated him, and I still do. Then I said goodbye to my friend.

My father was right. I went to work, worked hard, and came out on top. And what I got in return was worth far more than something that can fit inside an envelope.

A Surprise Gift

Susie Ballard

Larry definitely had a reputation that preceded him. Working with the Miller Group for over three decades, I've heard almost everything anyone could say about the man. He wasn't perfect, and he never claimed to be. But at his core, he was a man who I could only describe in one word: generous.

When I started working at the Miller Group, I was the second employee at Larry H. Miller Leasing, in the original Murray Toyota store. The leasing office was right next to Larry's, so we saw him on a daily basis, which was nice because it helped Larry to get to know us on a personal level. He would always greet us by name and ask us questions about our home lives, listening intently to what we had to say.

He got to know me so well that he knew that my husband and I went out of town on the weekends to go fishing and camping. To me, knowing that he was the owner of the businesses—and a man of great importance in the community—it was touching that he would take the time to get to know me enough to remember to ask how my weekend trips went.

I had been working for the Miller Group for about two years when I found myself unexpectedly in an extended hospital stay. My husband and I had gone camping to our familiar spot at Moon Lake up in the High Uinta Mountains. The trip started out as usual, but after a few hours, I started to not feel well. My body ached. We decided to pack up and head home. On our way down Parley's Canyon, my condition worsened, and I asked my husband to take me to the hospital. The pain had now reached severe levels. I ended up spending six days in a hospital bed, stuck with needles and endless tests to try to solve this mystery illness. Each result was the same: inconclusive.

As this was my first hospital stay, I didn't have much insight into how my insurance worked. After hearing countless insurance-claim horror stories, I was concerned about the amount of money that I was going to owe. I came home and several weeks passed, but I still hadn't received any billing statements for my stay. Confused, I asked Marilyn, who was Larry's administrative assistant at the time, if she knew where I should begin. She told me that she would check into it and get back with me.

A week or two went by, and I still hadn't received word, so I asked again. She told me that not all of the bills had come in yet and to just be patient. A few more weeks passed, and I feared that something had been miscommunicated and the thought of my debt going to a collection agency worried me. I needed to know a dollar amount, even if just a ballpark figure, so that I could adjust my household budget to accommodate this unexpected expense.

My husband worked construction at the time, and every winter he would be furloughed indefinitely. Knowing that our monthly budget was critical to our financial survival, I went to Marilyn again. This time she told me that everything had been taken care of and that I didn't need to cover my hospital stay. I stood there in shock, unsure how to process the remark. I asked how that was possible. She said, "It just is."

That still didn't clear anything up. Nothing could be that easy. I asked if I could know who took care of this for me so that I could thank them.

"Larry did," she smiled.

I was dumbfounded. I could not believe the generosity of this man. Being an employee of only two years, I would never have expected him to cover my bills, let alone a pricey hospital stay. It was then that I began to realize what an incredible man he was and that I was working for the best company I could ask for—one that really cares about its employees.

In the past thirty-one years that I have worked for the Miller Group, I have heard a lot of harsh criticism about the way Larry ran his company or the things he said to people. But with all of the criticism sent his way, those who work for Larry, or used to work for Larry, or know Larry at all, know that he was a remarkably giving man. Everything he did was in the best interest of the company and the communities that we have businesses in. And because of that man, many lives have been changed forever. The legacy of his generosity will outlast any condemnation.

FEELING AT HOME

David Allred

My friendship with Larry Miller began and ended with the story of a house.

I was hired as the first-ever public relations intern for the Utah Jazz during the 1982–83 season, later becoming the team's assistant PR director. The following year, I was given additional duties of overseeing the team's community relations, such as player appearances, youth programs, community outreach, etc. It was in this role that my relationship with Larry began.

I'd taken work off one morning in early April of 1985, as my wife and I were headed to sign papers for the purchase of our first home in Kaysville, Utah. After working for the Utah Jazz for four difficult seasons, both financially and on the court, this season began offering the fans and the front office some hope.

But with this success came rumors.

Was the rise of the Jazz from the depths of mediocrity to minimal competitiveness the opportunity for owner Sam Battistone to sell the team and move on? Word was that an ownership group from Minnesota was again talking about acquiring full ownership of the team and moving it to the North Star State. In spite of this, my wife and I still felt confident in my job security and with the purchase of our home in Utah.

Just before leaving for Kaysville to sign the closing documents,

I answered a phone call from Executive Vice President David Checketts. "Press conference at noon at the Salt Palace," he said. "You need to be there."

We put our plans for the home on hold and headed to the office. This was the first time I met Larry Miller. The front office staff was small then, so we were all quickly introduced to "the man who saved the Jazz." It was the start of a lasting relationship.

For the next eighteen years, almost every public and private community outreach effort, first by the team and later by the Miller organization, ran through me. Larry would often hear of a need and call me to reach out and help. He always preferred his charity be kept private. His faith had instilled in him a desire to serve but to do so without fanfare or recognition.

"I need the blessings," he would tell me on occasion. "Let's just make sure this gets taken care of."

As the team achieved greater success through the years and Larry's other businesses expanded, so grew the requests he would personally receive asking for help. His public visibility and accessibility made him vulnerable to thousands of requests each year. Most efforts were small, but many were life altering. I quickly learned of Larry's capacity to assess each one and then provide the means for assistance. Often, he and I were the only ones in the organization who knew of his anonymous efforts.

By 1993, the number of requests coming into the organization required the founding of Larry H. Miller Charities. Larry never let the bureaucracy label of organized charitable giving stand in his way of helping someone in need. It was not uncommon for me to witness someone receiving a phone call from Larry offering his guidance—sometimes financial, sometimes otherwise. Again, all without any public attention.

In 2002, though I was president of his charitable foundation, I became an unintentional recipient of Larry's generosity. My wife and I put off buying a home until 1992, when we purchased property and built our dream home in a neighborhood where we'd both grown up.

After ten years of living in our dream home and being just minutes from our parents' and siblings' homes, my wife suddenly asked for a divorce. As the following Jazz season began, I faced a difficult personal crisis on multiple fronts. I was moving out of my home and seeking a place to live. For my family, friends, coworkers, and my own self-interest, I wanted to give the impression that I could weather the end of a twenty-three-year marriage and the resulting complications.

Larry had been made aware of my divorce early, and it was not uncommon for him to call me "just to see how I was doing." On one occasion, he called and asked where I'd been living.

"With my parents," I answered, embarrassed. For two weeks, I'd lived back home, even though my ego wasn't going to let me do that for long.

"That will never do," he responded. "Walk to the back parking lot of the Delta Center in an hour. Gail will meet you there."

So an hour later, I met Gail, who proceeded to take me to a furnished apartment in downtown Salt Lake. "Larry and I want you to stay here as long as is needful," she said as she handed me the keys.

I lived there just two months until I closed on a home just minutes from my children. Larry wanted me to find a house in the neighborhood near my children and offered to help me with the down payment. For two months, it was a big adventure for my kids and me to spend time downtown. But it also gave me the time and space I needed to make critical decisions regarding my future. I ended my tenure with the Jazz that year, but I paid interest to Larry on the loan for my house, able to fully repay him in just a few years, after I had remarried and then re-sold the house.

For eighteen years, I had seen lives changed in subtle yet unequivocal ways by this Good Samaritan. I never expected the day I would experience his service firsthand when he offered me a way to rebuild my life and home. I am sure he now has a mansion on the other side.

LET ME HELP YOU DO WHAT YOU DO

Michael McDonough

The caller ID read, "Larry H. Miller." I thought it was odd for an auto dealership to call me out of the blue like that. After all, I wasn't in the market for a new car. In fact, at the moment, I didn't even have a full-time job.

I was a sound designer, specializing in creating and mixing sound for motion pictures, with twenty years of experience under my belt. I had worked on many movie and television projects up to that point, including about a dozen IMAX films. I had worked with the best in the business, doing projects alongside Academy Award-winning producers and directors.

I had just finished two weeks of sound mixing for an IMAX film about the building of Hearst Castle on the Central California coast. I had completed the job at George Lucas's Skywalker Ranch in Marin County, California, and then attended the world premiere of the film at the castle's visitor center.

The morning after the premiere, I found myself walking along the rugged beach of San Simeon. I guess I needed to think about my future in the sound business. Something told me that I needed to make a change, but I didn't quite know what direction to go. I had a wife and two daughters who depended on me, and I was certainly not the type to just quit a job without having a better opportunity present itself.

I climbed up on a large outcropping of rocks to watch the surf crash and spray in front of me. As I sat there and pondered what I should do, a thought came over me that was very vivid. I suddenly knew it would be the right thing to do if I were to leave my employment right away. Somehow I knew that if I did, everything would be all right. I talked to my wife, Marilyn, and she was very supportive of my decision.

A week after leaving my job, I was asked to create some unique sound design for the upcoming film *Star Trek: First Contact*. I didn't have a studio to work in then, so I made some calls. I found a company in San Diego that would lease me the new sound equipment I needed. We decided I'd use the basement as the makeshift sound studio, for lack of a better option.

That's when the phone rang, and it changed everything.

The call wasn't from the local Toyota dealership. It was Larry Miller himself. He said he had heard I'd left the production company where I was employed and felt the need to call me. For the next forty-five minutes Larry talked, and I listened. He said he was deeply concerned that Utah needed to keep a pool of experienced and talented people in the arts, and not lose anyone to out-of-state employment.

He realized sometimes artists, composers, sculptors, and even sound designers were better craftsmen than they were businessmen. "That's where I come in," he said. "Let me take the risk for you. Let me help you do what you do."

I'll never forget it.

That began a thirteen-year partnership with Larry Miller. Soon I had a beautiful sound facility at one of his buildings by the airport, where I could create sound for movies and television projects. Even though I don't think Larry ever quite knew exactly what I did, he seemed fascinated with it and wanted to support it. Just as he had said in that phone call, he wanted to help me and others do what we do.

One day Larry came into my mixing room and sat down on my burgundy leather couch. We talked for a while, and soon Larry was telling me his life story. He really opened up to me, recounting his years of working to establish his businesses and how it had taken so much of his time and energy. He said he had neglected spending enough time with his wife, Gail, and his children. The tears flowed as he told me of his regrets, and he said the opportunity to help raise his grandson was a second chance.

Over the years, I got to know a few of Larry's passions. One day, he invited me down to a project under construction in Sandy. I put on a hardhat and we walked around this immense cement structure. He showed me where there would be movie screens, an IMAX theater, and a restaurant featuring audio-animatronic puppets and a waterfall. Larry said they had no experience with movie theaters or restaurants but that he wanted to make something amazing for the community to enjoy. He wanted to give back. Soon I was in my studio putting together the soundtrack for a computerized show with singing toucans and cliff divers!

Larry was always fascinated by movies, and it wasn't long before he was looking into making them. He asked me for the names of several film producers I had worked with over the years. He spoke to a few people and ultimately decided to fund several movies based on The Work and the Glory, the bestselling book series by Gerald Lund about the early days of the Mormon Church. Larry invested heavily in these films and even outfitted my studio with the latest digital sound gear to help me finish the movies' soundtracks.

The movie business is notoriously tricky, even for experienced producers, and it was soon apparent that Larry would lose most of his investment in these films. I don't think he was used to losing money on this scale, and one day I just happened to be on the receiving end of his pent-up frustration. He yelled so loudly on my cell phone that I had to hold it out away from my ears!

I had never experienced this side of him, but he kept saying he wasn't mad at me. I guess he didn't know who else to yell at. A few days later, he called me back and apologized for his tantrum and even became emotional over his behavior. My admiration for him grew from this.

Right to the end of his life, Larry Miller gave back as much as he could. In the last phone conversation I had with him, Larry told me of the huge amount of money that he and Gail had committed in the next few years to charity. He was giving back right to the end.

He and Gail were amazingly generous to me and my family, and I'll never forget it. Every time I look at the top of the ten-story office building at Jordan Commons, I think of Larry in his office, looking out the window at what he and his family had built. We are all the better for Larry H. Miller.

A MAN OF VISION

Mayor Tom Dolan

When discussing Larry Miller, it is easy to use such words as driven, tenacious, intense, and motivated. These descriptions certainly are as accurate as they are deserved, but for me the word that best describes Larry is "humble."

I also consider him to be the guy who developed Sandy.

As mayor of Sandy City, I have appreciated the support Larry gave to the community through economic investment and the sharing of his time. There are countless stories. They range from his support of the Sandy Boys and Girls Clubs, to his ahead-of-its-time vision with the Southtowne Auto Mall, to expanding the Salt Lake Community College campus, to venturing into the entertainment business, to a score of things in between. Larry saw possibilities when others did not.

Shrewd, honest, innovative. Larry Miller was all of that. The best measure of a person's character, however, is not found on a balance sheet. Rather, it comes from within one's heart. Albert Schweitzer said it best: "The full measure of a man is not to be found in the man himself, but in the colors and textures that come alive in others because of him." Larry had the ability to bring out the best in those around him.

Larry and I first met in 1962 in Littleton, Colorado. In Littleton, we were in the same LDS ward. I remember vividly when, in a priesthood meeting one Sunday, Larry stood and bore his testimony. I will never forget the spirit I felt as he asked for forgiveness from anyone he had offended as he shared a renewed commitment to better gospel living.

His courage, honesty, and strength produced a touching experience for everyone in the room. It was his humility, though, that most impacted me. I became more introspective of my devotion.

When I was first elected mayor in 1994, Sandy City was attempting to develop an auto mall. At that time, only Riverton Motors and Merle Motors, a small used car operation, had relocated on the land set aside for the mall. Activity was slow in coming.

I decided to talk with Larry Miller, who owned a Chevy dealership in Murray, about planting a flag in Sandy City. Larry said he would think about the auto mall. A few months later he called me to say he had bought the rest of the future auto mall property. He went on to acquire Merle Motors and expand his own dealership into Sandy. In Larry's first month there, he sold more than a hundred cars.

That's vision.

It wasn't long before Ken Garff, the Miller Group's biggest auto competitor, wanted to locate in the mall as well. The trouble was Larry had purchased all the available land; Garff was shut out. But Larry wasn't afraid of competition, and he agreed to sell Ken land on the site. Larry was a very fair guy. Larry also knew an economic fact of life: more cars meant more people browsing, and some of his competitors' browsers would wander over to his lot.

Jordan Commons, a large commercial development, came along, and Larry built a cinema complex and an innovative restaurant. Many questioned his expertise in those areas, saying the movie and food businesses were a long way from selling cars. He proved the naysayers wrong with courage, creativity, and commitment.

And vision.

For Larry, it wasn't always just about personal profits. For example, he believed Salt Lake Community College's Sandy campus needed expansion. As it turned out, the city of Sandy had twenty acres of land available just west of Interstate 15. He didn't want simply to donate the funds to SLCC for the project; he wanted to construct it himself and, upon completion, donate the finished product to the college. He would hire his own contractor, build to his specifications, do it faster and better, and save the school millions of dollars in the process. The SLCC Miller Campus opened in 2001 and is home to the Miller Business Resource and Business Innovation centers, among numerous other programs.

Sandy City lost a good friend when Larry Miller died. He is an irreplaceable molder of Utah's future. He stepped up and embraced leadership, regardless of what some people thought about his ideas. For Larry Miller, if his vision seemed to be the right thing, he did it.

FAITH & SPIRITUALITY

AT REST

Robert Tingey

There are people I've met in life who, under any circumstance, seem to be at peace with their surroundings. Even when times prove difficult, they remain happy and calm. Larry was not one of those people.

I'd been working just a short time at the law firm Winder & Haslam in the mid-'80s when I walked past Dennis Haslam's office. "Hey, Robert," he called. "Come in and meet this guy." "This guy" turned out to be the new owner of the Utah Jazz. The guy I'd seen countless times on television or standing in our offices in his golf shirt and khakis. I thought to myself, *I'm going to like this guy.* It's not something I could ever explain; my gut reaction just told me that I would take to him easily.

It was clear from the start that Larry always had something on his mind. He was very precise, and he expected that in return. If the deal concerned a 5.243-acre piece of land, it was important never to round up, because he wanted to know exact numbers. It's how his mind worked.

The first time I ever spent any one-on-one time with Larry occurred when we were working on closing a deal in Phoenix. Haslam had asked me to shepherd part of the deal. Numbers were something I was comfortable with, so I spent a fair amount of time combing through the documents.

Then Larry called me just after five o'clock that day, which I later learned he did often. His mind never shut off from his professional responsibilities after the working day ended. It kept ticking away. He wanted to go over the settlement statement in detail. We spent over two hours on the phone together going over things line by line. To me, it was just part of my job, but I did get the impression that he was slightly disappointed when he couldn't find anything wrong with my numbers.

The next day, I was in my office with Haslam and told him, "Larry called me last night and we went over the settlement statement."

Instantly, a panicked look came over his face. "How did you do?"

"The numbers were all okay," I shrugged. "So, I guess I did all right."

Haslam looked both relieved and shocked at the same time. "Well, you just wrestled with the best and came out unscathed, so you should be proud of yourself."

It was then I knew Larry liked me in return. While it's easy to say that he liked almost everyone, if you could somehow prove yourself to him, you had his friendship and loyalty for life. No further questions asked.

Eventually, I came to work for Larry's organization. Most of our interaction was strictly business. As his enterprise continued its expansion, more and more deals needed to be settled. He always had legal questions. Sometimes he would call me into his office for a twenty-minute conference, only to go on for hours at a time. In a lot of respects, it was as though I were getting an MBA course in a lot of things. Larry's mind never forgot. He knew details and facts and could recall them quicker than anyone.

I suppose that's both a blessing and a curse. I never saw him able to kick back and relax much, and he constantly placed a lot of responsibility on his own shoulders. He felt a sense of duty and stewardship to the community unlike anyone else I'd ever met. For a long time it impressed me, but I honestly never knew why he felt such obligation.

This overwhelming sense of stewardship remained a mystery to me until the last months of his life. His illness had been apparent for a while, but it was when he was in a wheelchair that he invited many of his friends, family, and coworkers to his LDS ward chapel for a fireside. He wanted to share with us his life decisions and his spiritual decisions. Many of the stories I'd heard before. That night, however, he went deeper into his faith, explaining his decision to become a more active member in his church and give back to the community that had granted him so many opportunities.

He regaled us with stories of what he believed were divine interventions, guiding him back to his spiritual side. To many, these would seem like mere coincidences, but Larry looked at them as an answer to his ongoing prayers during this time of searching. His sense of service grew from the love of his church and family.

Still, even that night, his mind was racing. Although he'd written down a prepared speech, he had left it at home. But his ever-going intellect allowed him to retain most of it and share it with us as though he'd been preparing for months. Larry is the only man I know who could have pulled that off.

It was a unique experience to hear Larry verbalize the core of his being. What he said may not have had the same impact on the other two hundred or so attendees, but it resonated with me, and I felt honored that he would share something so personal. But my most spiritual moment with Larry was yet to come.

Months later, Larry was in the hospital. The doctors told him that there were some procedures they could perform that might extend his life for a few months, but they wouldn't be pleasant ones. Larry didn't want to go through that anymore, so he opted to go home, knowing he would only have a few more days.

Clark Whitworth, the organization's chief financial officer, and I went over to Larry's to have him sign a few documents. This was just a few days before he passed away. Gail answered the door. We went up to Larry's bedroom. I imagined myself in his position, wondering what I would be thinking about if I knew I were going to pass away in a matter of days. My mind would probably be focused on all the wrong things, all the mistakes I'd made.

As I studied his face, it was to my amazement that he wasn't thinking about any of these things. For the first time since I'd met him over twenty years earlier, I saw Larry at peace. He'd made peace with himself and with God. He was ready. At one point, he even said, "I'm ready and curious to know what awaits me on the other side."

I will remember Larry as a brilliant human being and as the hardest working, most passionate man I've ever seen. Seeing him finally at peace is part of his legacy that continues to last for me because it has granted me the knowledge and tools to be able to do the same when my time comes.

FIFTY LETTERS

Steve Miller

I was only eight years old when my father purchased a Toyota dealership in Murray, Utah, in 1979. I'd seen him make career moves, but when this one happened, I could tell something was different. It might have been the first time I'd seen my parents have even the slightest bit of anxiety over a career decision. But they were also excited, because it meant they'd be moving our family back to Utah.

As I'd spent my entire life growing up in Colorado, I certainly didn't want to move. But I had faith in my father that the decision he was making was for the greater benefit of our family. We soon packed the proverbial station wagon and moved to Utah, little aware of the magnitude of things to come.

Life was more or less normal for us during our first years in Utah as my dad's car business rapidly expanded. He was always working; that wasn't anything new. But nothing accelerated things more than when my father purchased half of the Utah Jazz. At first, I didn't understand his interest. Selling cars and owning a basketball team had next to nothing in common. But remembering how he'd been right about purchasing the first dealership and how I'd grown to love Utah, I believed in his decisions. As the Jazz and my father's other businesses gained prominence, he developed a reputation in the community of being superhuman, always managing multiple agendas, constantly running numbers in his head. To me, he was always just a man—a man who loved Utah. He had his share of faults and weaknesses, but he wanted the world to be a better place, and he felt he could make that happen.

Dad was like the boy at the beach throwing starfish back into the ocean in order to make a difference to the few he could help. Dad was content if he felt he could make a difference to just one person, but as his business gave him the means to do so, he never stopped at just one. He felt responsible to the community as a whole.

While Dad wasn't known to slow down very often, sometimes our family would vacation at our ranch in Idaho. Many times, he would ask my siblings and me if any of us would like to come fishing with him. Most often, I was the only one who said yes. My brothers and sister felt that fishing with my father was often just a ruse so he could preach a lesson, which wasn't always enjoyable for them. I can't say I blame them, because he was guilty of this, but I saw it as an opportunity my father wanted to provide.

Dad liked to troll out of the back of the boat, with a wet fly or wooly-bugger, and he would catch a lot of fish. But it's hard to say if he actually enjoyed fishing that much. It seemed he was more interested in *creating* the experience for me than in having the experience itself. Mostly, I think he knew I enjoyed fishing and wanted to give me the chance to do it. We spent a lot of days in that shoddy boat, and I look back on those memories with a tremendous amount of fondness.

I think this is an allegory for many of his endeavors. Before the purchase of the Utah Jazz, for example, my father didn't know much about NBA basketball. He enjoyed going to games, but more important to him was keeping the team in Utah for those who enjoyed going to the games even more than he did and what it meant to the state to have a professional basketball team. It wasn't about him. Even when it came time to build a larger arena to house the Jazz, he knew the cost would be great, but he recognized that the reward of enriching the community would far outweigh it.

The arena was a massive undertaking, and it was built right when it came time for me to serve an LDS mission at age nineteen. My father never pressured any of his children in religious ways. My two older brothers opted for different paths when they came of the expected mission age, but I knew it was something that I had always wanted to do. My dad created the runway and let us direct where we wanted to go, and he fully supported our decisions. Eventually, I was called to serve in Quebec, Canada. Though I was 2,000 miles away, this experience brought me closer to my father than any other.

He wrote me regularly. He'd tell me the goings-on behind the arena. He'd recap the Jazz games for me, letting me know how many points Malone had scored the night before. By the end of my mission, I collected about fifty handwritten letters from him, each one containing its own gems of advice and wisdom, and more important, a reminder of how much he loved me.

A lot of other lessons he taught me, however, came mostly through omission. When he became sick, my dad often spoke of his regret for not spending enough time with his family. I knew I didn't want to pay the price he did. But because of him, I'm able to attend my children's recitals and games. Family is my number-one priority.

Luckily, he did come to one of my events when it mattered most. In 2007, I was competing in the 206-mile bicycle race known as LoToJa, which runs from Logan, Utah, to Jackson Hole, Wyoming. It was the first time I'd competed in an event like this. His health had been declining, so the event coordinators allowed him to park near the finish line. With his poor vision, I'm not sure he could see me as I rounded the final bend, but I saw him. He knew how much it meant to me to finish that race. It's a moment I'll never forget and one I want to be able to repeat many times for my own children.

I venture to say that my father was misunderstood a lot of the time. He wore his emotions on his sleeve, but he was a good man who did a lot for others. So many times he would sign personal checks, paying off someone else's mortgage. There are still many acts like this I'm discovering years later. He and my mother wanted to keep their acts of service private. They didn't feel the need to brag about their good deeds to others.

My dad was a man of integrity who didn't want to have to cross the street to avoid talking to someone who felt wronged by him. Many of these lessons my wife and I teach to our children almost daily. We use informal moments to remind our children of their grandfather and the opportunities he created for us.

I still read through the letters he wrote me. They're one of my most valued possessions. You see fewer and fewer people like my father these days. I think one of the things that happens when people pass on is that they tend to be forgotten, some becoming obscure or taking on a different status than when they were alive. My dad's letters help me remember him for the man he was—just a man I sat with in a fishing boat in Idaho.

MEETING LARRY

Chris Hancuff

I worked for Larry for several years in ticket sales, never meeting him or hearing from him until the day it mattered most.

"Dad, Larry Miller called for you while you were out," my young son, Dannon, told me. As Dannon was known around our household as being a practical joker, I immediately dismissed it.

"Dannon," I said, "Larry Miller is way too busy to be giving me a call. I don't think he even knows who I am. You're pulling my leg."

I originally worked for the Golden Eagles minor league hockey team until Larry purchased them in the late 1980s. After that, I was in charge of ticket sales for the Utah Jazz as well as other events that came through the Delta Center. I'd seen Larry around the halls, of course, but we had never spoken to one another. There was no reason to believe he'd be calling me now.

That day, my wife and I had been out on an errand no parent should have to run. We were making funeral arrangements for my oldest son, Christopher, who'd just lost a battle to cancer.

It was the next day at work that I discovered that Larry really *did* call. That day he phoned my office to ask about my son and how everything had happened.

It's hard to explain to others about the pain you feel when one of your children is suffering. Christopher was just thirteen when he was diagnosed with a form of soft tissue cancer. After surgery to re-move the tumor and surrounding tissue, he spent eighteen months in chemotherapy and radiation treatment to prevent potential growth.

The rule of thumb is that after eighteen months of treatment, if you're cancer free for another eighteen months, you're consid-ered low-risk for a reccurrence. However, after fourteen months, Christopher told my wife and me that he was having chest pains when he breathed. We immediately took him to the doctor, hoping it wouldn't be anything serious.

Unfortunately, we were informed that the cancer was back at stage four, having metastasized into Christopher's lungs. The doctor told my son that he had a zero chance of survival. I'll never forget my son's reaction after the doctor left. He looked to his mom and said, "I guess there's more God wants me to learn that I didn't learn the first time around."

Even though he knew the odds were against him, my son wanted to fight it. He underwent chemo and radiation a second time, in addition to experimental procedures. But after six months and several more overnight hospital visits, my son's condition was worsening. The tumors in his lungs were bleeding to the point that even the hospital couldn't replace the blood fast enough.

Four days after his seventeenth birthday, my son passed away at Primary Children's Medical Center.

I relayed this to Larry over the phone and told him that the only comfort we had as a family rested in knowing that we would be able to someday see him again. As members of the LDS faith, we believe that families are sealed for all time and eternity, but waiting to see him again would still be a difficult process. Even over twenty years later, we still miss him every single day. Nothing can heal the pain of losing a child.

Larry and I spoke for over twenty minutes. With everything he had to do, in the middle of a busy Jazz season, it was very touching that someone in his position would find the time to listen to me and genuinely care about my family. He was in no hurry and let me do most of the talking. Before we hung up, he offered his condolences and told me to let him know if there was anything I needed. It's a moment I'll always remember.

A couple weeks after the funeral, my manager also asked me if there was anything he could do for my family. I told him that the engine to our family van needed some major mechanical work and had to be repaired. The estimate was three thousand dollars. It was a lot of money. With all the medical and funeral expenses, we simply didn't have it. I asked if maybe we could have it repaired at one of our dealerships for a decent price.

Thankfully, a dealership was able to repair the vehicle, but even with a discount, I still had no idea where the money was going to come from. When I went to pick up the vehicle from the dealership, I was handed the receipt and was surprised to see a balance due of zero. "How can this be?" I asked.

"Larry paid for it," they told me.

My gratitude to Larry at that moment was overwhelming. I didn't know how to thank him. I sent a thank-you card, but later I was finally able to thank him in person at one of our annual company recognition dinners. I'd been with the company for ten years and was one of a few being honored that evening at the Delta Center.

One of my managers stood up to introduce me. He was relatively new and was mostly winging his speech. It was then that Larry took the microphone from him and took over, complimenting me for my years of hard work and my dedication to the company as well as my value as a human being. It meant a great deal to me that Larry cared enough to personally thank me and recognize me in such a way.

Working for Larry's organization all these years has truly been an honor. He's helped my family in so many others ways. Four of my other children have graduated from college because of the company education fund. He's a man who genuinely cared about his employees.

I'll never forget my first interaction with Larry. It was under sad circumstances, but it's my happiest memory of him, one that will stay with me always.

Sneakers to Suits

Stewart Glazier

There are so many things that come to mind when people think of Larry Miller, and one of those has to be his casual attire. When you think of Larry, the image is of him in those white tennis shoes. That's why I remember so vividly when he traded in the sneakers for a suit.

I met Larry when he, Gail, and their family moved into the Pepperwood neighborhood of Sandy, Utah. I served as the bishop and later the stake president of the local organization of The Church of Jesus Christ of Latter-day Saints, and that meant I got to interact with members of the Church and occasionally invite people to serve in different capacities.

Later on in Larry's time in Pepperwood, we called Larry to join the High Council, a group of leaders that assists the stake presidency in communicating to and instructing the members of the stake. Larry was a bit reticent at first when we extended the call, partially because he never wore a suit. But Larry accepted the call, and I got to watch an interesting change in him as he went from sneakers to suits.

The calling stretched Larry in certain ways. It was kind of like getting a new suit. You want a new suit to fit, you want to feel comfortable in it, and that happens over time as you move a little bit. Larry soon became accustomed to the role. I enjoyed the relationship we had. In his business dealings, Larry was said to be very assertive, at the center of every discussion. In our meetings, he didn't talk a lot. He was very studious and respectful of the presidency and the other members.

One of my favorite Larry memories, though, happened when I approached Larry the businessman and asked him for some help. We had started a pioneer trek with the Church Education System (CES), a cross-country journey in which youth and families could retrace the steps of the Mormon pioneers. We had vehicles accompany the trek along the way, carrying supplies and providing assistance in case of emergencies. The CES teachers were often using their own vehicles, but it was tough on people's cars because following the footsteps of our pioneer ancestors required getting off the trail, and not all of the cars were built for that. We had had some cars break down, and we needed an alternative.

I reached out to Larry to see if he had any used trucks or SUVs that we could rent. That way we'd be equipped to handle the rough terrain as well as carry food and supplies. Larry was passionate about sharing the pioneer story, and he said, "Why don't I just let you use some?" He loaned us brand-new vehicles, seventeen to eighteen per trip. Year after year he made the trip possible, because there was really no other way to make it happen.

One time, a truck was heading up a muddy hill in a rainstorm and slid into another vehicle. We got the vehicles back, and the estimate was about $10,000 worth of damage. I thought, *CES is going to have to pay for all of this, and we're going to be in big trouble.* But that wasn't the case. Larry took care of it, and we didn't have to worry.

He truly enjoyed doing it because of his passion for Church history and pioneer stories. He enjoyed hearing what the youth learned and how they felt, and he often shared with me the letters that people wrote him, thanking him for his kindness. We still do the trek today, and the Miller family has continued to honor Larry by allowing us to use vehicles from the Miller dealerships.

Larry would often drive out and meet us on the trail, and we shared some special experiences there. I know those moments had a deep impact on Larry. We would follow along with the stories of the original trek by reading journal entries from pioneers that I had compiled in a book called *Journal of the Trail*. One day, I was listening to one of Larry's radio interviews, and he was asked if he had a book he would recommend, and he mentioned my book, adding, "Everybody ought to read it." I was humbled that he would mention it, especially with all of the other books he might have considered.

Over the years, he would occasionally invite me to join him at Jazz games, including at the height of the Jazz's successful run in the 1990s. We would also go to lunch and talk about Church history, cars, or business. I didn't know that much about his many different endeavors, so I would ask questions. It was interesting to listen to him talk about his story, all the way back to his start in the parts department in Colorado.

Eventually, Larry and Gail moved from Pepperwood to the Avenues, but I kept in touch through Greg, who was still in the neighborhood. When Larry began to get really sick, Greg said to me one day, "I'm going to get serious about exercising." We both knew that Larry had pushed himself so hard for so many years at the expense of taking care of himself, and that was contributing to his diabetes and related problems.

I used to ask Larry, "Why do you drive yourself so hard?" He would tell me he was doing it for the family, and I said, "Larry, you won't be around to be with your family." It's important to have balance, to take the time to nurture relationships. As men, we have to pay a little bit more attention to our sweethearts and our children. We can certainly learn a great deal from Larry's life, including the lesson of the importance of having that balance.

I had a chance to have a final visit with Larry and Gail. It was after his legs had been amputated below the knees due to complications from his diabetes. Larry was in a wheelchair but in good spirits, and we spent time talking about our long friendship and experiences together.

Larry was a very service-oriented, caring person. From wanting to be a faithful high councilor to providing a means whereby hundreds could enjoy the special and faith-building experience of walking in the pioneers' footsteps, Larry was always helping. He had a burning fire, a dedication to keep things going. He wouldn't take no for an answer, and he was up for any challenge, even when his stake president asked him to trade the sneakers for suit jackets.

PIONEERS AND LIME CRUSH

A. Lynn Scoresby

Whether it was 936 bottles of Canadian soda or his valuable time and attention, Larry Miller loved to give.

As a management trainer and consultant to the Larry H. Miller Group, I had the opportunity and privilege of spending time with Larry. During that time, I noticed some of the things that made him a truly talented and remarkable man. There were so many dimensions of Larry as an individual and as a businessman, but the stories that come to mind are very different stories about ways he gave of himself.

Larry had asked if I would join his annual managers meeting and make presentations about the importance of marriage and family, as well as provide management training. My wife, Dorothy, and I had attended these conferences over the years and traveled to many places we would not have visited on our own. One of these was Lake Louise in Banff, Canada—a truly beautiful place. Three or four times during that visit, Larry and I walked along the path next to the lake while he talked to me about his vision for the company and where he felt progress was needed.

At some point in these conversations, I learned of his penchant for Lime Crush soda, which he said was no longer produced in the United States but *was* available in Canada. He said that he was going to find the plant where it was bottled and purchase some. I didn't think much about it at the time, but apparently he did just that. During his stay in Canada, he tracked down the distributor and asked for a pallet to be delivered to Salt Lake, thinking it would be something like twelve boxes with twelve bottles each.

A few weeks later, I was in his Murray office at the Chevrolet store when he received a telephone call. He told his secretary to defer the call, but she persisted.

"Umm, you might want to answer this one."

He complied, and I watched as the expression on his face changed from calmness to consternation. Finally, he said, "Just bring it to the Chevrolet store, and put it in the parts storage."

He concluded the call and looked at me sheepishly. He told me about his order for a pallet of Lime Crush. The call was from the Canadian delivery driver—who had 936 bottles of soda on the truck ready to be delivered!

For the next several meetings, I'd often ask how he was doing in terms of getting rid of the soda. He once announced, "I have good news." He told me he had given a few cases to some group planning a party. Once I helped out by giving some to a church group. We were making progress.

It was at about that point when Larry and Gail hosted a dinner party. Dorothy and I felt honored to be invited. In attendance were Michael Ballam, the singer and director of the Utah Festival Opera; David Linn, a budding artist who had painted *Helping Hands*; and Al Rounds, a successful watercolorist who had painted some of the Millers' favorite artwork of early Salt Lake City. At the Millers' request, we each had to bring a product of our own creativity and share it with the others. It was a lovely evening and truly memorable.

After we shared our gifts, Larry and Gail went out of the room for a moment, and someone asked, "What do you think they will share?" I was quite sure I knew, so I proffered my guess: "It might be lime soda." As it turned out, we all received a case of Lime Crush along with a basketball signed by all the Utah Jazz players. I have the basketball in my office, and it still impresses visitors when they see who signed it. But the real haul was the Lime Crush, especially because I knew the history behind it.

But the greatest gift Larry bestowed upon people had nothing to do with lime soda or basketball paraphernalia. It was the way he gave his own time and attention.

When I began working as a consultant to the company, I asked Larry if he was willing to let me have access to him whenever I wanted. That was a lot to ask of someone as prominent and busy as he was. I promised I would not abuse it but felt it would be useful to inform him about what I learned and any potential problems I saw as I traveled around working with his management teams. He agreed and kept his promise, but I learned that the term "access" had a different meaning than I had intended.

When I called and asked to talk, he almost always was able to speak to me. And I learned firsthand on many occasions that this was true for many people. Larry gave access to his friends, to ward members, to people who needed help, to customers who had complaints, and to strangers who just wanted to visit for a moment. In light of how busy he was, this was pretty amazing to me.

His schedule of people to see and work to do was extensive. On his desk, he organized all the phone messages he got in the order they were received. He lined the messages up on one side of his desk and moved each to the other side once he had returned that call. His goal was to get through the list every day, but most of the time, unless the list was short, he did not make it. On some days, the line of phone messages stretched fully across his big desk.

On several occasions when I called, he wanted to get out of the office, so we went to lunch. We went to the cafeteria at a nearby hospital because "Earl's clam chowder was the best." When we went to Ruth's Diner up Emigration Canyon, he spoke to the server by name and inquired about her family. We once went to a Mexican restaurant south of the office, and he spoke to both the manager and the server by name and inquired about how the business was doing. During some of these meals, well-wishers would stop by to talk about a recent Jazz game or ask questions about him. He was always gracious.

This was not all. He knew about struggling artists and purchased paintings from them. He found ways to use his business to help people in landscaping, printing, travel, insurance, food production, media design, business consulting, accounting, cars, farming, and many other fields.

It took me a while to catch on to why he was like this, but one day it became clear. We traveled up Emigration Canyon and stopped at a clearing on the north side of the road. We sat in his car while he explained where he thought the Mormon pioneers had stayed the night, and he became a bit emotional while talking about the story.

Later on, he and Gail financed the building of the fire station at This Is the Place Heritage Park to honor Jesse C. Little, a pioneer relative who was one of Salt Lake City's first firemen. While watching the presentation and the glow on their faces that night of the dedication, I realized that I was watching something greater than people just donating money to a worthy cause. They were giving access to people because they felt a shared responsibility to do so. Caring for one another was the rich tradition and heritage of all early pioneers, and Larry and Gail did the same to honor that legacy.

THE WORK AND
THE GLORY

Scott Swofford

Is this going to be business or charity?"

That was Larry's greeting as I answered the phone in the fall of 2003, after a decade of not working together. I immediately knew his voice and I knew the only acceptable answer: business. Knowing he had myriad charitable efforts underway, I wasn't anxious to add to that pile.

"It has to be business, because there are nine books, and no philanthropy is going to fund nine films," he agreed. "If I do this, it's not for the money, but if you want it to continue, they have to break even. Are we clear about that?"

"Yes, sir," I said.

"Will they be good? Because you have no idea how many film pitches people try to give us."

I had been a producer of films for over two decades at that point, many of which had gained prominence in the LDS community. "They will be the best films this culture has produced to date," I answered.

"Okay," he replied. "Let's set up a meeting."

That was Larry's initial leap of faith and devotion into the *Work and the Glory* experience. I knew he loved and had been an early confidant of author Gerald N. Lund during the creation of the book series, and it had sold over two million copies at that point. I was confident we had a winner, but the expense was significant—much greater than any LDS film to date. *The Other Side of Heaven* was the frontrunner at the LDS box office with just under a five million gross, and our projections needed only twenty-five percent more attendance than that to break even.

The initial meetings with Larry were full of challenges and due diligence. Our production accountant, formerly a certified fraud auditor for the state, said he had never been grilled so hard. Eventually, Larry said he believed in the material and the story we were trying to tell and granted us the green light.

Larry never came to the set, but his wife, Gail, and their grandson, Zane, did. Larry would call often, at odd times, asking very searching questions about decisions we were making. When the first film was finally in rough edit form, I took the copy under my arm to Larry's basement screening room for his first look. He had invited his family and a few business associates. At the final fade out, everyone was quiet. Everyone but Larry. He stood and was his characteristically emotional self.

One of the most powerful impressions he made was when he said, "It's a home run with me." Larry, our financier and visionary, had approved.

President Gordon B. Hinckley attended the premiere, waved his cane in acceptance, and the film opened strong, but it didn't quite beat *The Other Side of Heaven* at the box office. Video releases and pay-per-view sales were still to come when it was time to consider the next film in the series. We didn't know how the story would continue.

We sat at the table in his office, and he looked us in the face. "There is value in this project beyond the balance sheet," he said. "I think it will change lives, and be a force for good, but I can't put my business in jeopardy if it can't sustain itself. Can you make it work with another try?"

I paused. "I believe we can," I said. And I really did.

"Well, then, let's do it. It's up to you. Are you up to it?"

Now it was my turn to be emotional. I was moved by his faith in our work, and in us personally, but I knew he also felt a sense of mission. He told me once that doing the right thing was never a risk he would refuse to take, that his measure of what mattered was bigger than money.

Before the endeavor was complete, there would be three films. The total expense for Larry came out to be almost nineteen million dollars. Paramount Pictures released the home video. Showtime aired the series. Critical acceptance was almost universal. National press was abundant. Revenue, however, was not. Contrary to everyone's expectation, people did not come in significant numbers.

For whatever reason or theory, *The Work and the Glory* series never achieved financial success. Larry was not ambiguous when he expressed his displeasure with our lack of financial success. Clearly, he was angry with me. I knew Larry was not angry just because we weren't profitable, but also because he knew the power of the stories in those books, and we had made it impossible to keep telling them through the visual medium. No amount of apologizing was useful. He'd trusted me, and I hadn't delivered as promised. Even though it was business, it was also a personal loss to him.

He didn't speak to me for years.

It was during that time, however, that Larry received many letters and responses to the film, detailing that it had dispelled myths and misperceptions about Mormons and changed many lives. One woman had personally written him to inform him of her skepticism of the LDS religion until viewing the films. She had since converted to his cherished faith. It was through this that Larry began to understand the worth of a soul and reaffirmed his belief that the movies we made were important.

In 2008 I ran into him in a Salt Lake City delicatessen, and I couldn't decide if I would honor or anger him by saying hello. He was ill at the time, unable to walk. Gail saw me coming and announced my presence, as his vision was failing him. I slowly approached the table and tried to gauge his reaction. He took my hand, shook it, and then patted it and told me he was grateful for the experience we'd had together and encouraged me in the work I was currently doing.

It was this act of love and courtesy that moved me greatly, because he worked so hard to be a man of integrity and fairness, and it would have been completely fair to never speak to me again after losing so much money. And yet he proved to me that the gruff exterior masked a humble and remarkable servant of God and man.

With every excuse to be angry—in fact, almost nineteen million reasons—Larry chose, in what would be his last interaction with me, to forgive and to learn. It is one of my life's few such reconciliations. It continues to inspire me in the way I deal with others. It was a type of the treatment I hope for at the hands of Him whom I admire most, when someday I stand where Larry has now stood.

THE PATRIOT

Steven L. Neal

In the middle of a busy clinic day in the spring of 1999, I was interrupted by an unexpected phone call.

"Hi, this is Marilyn Smith for Larry H. Miller. Is this Dr. Steven Neal?"

"Yes."

"Larry really liked your bronze statue *The Price of Liberty* in the museum art show and would like to buy it."

Silence.

"Hello? It is for sale, isn't it?"

"Is this the Larry Miller who owns the Utah Jazz?"

"Yes."

"Well, tell him I'd be honored to sell it to him, but he'll have to have dinner with me." That was the beginning of my friendship with Larry. The catalyst for him entering into my life was his love of liberty and those ideals that make America great. True to his word, Larry and Gail met my wife, Susan, and me for dinner at the Little America in Salt Lake City. Being from Oregon, I didn't know what he looked like, but I quickly realized everyone else in the restaurant did. And he indeed purchased the bronze statue *The Price of Liberty*, displaying it in his living room.

To his delight, Larry often would have me recite the meaning of the images sculpted in bronze. The scenario comes from the pages of the *Book of Mormon*. Moroni, a patriot and military leader of an ancient civilization, calls for recruits to defend against an impending invasion. He takes off his coat, rends it, writes on it, and places it atop a pole in flag-like fashion. A baby, who represents us as America's progeny, is held up by a patriot forefather in 1776 dress so he can grasp the banner fluttering in the breeze.

The inscription on the banner reads: "In memory of our God, our religion, and freedom, and our peace, our wives, and our children." If you want to know what was written in Larry Miller's heart, it assuredly is much the same motto. He felt deeply about those things, which is why this piece of art excited him so. I used to tell him we should make a giant sculpture of it and cast *him* as the patriot.

Larry Miller loved the Constitution. He believed it to be divinely inspired. In one of our earliest conversations, Larry asked if I had read *Miracle at Philadelphia*, by Catherine Drinker Bowen. I had not.

"It's a wonderful book," he said. "It tells the story about the ratification of the Constitution. There were so many things working against its ratification that it truly was a miracle it actually happened. I'll send you a copy of the book."

I read it cover to cover. In a subsequent conversation, Larry relayed that one of his favorite parts was when signer Benjamin Rush exclaims, "The fact that twelve states could form a union against local prejudices and opposing interests in only ten months was a solitary event in the history of mankind. 'Tis done! We have become a nation!'"

In the early 1990s, the two of us became involved in a seven-year Mormon Battalion Association project. He handled the financing, and I created the sculpture. Members of the nineteenth-century battalion were draftees called to leave their families a half continent behind to fight for the United States in the Mexican-American War of 1846. The battalion had played a large role in the history of California and Utah but had received little recognition for it—certainly not in California history books. We made the sculpture larger than life as, indeed, the battalion's actions had been. It was twelve feet tall in two compositions. Battalion members marched for their nation, their families, their religion, their peace, and their freedom, much like the *Price of Liberty* motto.

I asked Larry to pose, holding the American flag in the second of the two pieces. It wasn't the first time I'd ask Larry if he would consider being sculpted—he had declined an earlier request. This time he agreed. I initially sculpted Larry from photos I took while sitting in his living room. Gail provided personal details for the finishing touches.

Everything had to be re-sculpted in the enlarging process, though, and Larry invited me to his Jordan Commons office to craft the enlarged version while he went about his business routine. In between his endless phone calls or conversations with hundreds of different parties, I would have him momentarily look up to catch the exact line of a portion of his forehead, chin, or mouth. He would go over the shooting percentages of Jazz players while I worked.

"That's really starting to look like me," he said.

I shrugged.

"No, really, I'm not blowing smoke."

Later that day, we took the oversized head down to his Lexus dealership in Lindon, where I stored the piece in a service bay. Given the size of the piece, the service bay was the only place I could work on it, and there it resided for a year and a half, until one day I climbed up the ladder and placed Larry's bust on "The Patriot."

Larry smiled. It was the last time I saw a vigorous Larry Miller. A couple of months later, he had the heart attack that started a cascade of events resulting in his untimely death. The statue *Duty Triumphs*, featuring Larry Miller as the Patriot holding a draped American flag and sporting a Paul Revere ponytail, stands at This Is the Place Heritage Park in Salt Lake City.

As ninety percent of the members of the Mormon Battalion had no shoes by the time they finished their march from Ft. Leavenworth, Kansas, to San Diego, California, Larry's feet are wrapped in the makeshift rawhide strips from stock animals that died on the original trek. The finished bronze sculptures were un-veiled by Gail Miller and Elder M. Russell Ballard on August 21, 2009, six months after Larry died.

In fitting tribute, I made a copy of the Patriot's head, sheared off Paul Revere's ponytail, and recast Larry's bust in bronze for the Energy*Solutions* Arena. Sometimes people ask me if I should have made the sculptures smaller. I think of men like those in the Mormon Battalion and Larry Miller and answer, "Absolutely not."

THE BRIDGE BUILDER
AND BROTHER JOSEPH

David Brown

A popular LDS hymn testifies that "millions will know Brother Joseph again." Thanks to my great friend and bridge builder Larry Miller, they do. In 2000, Larry became involved in a project that would help people both in and outside of the Church better understand its first prophet, Joseph Smith. And it all started with a friendship that had begun nearly three decades earlier.

Larry and I first met in 1972. I had been called to serve as the bishop of the Colorado ward where Larry and his wife, Gail, lived. As a new bishop, I was determined to meet every member of the ward, especially those who were less active, and Larry certainly fell into that category.

When we met, I challenged him to give the Lord a chance—to attend church with his family and to pray.

"It couldn't hurt," was Larry's response. Thus started a long process that involved many other special friends who led him back to full activity with the Church. That was also the start of a wonderful friendship between Larry and me.

The Millers have remained dear friends to my wife, MelRae, and me ever since, which gives me special insight into the building of the business empire that hadn't even started when I first knocked on Larry's door. Larry was extremely bright, creative, aggressive, decisive, and hardworking. He was a serial entrepreneur, always building.

My wife and I were invited to join the Millers and thousands of their employees in celebrating the twenty-fifth anniversary of the Larry H. Miller Group of Companies, which was founded when Larry and Gail purchased their first Toyota dealership in Murray, Utah. Everyone in attendance received from Larry and Gail a gift: a small sculpture of a bridge crossing a ravine, which Larry said describes his philosophy of life and his desire to leave this world in a better condition than when he arrived.

Then he read the following words written by the poet Will Allen Dromgoole, which Larry said speaks of each generation's responsibilities to its successors:

The Bridge Builder

An old man, going a lone a highway,
Came at the evening, cold and gray,
To a chasm, vast, and deep and wide,
Through which was flowing a sullen tide.

The old man crossed in the twilight dim;
The sullen stream had no fear for him;
But he turned, when safe on the other side,
And built a bridge to span the tide.

"Old man," said a fellow pilgrim, near,
"You are wasting strength with building here;
Your journey will end with the ending day;
You never again must pass this way;
You have crossed the chasm, deep and wide-
Why build you this bridge at the even tide?"

The builder lifted his old gray head:
"Good friend, in the path I have come," he said,
"There followeth after me today,
A youth, whose feet must pass this way.

This chasm, that has been naught to me,
To that fair-haired youth may a pitfall be.
He, too, must cross in the twilight dim;
Good friend, I am building this bridge for him."

Larry was such a consummate builder. He built a billion-dollar business empire and constructed places for his community to come together, such as the Delta Center, Miller Motorsports Park, the Megaplex Theatres, and Franklin Quest Field. He would spread his entrepreneurial wings to pursue what may have seemed like wholly unrelated businesses, but he always linked them together in a brilliant way.

But of all the things he built, Larry frequently mentioned to me that he hoped the Joseph Smith Papers would be his legacy. In the spirit of building bridges, he wanted to help the generations to come to gain an understanding and ultimately a testimony of the Prophet and founder of The Church of Jesus Christ of Latter-day Saints.

In 2001, I was preparing to serve as the director of the Historic Kirtland Visitor Center, an important site in the history of the Church and the story of Joseph Smith. I wanted to learn more about the Church's history in Kirtland, Ohio, and I happened to meet senior Church historian Ron Barney, who was extremely helpful and provided a fountain of knowledge. He offered to arrange a private showing in which some of my close friends and family could join me to see some important Church history artifacts such as the original manuscript of the Book of Mormon, the original Book of Commandments, Joseph Smith's journal, and several other precious pieces from the Church's archives.

Larry was among the small group of friends I invited to this unique engagement, and he told me how special it was because it happened to fall on the anniversary of his first date with Gail. He was totally impressed by what we were shown. He met Ron, who mentioned to him some of the work he'd been doing on a project called the Joseph Smith Papers.

I left for Ohio the next day, but Larry was hardly done exploring. He mentioned to Gail, "There's something I need to be doing here."

He contacted Ron to figure out how he could help, and it became clear which project needed the most assistance. Ron and others were working to create a comprehensive Joseph Smith history, but they needed more researchers and more funding. They were trying to produce a set of books that would include unpublished letters, personal diaries, important sermons, and much more. That's when Larry said to Ron, "Let's do this."

Several months later, I answered my phone in Kirtland and heard Larry's voice. "You would never believe what it was that you got started," he said with excitement. In the intervening months, Larry had committed millions of dollars to the project. Multiple volumes of the Papers have been published, and a companion documentary TV series aired on Larry's KJZZ-TV in 2008 and 2009 and later became available on DVD. The project is still underway, and Gail and the Miller family continue to honor the commitments Larry made. Indeed, Larry and Gail are helping millions "know Brother Joseph again."

Even for a man whose legacy includes dozens of high-profile successes that impacted countless lives, perhaps his crowning achievement was the Joseph Smith Papers. He believed that anyone who took the time to prayerfully read, study, and ponder about Smith's life would come to know and respect that he was indeed a prophet of God.

I'm incredibly grateful for the thirty-seven years of friendship that started in Larry and Gail's Colorado home. Larry was an incredible entrepreneur, a lifelong friend, a deeply religious man—and a builder of bridges.

REFLECTION OF PIONEER TREK

Elder M. Russell Ballard

My family, along with the Larry and Gail Miller family, had a very special experience in 2001 as we were guided over the Mormon Trail by Church history experts Stewart Glazier and Gerald Lund.

Pioneer trek is an experience many Latter-day Saints embark upon to recreate the experiences of early Mormon pioneers as they crossed the Midwest with their wagons and handcarts, battling a number of different obstacles in their quest to gather in the West. Today, families and individuals retrace their steps, seeking to understand and honor the strength and sacrifice of their forebears in the faith.

As our families pulled handcarts over the steep, rocky path known as Rocky Ridge, we contemplated the faith and willingness of our pioneer forefathers to withstand the rigors of this journey from Illinois and Iowa into the Salt Lake Valley. Repeatedly, the thoughts of this sacrifice brought Larry Miller to tears as we read from their history regarding their struggle for survival.

At Martin's Cove, which is a place of stillness and solemnity, we all reflected on the sacrifice and sanctification that came to those in the Martin Handcart Company. The company was comprised largely of British and Scandinavian converts whose journey to Utah started late in the year. Because of their late departure, wintry and treacherous conditions had set in by the time they reached a small cove in what is now Wyoming.

We looked across the cove and saw green spots where some of the Saints who didn't survive were likely buried, and Gerald would read from the company's accounts. These were extremely spiritual moments, and tears welled up in the eyes of many, including Larry.

Later, I stood side by side with Larry, looking down from a nearby ridge called the Eminence. This ridge overlooks the Sweetwater River, where another group of immigrant pioneers, the Willey Handcart Company, met similar struggles. We reflected upon what happened to the Saints who were suffering and praying for rescue. Rescue teams were dispatched from the Salt Lake Valley, and as we stood at the Eminence, we read the accounts of joy from when the rescuers came over the mountains, bringing both supplies and hope.

"Shouts of joy rent the air," wrote pioneer John Chislett of the moment their rescuers arrived. "Strong men wept till tears ran freely down their furrowed and sun-burnt cheeks . . . That evening, for the first time in quite a period, the songs of Zion were to be heard in the camp, and peals of laughter issued from the little knots of people as they chatted around the fires."

Another pioneer encamped in the area, Mary Ferguson Scott, rose to her feet when she saw the company of rescuers approaching. "I see them coming, I see them coming!" Mary exclaimed. "Surely they are angels from heaven."

We reflected that perhaps there had never been a greater rescue than the rescue of the pioneers by the faithful men who risked their own lives to save those who were in such hopeless circumstances. These experiences had deep meaning and touched Larry in a very tender way.

As we stood together on the Eminence, I reminded all who were in the group, "We must not lose sight of the greatest rescue ever made. That was in Gethsemane, the Savior's rescue of all those who would repent and come to Him."

On this occasion I came to know of the deep spiritual sensitivity that Larry Miller had for those who blazed the trails, making it possible for him and his family to be able to do the good things they do in the state of Utah and the city of Salt Lake.

We had known the Millers for a long time already. I, too, grew up in the car business, so I had a common relationship with Larry that evolved into a strong friendship over the years. Larry would visit me and we'd talk about business, about gospel questions, about the Joseph Smith Papers project and a number of other topics. The experiences we shared while following in the pioneers' footsteps cemented a strong friendship and showed me that Larry was a deeply spiritual man.

He also deeply loved the community, and both he and Gail have been great contributors to the people around them. Gail keeps this legacy intact as she continues to lead the humanitarian side of the organization. She contributes to worthy causes and makes a difference in the lives of a great many people.

We remained close, and I was able to spend time with Larry, Gail, and the family toward the end of his life. I visited him several times to try to lift his spirits after his amputation and throughout the period of illness that followed. I had the opportunity to feel the power of testimony and love that my dear friend had for his family, for Gail, for our community, and for his church. His faith and trust in God carried him safely to the end of his journey in mortality, for which I will always thank him.

On my last visit to Larry, his whole family was gathered around in his room at the Huntsman Cancer Institute. Larry was still able to converse, but it was obvious his time was limited.

I took hold of his hand. "It's time to shift and think about where you're going," I told him. "You have friends and family you're going to meet, and it's going to be a glorious and great experience." It is a tender memory, the last one I have of my friend Larry.

People know a great deal about Larry's business success and public persona. I feel blessed to have seen a side of Larry that was there when all the business meetings were over and the cameras were off. He was a devout, faithful Latter-day Saint. There was an inward spirituality about him that not everybody saw. He felt it. He knew it. He loved the Church; he loved the Lord.

LOVE

LOVE STORY

Gail Miller

Of all the stories that could be written about Larry Miller, mine has to be unique. I was married to him for forty-four years. I knew him at his best; I knew him at his worst. I knew his joys, his sorrows, his hopes, his dreams, his bitter disappointments, and his greatest accomplishments. I could tell many stories, but I have chosen to tell our love story.

We were two kids when we met—twelve years old, seventh graders in junior high school. I was tall and lanky, he was short and stocky. We were not immediately attracted to each other but as we "matured" to ninth graders, a spark ignited, and we began to date. There was something about him that was irresistible, almost a teddy bear-like quality that made me want to hold him close and protect him, and yet he was strong and rugged at the same time. He loved the outdoors, he loved sports, he loved adventure. He was intelligent, healthy, and sun-kissed. He had sparkling, intense blue eyes and curly blond hair. His shoulders were broad and his arms were very muscular.

I could tell Larry was very smart, but I could also see that he would rather play than apply himself in school. Throughout our high school years, he earned a reputation that made teachers dread having him in their classes. One teacher told him to stay away, study some scientific anomaly, come back at the end of the term and report on it, but "don't come to class." Larry obeyed, gave an acceptable report, and passed the class with an average grade while avoiding the regular curriculum. I think Larry came out the winner. All of his teachers liked him but preferred to avoid the disruption he caused in the classroom. Larry was charismatic, fun to be around, very social, and loved to talk—about anything and everything.

From the very beginning, Larry was a romantic. He saved every memento from every date, including wrappers—gum was the only treat we could afford after we'd pay the price of a movie ticket—and he often wrote sweet notes of affection to me. As time went on, we became "exclusive," and everyone in school knew I was "Larry's girl" and that trying to date me would incur his wrath.

After graduation from high school, we continued to spend every spare minute with each other. For a long time our dates were "walking dates" because we lived close to town and neither of us had a car. Once in a while we could borrow his parents' car if we wanted to go somewhere that required more than foot power. But walking provided the opportunity to get to know everything about each other, and we became best friends. It was inevitable, with all the time we were spending together, for us to fall in love.

As smart as Larry was, he was a slow learner, and after six years of dating, I began to get impatient waiting for a marriage proposal. I had a job that gave me the opportunity to take a vacation in March of 1965. Instead of waiting any longer, I took matters into my own hands and proposed to him. If he was willing to take the next step and get married, I was ready, but if not, it was time to part company. He saw the light, and we became husband and wife.

It was a nice wedding, with lots of friends and family in attendance. Our children began to come the following year: First, a boy; second, a boy; third, a boy; finally a girl, and then another boy. Our family was complete.

His love notes continued throughout our marriage. I saved and cherished each one. For every holiday, every birthday, every special occasion, he wrote a letter or card or note to express his delight and his feelings of love and gratitude for me and for his children. He felt blessed to be their father. It was important to him to document important events in letters, to give hope and encouragement when times were tough, to share the things that were of importance to him and tell me his hopes and dreams for the future. At times he composed poems expressing his deepest love for me, and at other times he would express the joy of sharing his "favorite things" with me, such as the song of the finches in our front yard. We had our secret phrases that meant we understood each other. We had times when we finished each other's sentences as if they were our own. Or, we would begin talking about the same thing at the same time, confirming the unity of our hearts.

Life was not always easy. Our journey together had many hills to climb and many valleys to wander through, but the one thing I never questioned was Larry's love for me. We were dedicated to each other, we were unified in our destination, and we worked together to accomplish what was most important to us. We learned from each other the value of a special relationship. We learned that life was not meant to be lived without love, without joy, or without hopes and dreams. It is much more meaningful if you share those things, and we did. We also learned that life is not meant to be lived for yourself. Sharing your life with someone you love is what brings true happiness. Whether it is through a kind word, a small act of service, being true to the values you cherish as the foundation of your life, or doing something so spectacular that it can't be put into words, all of these things become more meaningful when you can share them with the person you love. I know we had a special love. It survived all the tests of time. It will live throughout eternity.

I'd like to share one of the last notes he wrote to me before he passed away on Feb 20, 2009:

Mother's Day
May 14, 2006

My Darling Gail,

Each year of our 47+ years together has had its challenges, its excitements, its victories and achievements, and each its own flavor. That statement is certainly true of the last twelve months, as well, in its very own unique ways.

On one hand I think of what we've been through together with my leg wound, our family trip to New York, the effects of type II diabetes on me, our "adventure" with Zane in the Lexus on the racetrack, the development of the racetrack itself, our first grandchild to announce her marriage—and I could go on for a while.

I think the main message that I want to convey to you in this letter is that unquestionably there have been factors in my life, the last year and longer, that have limited me in many ways, some significantly, from doing things with the energy, drive, and capacity that I've been used to all of my life. I think that more than anyone, you are aware of these changes.

I don't mention them to complain, however. I simply want to acknowledge them, then write about the positive trade-offs.

Because of the limiting factors that I described above, I've had to slow down, physically and emotionally, so as to be able to "stay within" myself and to be able to continue doing the things I think are most essential to do with my more limited physical and emotional energy.

In slowing down to adjust to this, I've been able to enjoy certain things more than ever before in my life. The song of the finches seems more cheery and musical (they sing for you, you know). The flowers in our garden have never looked more beautiful, the flowering trees and shrubs have never looked so rich and colorful, and the call of the quail and song of the robins brings me greater joy than ever. I enjoy walking in City Creek Canyon more than ever, as well as the sunsets as seen from our home, and the moonlight. These are all beautiful reminders to me of Heavenly Father and His love for us.

However, as beautiful and special as all these things are, they only serve as backdrops for the things we share together.

Again, because of a more limited capacity in other ways, I find my-self constantly comforted, pleased, and/or excited by the sound of your voice. I love our greetings to each other at different times of the day, our walks together, our talks together in which, maybe more than ever, we talk of love, hopes, dreams, goals, children, grandchildren, etc.

When I have quiet moments and reflect on what we've shared in doing together throughout our lives, I can scarcely comprehend it.

On this Mother's Day, know that I truly honor, revere, and love you. I still believe you may be the most loved woman, by her husband, who ever lived.

Thank you for understanding me. Thank you for taking such very good care of me. Thank you for your patience with me. Thank you for sharing life with me. Thank you for loving me.

> *With ALL my love and respect eternally,*
> *Larry*

*Larry's mention of 47 years refers to our first date on Jan 30, 1959, a date he always remembered and celebrated with as much importance as the day we got married.

ACKNOWLEDGMENTS

I offer my gratitude to everyone who contributed a story about Larry, even the ones that weren't included in this book. Thank you for helping to keep Larry's memory alive. As the poet Thomas Campbell said, "To live in hearts we leave behind is to not die." Each story—published or not—has tremendous value to the Miller family and to Larry's legacy.

Thank you to the employees of the Larry H. Miller Group of Companies for the work you do every day to fulfill our mission, "To Enrich Lives." I hope this book helps you better understand the kind of man Larry was and that it inspires you to live and work according to the Group's core values of integrity, hard work, stewardship, and service.

Thank you especially to my immediate family—Gail, Greg, Roger, Steve, Karen, and Zane—and to your spouses, and all of generations "3.0" and "4.0." You were this book's original audience, and this book wouldn't exist without your positive influence, faith, and support.

Thank you to the Miller Inspiration team—Robert Bell, Andrew Johnson, Jack Sanford, Andrew T. Wankier, Carisa Miller, Brett Hullinger, and Michele Nell. For as long as I can remember, I've wanted to work with a creative team of dedicated professionals doing enjoyable work that matters. I'm grateful to you for being that team.

ACKNOWLEDGMENTS

Thank you to everyone at Deseret Book and Shadow Mountain—Sheri Dew, Chris Schoebinger, Tracy Keck, and Richard Erickson. In our first meeting about this project, Sheri said, "Reading these stories made me want to be a better person." I hope that others will feel the same way. Thanks to the Deseret Book team for helping the book make its way into readers' hands.

Thank you to others who played a role in the development of this project—Dan Clayton, Jody Genessy, Jay Shelledy, and Page Wiren for your skillful editing; Doug Robinson and Stanton Huntington for your early strategy and advice; Patty Aubery and Jack Canfield for your inspiration and vision; and Robert Tingey for your legal counsel. Thank you to everyone who read drafts of stories and provided feedback. This is a better book than it would have been without you.

Thank you to the team at BYU who video recorded oral histories and to the transcriptionists at REV.com.

Thank you to the American Diabetes Association for being the book's charitable partner. Larry would have lived much longer if he'd done a better job managing his diabetes. My hope is that this project will inspire its readers to take better care of their health.

Thank you to my wife, Heather Dawn, and our kids, Abbie, Zack, Elizabeth, Leo, Lola, and Maya, for your love and patience when the writing process took away from our family time.

Thank you, Larry, for living an exemplary life and for encouraging each of us to ask the question, "What manner of man—or woman—ought ye to be?" And finally, gratitude to the Creator, with whom all things are possible.

—Bryan Miller

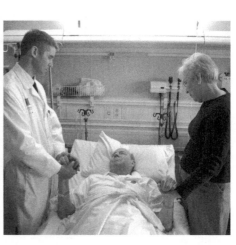

Larry H. Miller passed away at
sixty-four due to complications from diabetes.

He would have lived longer—and had
a better quality of life—had he done more to
manage this treatable disease.

Take care of yourself. Eat right. Exercise.
Visit your doctor.

BRYAN MILLER

SPEAKER • AUTHOR • TRAINER • COACH

AS A SPEAKER, Bryan is a gifted storyteller and has entertained and inspired thousands of people nationwide. He has spoken at leading companies and universities, and in 2015 he presented to a capacity crowd at the SXSW Interactive Festival in Austin, Texas. His talks encourage people to live passionately and purposefully and to go beyond society's often hollow definitions of success.

AS AN AUTHOR, Bryan is working on his next project—a book of stories about life purpose.

AS A TRAINER, Bryan delivers world-class workshops designed to help people achieve POWER, PRODUCTIVITY, and PEACE in every area of their lives.

AS A COACH, Bryan works with individuals and teams to optimize their performance both personally and professionally.

Here are a few things people have said about working with Bryan:

"Bryan's message was simple yet profound—no matter what our circumstances, we can find personal and collective meaning through service to our community."
—EVENT ORGANIZER

"I woke up feeling devastated, and Bryan's workshop gave me hope."
—WORKSHOP PARTICIPANT

"Bryan's coaching gave me new energy and focus."
—COACHING CLIENT

For more information about Bryan, visit www.bryanmiller.com.